DRIVING TOURS
FRANCE

Macmillan • USA

Original photography by Barrie Smith

Revised second edition 1995

First published January 1991

Edited, designed and produced by AA Publishing.

© The Automobile Association 1991.

Maps © The Automobile Association 1991

ISBN 0-02-860451-2

Published in the United States by Macmillan Travel
A Prentice Hall Macmillan Company
15 Columbus Circle
New York, NY 10023

Macmillan is a registered trademark of Macmillan, Inc.

Color separation: Mullis Morgan Ltd, London

Printed and bound in Italy by Printers SRL, Trento

Title page: *La Grasse, near Carcassonne*

Opposite: *A citizen of Beynac*

CONTENTS

INTRODUCTION

This book is not only a practical touring guide for the independent traveller, but is also invaluable for those who would like to know more about the country.

It is divided into 6 regions, each containing between 3 and 5 tours. The tours start and finish in major towns and cities which we consider to be the best centres for exploration. Each tour has details of the most interesting places to visit *en route*. Side panels cater for special interests and requirements and cover a range of categories – for those whose interest is history, wildlife or walking, and those who have children. There are also panels which highlight scenic stretches of road and which give details of special events, crafts and customs. The numbers link them to the appropriate main text.

The simple route directions are accompanied by an easy-to-use map of the tour, and there are addresses of local tourist information centres in some of the towns *en route* as well as in the start town.

Simple charts show how far it is from one town to the next in kilometres and (miles). These can help you to decide where to take a break and stop overnight, for example. (All distances quoted are approximate.)

Before setting off it is advisable to check with the information centre at the start of the tour for recommendations on where to break your journey and for additional information on what to see and do, and when best to visit.

ENTRY REGULATIONS
No visas are required for nationals of EU countries (except Turkey), USA, Canada, Japan, New Zealand, Singapore and South Korea. Visas required for all others. Check, though, with a travel agent or the French Government Tourist Office, since visa policy is subject to review.

CUSTOMS
Since 1 January 1993 there is no limit on the importation into one EU country of tax-paid goods purchased in another, provided that these goods are for personal use. However, all EU customs authorities have fixed indicative limits on alcohol and tobacco. Beyond these limits the importer must be able to prove that these goods are for personal use: 800 cigarettes or 400 cigarillos; 200 cigars or 1kg of tobacco; 10 litres of alcohol over 22 per cent volume (or 38.8 deg proof) plus 20 litres not over 22 per cent volume (eg fortified wine), plus 90 litres of still table wine (60 litres of sparkling wine); no limit on perfume, toilet water or coffee

If purchased in duty free shops or outside the EU: 200 cigarettes or 100 cigarillos; 50 cigars or 250g (9oz) of

Left: Le Croisic Harbour, in the Loire-Atlantique region
Right: The River Rance at Dinan

tobacco; 1 litre of alcohol over 22 per cent volume (or 38.8 deg proof) or 2 litres not over 22 per cent volume or fortified or sparkling wine, plus 2 litres of still table wine; 60ml of perfume and 250ml of toilet water; 500g of coffee or 100g of tea. No alcohol or tobacco for under 17s.

EMERGENCY TELEPHONE NUMBERS
Police tel: 17
Fire tel: 18
Ambulance: 15.

HEALTH
There are no special health requirements or regulations. Visitors other than EU citizens, where there may be reciprocal medical services available, are advised to take out medical insurance.

CURRENCY
The unit of currency is the franc, divided into 100 centimes. Coins are in denominations of 10, 20 and 50 centimes, and 1, 2, 5, 10 and 20 francs; notes in denominations of 20, 50, 100, 200 and 500 francs.

CREDIT CARDS
International credit cards are accepted widely throughout France, though not so much in rural areas. They are not accepted at some petrol stations.

BANKS
Normal banking hours are 9am to noon and 2pm to 4pm weekdays. Banks are closed either Mondays or Saturdays and on Sundays and public holidays.

Banks close at noon on the day before a national holiday, and all day on Monday if the holiday falls on a Tuesday.

TIME
France follows Greenwich Mean Time (GMT) plus one hour, with clocks put forward for a further hour from late March to late September.

POST OFFICES
Normal opening times for main post offices are 8am to 7pm on weekdays, and 8am to noon on Saturdays, though some small offices may close for lunch. Stamps may also be bought in tobacco shops (*tabacs*) or cafés marked with a red cigar sign. Letter boxes (*boîtes aux lettres*) are yellow.

TELEPHONES
Insert coin after lifting the receiver; the dialling tone is a continuous tone. To make a local call use a 1 franc coin or a *jeton*. Most telephone booths now take phonecards (*télécartes*). Buy them at 50FF or 120FF from post offices, tobac-

TOURIST OFFICES
Where no address is given for a separate tourist information office, enquire at the **Mairie** (mayor's office) in a village or small town, the Hôtel de Ville (town hall) in a larger place, or perhaps the **Syndicat d'Initiative** office. In some places the tourist offices open only seasonally, and the Mairie or Town Hall will handle enquiries out of season.

USEFUL WORDS
The most useful phrase in French is s'il vous plaît or please. You will get a lot further using it after every request than if you leave it out. The following words and phrases are helpful in finding your way about.

English   French
bridge   pont
bus   autobus
car park   un parking
I need petrol   j'ai besoin d'essence
my car has broken down   ma voiture est en panne
oil   huile
petrol   essence
the road for   la route pour
traffic lights   les feux
tyres   les pneus
underground   Métro
after   après
behind   derrière
before   avant
here   ici
left   à gauche
near   près
opposite   en face
right   à droite
straight on   tour droit
there   là
where?   où?
where is?   où est?
at what time   à quelle heure?
I do not understand   je ne comprends pas
do you speak English?   parlez-vous Anglais?
help!   au secours!
how much is it?   ça coute combien?
I'm sorry   pardon
thank you very much   merci beaucoup
do you accept credit cards?   acceptez-vous des cartes de credit?
money   argent

Rocamadour has been a city of pilgrimage since the Middle Ages. Medieval buildings cling to the spectacular rock face like jewels in a crown

GREAT BRITAIN

English Channel

BRETAGNE

●Quimper

Bay of Biscay

SPAIN

EMBASSIES

British Embassy: 35 rue du Faubourg St Honoré, 75383 Paris Cedex 08 tel: (1) 42 66 91 42.
Canadian Embassy: 35 avenue Montaigne, 75008 Paris tel: (1) 47 23 01 01.
US Embassy: 2 avenue Gabriel, 75382 Paris Cedex 08 tel: (1) 42 96 12 02.

ELECTRICITY

220 volts (50 cycles AC) is now the norm, with the standard continental two-pin round plug, making an adaptor essential for British and American appliances.

conists and newsagents. For international calls out of France dial 19, wait for a new tone, then dial the national code, followed by the local code, omitting the initial 0, and then the number.

MOTORING

Speed limits

Built-up areas 50kph (31mph).
Outside built-up areas on normal roads 90kph (56mph); on dual carriageways separated by a central reservation 110kph (68mph); also motorways without tolls.
Toll motorways 130kph (80mph). The beginning of a built-up area is indicated by a sign with the place-name in blue letters on a light background; the end is signified by a thin red line diagonally across the place-name sign. Unless otherwise signposted, follow the above speed limits.

Breakdowns

If your car breaks down, try to move it to the side of the road so it obstructs the traffic flow as little as possible. You are advised to seek local assistance as, at present, there is no nationwide road assistance service in France. On

autoroutes, ring from emergency phones located every 2km (mile) to contact breakdown service.
The use of a warning triangle or hazard warning lights is compulsory in the event of an accident or breakdown.

Accidents

If you are involved in an accident you must complete a *constat l'amiable* before the vehicle is moved. It must be signed by the other party, and in the event of a dispute or a refusal to complete the form, you should immediately obtain a *constat d'huissier*. This is a written report from a bailiff (*huissier*).
The police are only called out to accidents when someone is injured, a driver is under the influence of alcohol or the accident impedes traffic flow.

Documents

A valid driver's licence, not provisional, is required. The minimum driving age is 18. An international

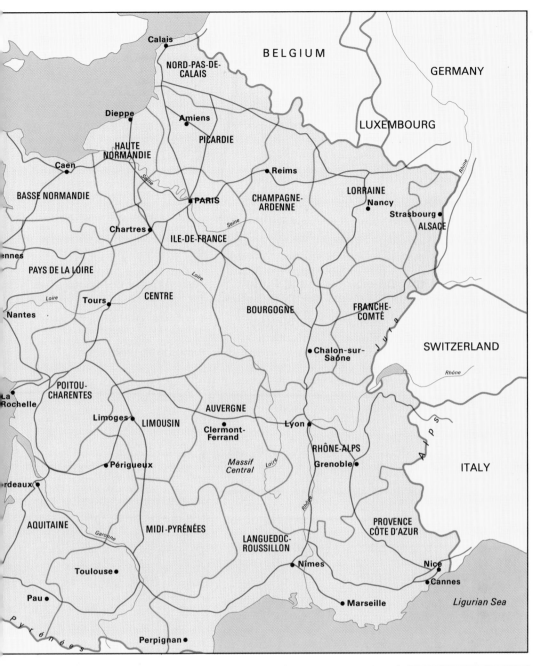

licence is not required for visitors from the US, UK or Western Europe. You also require the vehicle's registration document, plus a letter of authorisation from the owner, if not accompanying the vehicle, and the current insurance certificate (a green card is not mandatory but remains internationally recognised and can be helpful). Also, a nationality plate or sticker is required.

Car hire and fly/drive
If you are not taking your own car, you can make arrangements to hire before departure. Many package holidays include car hire as an option. The main car hire companies are represented in France.

Driving conditions
Keep to the right (*serrez à droite*). Though main roads have priority (*passage protégé*), right of way is otherwise given to vehicles coming in from the right (*priorité à droite*). The *priorité* rule no longer applies at roundabouts, which means you give way to cars already on the roundabout.

Mountain tours, including the ones in the South of France, call for a properly serviced and not over-laden car. Especially in these areas, petrol stations may be far apart. Unleaded fuel is now widely available all over France.

On the Clermont-Ferrand, Pau and Grenoble tours, roadside notices displaying either *Ouvert* (open) or *Fermé* (closed) will show the road conditions ahead. Do not make for a road notified as being closed.

The wearing of seat belts in both the front and back is compulsory and children under 10 years of age may not travel as front seat passengers.

Route directions
Throughout the book the following abbreviations are used for French roads:
A – Autoroute
N – Route Nationale
D – Route Départementale
C and V – smaller roads.

PUBLIC HOLIDAYS

1 January – New Year's Day
Easter Monday
1 May – Labour Day
8 May – VE Day
6th Thursday after Easter – Ascension Day
2nd Monday after Ascension – Whitsun
14 July – Bastille Day
15 August – Assumption Day
1 November – All Saints' Day
11 November – Remembrance Day
25 December – Christmas Day

8

NORMANDY & BRITTANY

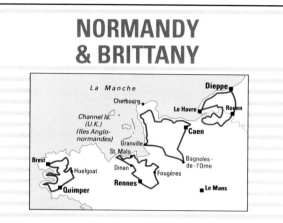

The wonder of Normandy is that it has rebuilt itself after the shattering bombardments and tank and infantry battles of World War II into a region of cheerful holiday resorts, attractive farmlands and archetypal rustic villages. Here and there, you will pick up eerie echoes of an earlier invasion which went the other way, from Normandy across the English Channel.

In the racial mix of northern France, the original Normans were Norsemen – Vikings who swept down from Scandinavia and, in the 10th century, had the dukedom of Normandy created for them. William the Conqueror was Duke of Normandy, with a legal claim to the English throne, long before he invaded England in 1066.

From that point on, the histories of Normandy and England intertwined. The English royal house had vast possessions in and around Normandy, and was constantly involved in French marriages. You will have to keep a firm grip on history to appreciate just why some Normandy towns were fortified by the Normans against the English, the English against the Normans, of the Normans against other independent forces in the previously fragmented country which we now call France.

The Normandy coastline is a succession of resorts. Look for the seafood restaurants in the fishing ports. Inland, the livestock farms supply a cuisine which is rich in butter, cheeses, cream and hefty helpings of meat. Apples and pears are major crops. The wooded farmlands of Normandy create some of the most beautiful landscapes in northern France.

Brittany becomes more Breton as you move further west. The place names and family names make that clear. A wonderful coastline and an airy, high-level interior are linked by a wooded middle district which could easily be in Devon or Cornwall.

Waves of colonists from Britain started arriving in the 5th century. Britain and Brittany, Briton and Breton are all from the same basic word; but the close connection was lost long ago.

Bretons, particularly in the west, retain a feeling of 'apartness' from the rest of France, and you will not be long there, especially in the breezy hill country or looking at great stone monuments of ancient days, before being aware of something Celtic in the air. Traditional costumes and religious processions, not always as well supported as they have been in the past, underline the differences in culture and background.

In both Brittany and Normandy, regional nature parks are very well organised, with wildlife reserves, museums of traditional ways of life and places where you can see products such as bread and cider being made in the old pre-industrialised way. They taste delicious! Enjoy them with a Camembert, best-known of the excellent Normandy cheeses.

Caen

You cannot miss William the Conqueror's influence on Caen, which has risen again from the devastation of 1944. Its centrepiece is not some elegant square, but the château of the dukes of Normandy. Inside this massive fortress, founded by William in 1060, you will find the Musée des Beaux-Arts with its splendid collection of French and Italian paintings, and the Musée de Normandie, devoted to archaeology, history and traditional life. William also endowed the monastery of the Abbaye aux Hommes, just as his wife built the original convent of the Abbaye aux Dames. William's tomb is in the Church of St-Étienne at the Abbaye aux Hommes, which now serves as Caen's Hôtel de Ville. The Musée de la Nature here concentrates on the wildlife of coast and country. The Mémorial-Musée pour la Paix has impressive displays and audio-visual presentations charting the rise of Facism, the collaboration of the Resistance and the D-Day landings through to the present day.

Dieppe

Like Caen, Dieppe has erased most of the scars of World War II. Its harbour area includes ferry, freight, fishing and pleasure ports. Morning fish stalls are set up by the roadside.

Cherbourg has been a key French port throughout history

The best view of Dieppe is from the 15th-century hillside château. It houses a fine museum and art gallery with extensive maritime rooms and a glorious collection of ivories, including a full-rigged ship with billowing sails.

Rennes

Rennes is the historic and flourishing provincial capital of Brittany. The River Vilaine runs through it, but, from the tourist office in the Quai Lamartine, there is no water to be seen. Here, the Vilaine has been roofed over to provide a car park. Another quay, this time named after the writer Émile Zola, is the address of the Musée des Beaux-Arts with its rich display of paintings, drawings, engravings and sculptures, many confiscated from religious houses during the Revolution. Rubens, Gaugin, Sisley, Boudin and Picasso are all represented. In the same building is the Musée de Bretagne, which traces the history of Brittany from prehistoric times.

Quimper

Quimper is more Breton than Rennes. The Musée Breton is here, completely refurbished. The pleasant old quarter centres on a square dominated by the twin spire of the cathedral, St-Corentin. Here is an architectural curiosity: the 15th-century nave is accidentally out of alignment with the 13th-century choir. Quimper's Musée des Beaux-Arts, totally renovated to include

The graceful approach to the twin-towered cathedral of St-Corentin at Quimper. Parts of this structure date from the 13th century

audio-visual presentations, is well provided with 17th-century Flemish paintings. In the same era, Quimper itself began the production of the glazed pottery for which it is still famous. Factories and ceramic artists' workshops welcome visitors.

3 days – 456km (283 miles)

LEGACY OF D-DAY

Caen • Pegasus Bridge • Arromanches • Bayeux
Plage d'Omaha • Valognes • Barneville-Carteret
Granville • Villedieu-les-Poêles • Bagnoles de l'Orne
Clécy • Caen

Normandy is a land of apples and cider, of spacious sands, of lovely inland *bocage* country with hedges and tree-lined fields, but behind the peaceful present-day scenes the region hides a devastated past. In June 1944 the huge invasion force of Operation Overlord stormed the German defences – British and Canadian troops at the beaches renamed Sword, Juno and Golf, Americans at Utah and Omaha. D-Day is the theme of memorials all over the district. Caen suffered tragically in the bitter fighting which liberated Normandy. Fiftieth anniversary celebrations in 1994 placed Caen in the spotlight, resulting in a considerable revamp of the museum for peace – Le Mémorial.

A memorial to D-Day heroism at Pointe du Hoc near Omaha Beach

[i] Place St Pierre Caen

Leave Caen on the D513 as for Cabourg. Go left on the D37 then take the D514 as for Ouistreham to Pegasus Bridge.

Pegasus Bridge, Normandy

1 In the eastern sector of the D-Day landings, the years of planning and training came down to one amazingly audacious feat. Just after midnight on the morning of 6 June 1944, three gliders with no room for a conventional approach suddenly crash-landed beside this ugly but vital little tilting bridge on the Caen–Ouistreham canal. British troops poured out and after four minutes' fierce fighting secured the bridge. They held it until reinforcements arrived, most decisively the Commandos led by Lord Lovat, who reached here exactly two-and-a-half minutes behind schedule after fighting their way inland from Sword Beach. Three columns in the scrubland southeast of the bridge show where the gliders landed. On the west side, a **museum** tells the story of that dramatic engagement. In November 1993 the original Pegasus Bridge was removed to be replaced by a wider, stronger bridge more appropriate to modern traffic.

Take the D35 to Douvres then follow the 'Bayeux' signs. Go right on the D79 to Courseulles, then right on the D12 and follow signs to Arromanches.

Arromanches, Normandy

2 Without massive supplies, the D-Day landings could not have developed into an advance across the whole of France. Arromanches was the scene of one of the greatest engineering feats of the war – the building, from thousands of tons of prefabricated parts shipped across the Channel, of Port Winston, the giant Mulberry (artificial) harbour. It threw a 5.7km (3½-mile) breakwater round the sea approaches to Arromanches, from which pontoon bridges reached to the shore, and was operational within 12 days.

Today, Arromanches is a busy but unremarkable little resort on a bay between all but vertical cliffs. A viewpoint on the eastern cliff overlooks the many sections of the artificial harbour which remain offshore. On the seafront, the lively and well-presented **Musée du Débarquement** illustrates with working models, films and photographs the creation and operation of 'the key to the liberation of France'.

[i] Rue du Maréchal Joffre

Leave Arromanches for Bayeux on the D516.

Bayeux, Normandy

3 Most of the fine historic buildings here, recently restored, survived the 1944 campaign. You can stroll through old streets and over narrow

Fine stained glass in Bayeux Cathedral, a splendid example of Norman Gothic architecture

bridges, admiring the gleaming stonework of the mills on the River Aure. On the ring road, the **Musée de la Bataille de Normandie** is 'guarded' by British, American and German tanks. Everything in Bayeux, however, pales in importance beside the priceless 11th-century tapestry, displayed in the **Centre Guillaume le Conquérant**, with its lively scenes of the Norman Conquest of England. Weavers and lacemakers still have studios in the town.

Alongside the cathedral, the **Musée Baron Gérard** shows paintings, lacework and ceramics. It opens from a little courtyard shaded by the famous 'liberty tree', planted according to the Revolutionary calendar (France's official calendar from 1793–1805) on 10 Germinal of the year V – otherwise 30 March, 1797.

ⓘ Pont St Jean

Leave Bayeux on the D6 to Port-en-Bessin. Go left on the D514 for Plage d'Omaha.

Plage d'Omaha, Normandy

4 Most side roads to the right of the D514 here reach memorials and above, the Americans' principal **D-Day landing beach**, although signs for the Plage d'Omaha lead to a holi-day camp area. Look for **Wn 62**, a high-set German strongpoint above the shoreline. There are American monuments here as well as explanations of the D-Day action and the fearsome German defences.

The American **military cemetery** for the men lost during the landings is close by, and there is an **Exposition Omaha** – housed in a prefabricated wartime building bizarrely described in some French guidebooks as a ship – at the village of Vierville.

Continue on the D514 then go right on the N13 as for Cherbourg and continue to Valognes.

Valognes, Normandy

5 In its 17th- to 19th-century heyday, Valognes was 'the Versailles of Normandy'. Aristocratic families owned town houses here, and there was a high-flying social life. The bombardments of 1944 wrecked the centre, which has been rebuilt, and also destroyed part of the **Church of St Malo**. Now a modern reinforced concrete nave and tower stand beside the 14th-century chancel.

However, several of Valogne's mansions survived. The elegant

FOR HISTORY BUFFS

4 Turn right off the D514 after Omaha Beach for **Pointe du Hoc**, to learn about the desperate struggle of the American Rangers to scale the cliffs on D-Day. Later, the landings were re-staged here for the film *The Longest Day*.

5 Ste-Mère-Église near Utah Beach was the first French town liberated on D-Day. A **museum** to the 82nd US Airborne Division describes the action and how it is commemorated, and explains why the figure of a paratrooper hangs from the church tower every summer.

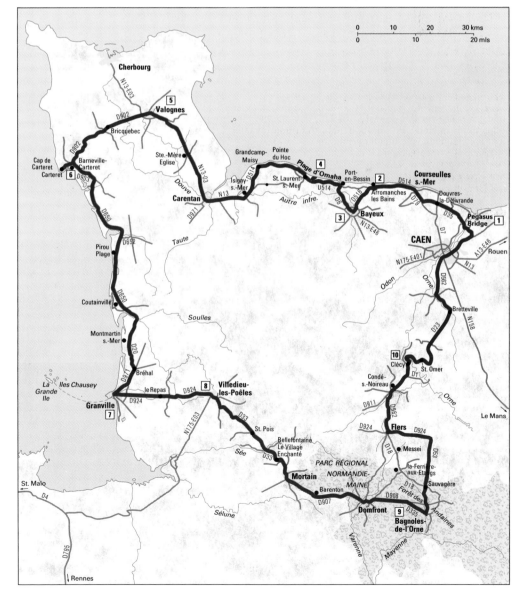

BACK TO NATURE

2 In the busy resort of Courseulles, part of Juno Beach on D-Day, the **Maison de la Mer** features aquariums with seahorses and conger eels, and a splendid display of shells.

6 Until early this century, the huge sand dunes north of the Cap de Carteret were moved steadily inland by the wind, engulfing roads and a mill. You can see how, classified as a nature reserve, they have now been stabilised by the planting of marram grass thickets. Look for birds such as Dartford warblers and stonechats as well as numerous lizards.

SCENIC ROUTES

While many places on this tour offer beautiful coastal views, the inland roads generally beat the ones near the coast for scenery. The **D33** after Villedieu-les-Poêles, alternating between ridgetop and valley floor, runs through gorgeous Normandy countryside. High above Clécy in the valley of the Orne, the **Route des Crêtes** sums up, without reaching any Alpine levels, the appeal of the Suisse Normande.

RECOMMENDED WALKS

6 At Barneville-Carteret, start from either of the beaches flanking the **Cap de Carteret** along the exhilarating **Sentier des Douaniers** (the Excisemen's Path), which contours the lichen-clad cliffs and passes the site of an 18th-century coastal gun battery.

9 Stop off on the way to Bagnoles and ask at the Mairie (town hall) in St Pois on the **D33** for the **Circuits Pédestres** leaflet. It describes a series of waymarked walks in the beautiful Normandy countryside. They explore the falls in the valley of the Glanon stream, granite quarries and the viewpoint ridge of Mont Buon.

18th-century **Hôtel de Beaumont** is open to visitors. The **Hôtel de Thieuville** houses the **Musée de l'Eau de Vie et des Vieux Métiers**, whose two main subjects are brandy and leatherwork. An annexe has displays on the French Revolution with some unusual themes, such as the role of scientists in Revolutionary times.

Close at hand the **Musée du Cidre**, once a dyer's workshop, then a barracks and then a smithy, concentrates on apples and cider-making.

ⓘ Place du Château

Leave Valognes for Barneville-Carteret on the D902.

Barneville-Carteret, Normandy

6 These two little towns, administratively linked together, form a family holiday resort with excellent sands, a spectacular rocky headland and a very sheltered tidal river harbour. This is a pleasant walking and watersports area, and summer ferries sail to the Channel Islands. Make for the lighthouse on **Cap de Carteret**, a wonderful viewpoint towards Jersey, Sark, Herm and, on the northern horizon, Alderney.

Take care at any family bathing parties. Every year people ignore the notices warning that, while the town beaches have a lifeguard service, the quieter one north of the Cap does not. There, it is all too easy for youngsters to be taken well out of their depth.

ⓘ Place Flandre-Dunkerque Carteret; Rue des Églises, Barneville

Leave Barneville as for La Haye-du-Puits on the D903, then keep right on the D650. Go straight on along the D20, to Bréhal, then right on the D971 and into Granville.

Left: Granville is part historic fort, part seaside resort with wartime relics. Daily boat trips visit the Channel Islands. Below: Keen cooks should invest in hand-made copper pans at Villedieu

Granville, Normandy

7 Like Monaco, Granville expanded from a fortified town on a promontory rock. Originally, thanks to the contortions of history, it was fortified by the English against the French! The story of the town is illustrated in the **Musée du Vieux Granville**, just inside the preserved drawbridge gateway of the **Haute Ville** (High Town).

The 15th-century **Notre Dame Church** stands among the alleyways of the High Town; a good **aquarium** here includes shell and mineral collections; and there is a very attractive path along the cliffs below the lighthouse. Views open up of the low-lying Chausey archipelago. Ferries sail to La Grande Île, with its château built by motor magnate Louis Renault.

On no account miss Granville's **Jardin Public**. Its lush lawns, pine trees and beautifully laid out flower beds surround the pink-and-white villa once owned by couturier Christian Dior. In early August, a 'Pardon of the Sea' melds religion with spectacle.

ⓘ Cours Jonville

Leave Granville for Villedieu on the D924.

Villedieu-les-Poêles, Normandy

8 If every place-name tells a story, how to explain Villedieu-les-Poêles – 'God's Town of the Pots and Frying-pans'? The Knights of Malta (a military religious order) established here in the 16th century, called the place Villedieu, and it became a famous centre of craftsmen and metalworkers.

That great tradition continues. Here you can watch hand-beaten copper being worked at the **Atelier du Cuivre**, pewterware at the **Maison de l'Étain**. At the extremes of Villedieu's historic product range, the Fonderie des Cloches is a bell-foundry open to visitors, and the **Maison de la Dentellerie** displays the lacework for which the women of the town were well-known all over northern France.

At the mouth of the River Bisque, Granville offers a casino, a golf course and a haven for yachts. It has acquired the nickname 'the Monaco of the North'!

ⓘ Place des Costils

Leave Villedieu on the N175 as for St Hilaire. Go right on the D924 and D999, then left on the D33 and continue through Mortain. Turn left on the D907, go through Domfront-centre then follow 'Bagnoles de l'Orne' signs along the D908 and right on the D335.

Bagnoles de l'Orne, Normandy

9 Retaining its old prominence as the most popular spa town in the west of France, Bagnoles, with the linked **Tessé la Madeleine**, lies among woodlands rising from the banks of the La Vée river. People come here for bath cures and to 'take the waters', but Bagnoles also offers excellent sporting facilities: golf, tennis, swimming, horse and pony riding, fishing and archery.

Wooded walks extend through the parks of the spa buildings and the château at Tessé. One fine viewpoint path leads to the **Roc du Chien** (the Dog's Rock) above the narrow river valley where the spa itself is located.

Bagnoles' **casino** backs on to a very pleasant lake where pedaloes can be hired. Close to the lake there are several restaurants specialising in the substantial Normandy cuisine.

ⓘ Place de la République

Leave Bagnoles for St Michel-des-Andaines on the D386. Go left and right on the D53 and continue to Flers. Go right as for Caen along the D962, then take the D562 to Clécy and turn off for Clécy-centre.

Clécy, Normandy

10 The River Orne at Clécy makes a dramatic curve below the wooded cliffs of La Suisse Normande (Norman Switzerland). Clécy is the main resort in this district whose name should not lead you to expect a Swiss-like landscape of lakes and mountains; but it is one of the most beautiful parts of inland Normandy nevertheless. In the pleasant town centre with its 18th-century houses, look for the **Musée Hardy** which displays the work of a local artist. An exhilarating walk climbs to the magnificent viewpoint of the **Pain du Sucre** (the Sugarloaf), high on the cliffs overlooking the Orne. The 16th-century Manoir de Placy houses the **Musée des Antiquités Normandes**, with a miniature railway and a train museum in the grounds.

ⓘ Place d l'Église

Leave Clécy on the D133c, then go left as for St Rémy. Just over the brow of a hill, go sharp right and follow Routes des Crêtes to St Omer. Avoid St Rémy itself. In St Omer turn right as for Pont d'Ouilly. Ignore the 'La Suisse Normande' turning. Go left at a stop sign to Bretteville and follow the D23. In Bretteville turn left on the D132, left at a give way sign, then return to Caen on the D562.

Caen – Pegasus Bridge 13 (8)
Pegasus Bridge – Arromanches 30 (19)
Arromanches – Bayeux 10 (6)
Bayeux – Plage d'Omaha 20 (12)
Plage d'Omaha – Valognes 72 (45)
Valognes – Barneville-Carteret 32 (20)
Barneville-Carteret – Granville 79 (49)
Granville – Villedieu-les-Poêles 28 (17)
Villedieu-les-Poêles – Bagnoles de
 l'Orne 77 (48)
Bagnoles de l'Orne – Clécy 48 (30)
Clécy – Caen 47 (29)

SPECIAL TO...

9 Normandy is famous for its apples and pears. The region's rich tradition in apple- and pear-growing, and the making of cider, are all explained in the **Maison de la Pomme et de la Poire**. Reached by turning right after Barenton on the D335, it has indoor displays as well as a walk through an orchard specially planted with many varieties of apple and pear trees.

9 At Bagnoles de l'Orne is the **Musée des Sapeurs-Pompiers**, which shows off France's finest collection of horse-drawn and hand-pumped fire engines. Look for **La Distinguée**, which operated as long ago as pre-Revolutionary times.

FOR CHILDREN

9 On the way from Villedieu-les-Poêles to Bagnoles, turn off the D33 for **Le Village Enchanté**, a beautiful estate where fairytale tableaux are laid out in the woodland.

10 In Clécy, 20-minute programmes at the **Musée du Chemin de Fer Miniature** show off more than 180 locomotives operating on the biggest model railway layout in Europe.

3 days – 434km (270 miles)

GREEN & PLEASANT NORMANDY

Dieppe • Varengeville-sur-Mer • Fécamp
Étretat • Le Havre • Caudebec-en-Caux
La Haye-de-Routot • Marais Vernier • Honfleur
Le Bec-Hellouin • Rouen • Dieppe

West of the cross-Channel port and fishing town of Dieppe, the white cliffs and deep valleys which slice into them are hidden from the main roads, but this tour twists along the coast to some very attractive holiday resorts favoured by the French themselves. Then it turns towards the tidal stretch of the River Seine, whose sweeping curves are industrialised in some places but border such fine inland landscapes as the Forêt de Brotonne and the delicious Marais Vernier. Some of the area is included in the regional nature park of Brotonne, where you can discover the secrets of traditional trades like bread-making and the transforming of apples into cider and Calvados.

RECOMMENDED WALKS

1 At Varengeville, three very attractive colour-coded walks follow pleasant country lanes and footpaths behind the great chalk cliffs of the coast. They all meet up close to the Parc Floral des Moutiers.

SCENIC ROUTES

From Dieppe westwards, the route runs along the rich farmland plateau then darts down breaks in the chalk cliffs to villages and harbours by the sea.

FOR CHILDREN

3 By the beach at Étretat, look for the children's playground with games, a roller-skating rink, a model boat pond and an aquarium.

ⓘ Pont Jehan Ango, Dieppe

Leave Dieppe on the D75 to Varengeville.

Varengeville-sur-Mer, Normandy

1 You might be deep in the heart of an English county here, with villas and cottages in discreetly private grounds, wooded and grass-banked lanes, and half-timbered farms fitted like jigsaw pieces in between. There is a wonderful English-style landscape garden at the Parc Floral des Moutiers, the garden of the house called Bois des Moutiers created by the architect Sir Edwin Lutyens and landscape gardener Gertrude Jekyll. Up on the farmland plateau, the Manoir d'Ango is a

The abbey at Le Bec-Hellouin takes its name from a medieval knight who became a man of God

Renaissance manor house with a beautiful dovecote.

At the foot of the Petit Ailly gorge you can wander along the stony shore under the towering cliffs. The artist Georges Braque, a founder of Cubism, is buried beside Varengeville's parish church, for which he designed one of the stained-glass windows.

Continue on the D75, then go into St Aubin and follow signs to St Valery, leaving it on the D925. Turn right to Veulettes-sur-Mer on the D79 then follow the signs to Fécamp.

Fécamp, Normandy

2 A fishing, freight and pleasure port at a dip in the cliffs, Fécamp has a shingle-bank beach and some remarkable places to visit. The Palais Bénédictine is the home of the liqueur of the same name, a distillation first carried out by monks of the Benedictine order, of 27 aromatic plants and spices whose precise recipe is a very closely guarded secret. There is a museum in the palace – a glorious 19th-century architectural confection of Gothic and Renaissance styles – which traces the history of Benedictine and also displays items of religious art, furnishings and, in the Gothic hall, a magnificent oak and chestnut ceiling built by Fécamp shipwrights. The early Gothic abbey church, La Trinité, is enormous, its nave one of the longest in France.

As well as a fine art museum, the town also has the Musée des Terre-Neuves. While going back to the Vikings, who colonised this coast, it concentrates on the years when the local fishing fleet used to spend months among the great cod banks of Newfoundland.

ⓘ Rue Alexandre le Grand

Leave Fécamp on the D940 as for Étretat, then go right on the D211 through Yport and follow the D11 to Étretat.

Étretat, Normandy

3 Nowhere on this coast matches Étretat for location. It lies behind a beach at the foot of a wooded valley.

The gardens at Fécamp, birthplace of the writer Guy de Maupassant

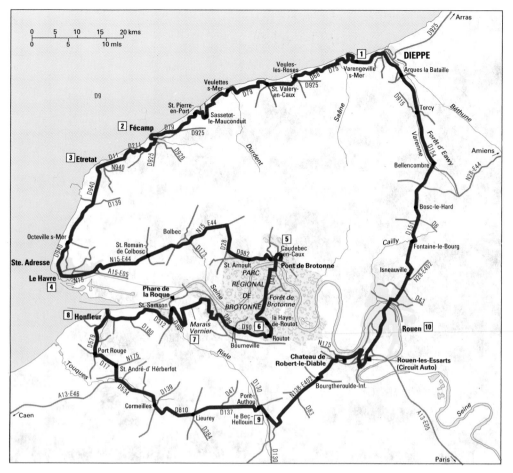

To north and south rise tall white cliffs with weathered-away natural arches and a great isolated needle rock a little way off shore.

Paths climb to the cliffs called **Falaise d'Amont** north of the town and the **Falaise d'Aval** to the south. Amont probably has the finer overall view, as well as a **seafarers' chapel** with fish carved in the stonework, and a **museum** to the aviators Nungesser and Coli, whose plane was last seen over Étretat before disappearing during the first attempt in 1927 to fly the Atlantic from east to west. There is also a dramatic memorial to them, with a mosaic tricolour of France.

[i] Place Maurice-Guillard

Leave Étretat on the D940 to Le Havre.

Le Havre, Normandy

4 Parts of Le Havre look curiously all of a piece with their postwar reinforced concrete buildings. The explanation for this is that the town was reduced to rubble in 1944, and had to be largely rebuilt after World War II.

Now it is once again a major freight and ferry port – the second busiest in France, occupying not only the traditional harbour area but also miles of riverside along the Seine. You can take a harbour cruise.

A splendid fine arts museum, **Musée des Beaux-Arts André-Malraux**, shows works by Renoir, Pissarro, Sisley and Dufy among others. The **Musée de l'Ancien Havre** illustrates the history of the town. Perhaps the best view of Le Havre is from the high-set **fort** at Ste-Adresse, a suburb to the northwest,

which housed the Belgian government in exile during World War I.

[i] Place de l'Hôtel de Ville

Leave Le Havre on the N15 as for Rouen. Turn right for Trouville on the D40, then go straight on along the D29 and D28. Follow the D28 left as for Anquetierville, but bear right to avoid the village. Turn left at the T-junction for Caudebec.

Caudebec-en-Caux, Normandy

5 Just downstream from the Pont de Brotonne suspension bridge which soars over the Seine, Caudebec is ideally situated to show off the commercial life of the river, to and from the container port at Rouen. The **Musée de la Marine de Seine** covers the history of river boats and river traffic.

Look for the remarkable Church of **Notre Dame** in 15th- and 16th-century Flamboyant Gothic style. It has a lovely fretted roof and a west frontage like lacework in stone, with 300 now heavily weathered figures of saints, prophets, musicians and gentlefolk of the town.

A stunning memorial beside the main road commemorates the Caudebec-built Latham seaplane which was lost in 1928 during a rescue mission in the Arctic. Roald Amundsen discoverer of the South Pole, was one of the crew.

[i] Quai Guilbaud

Leave Caudebec on the D982 then turn left to cross the Pont de Brotonne. Go right on the D65, left on the D40, then bear left to La Haye-de-Routot.

FOR HISTORY BUFFS

On Dieppe seafront, look for the memorial to the disastrous raid of August 1942, by a force of mostly Canadian and Scottish troops. The bitter lessons learned from its failure were put into practice on D-Day. Appropriately, Canadians liberated Dieppe in 1944.

4 In June 1940, while most of the British troops in France were being evacuated from Dunkirque, the 51st Highland Division was ordered to pull back to Le Havre. In this sacrificial manoeuvre, which helped to divert 10 German divisions, the Highlanders fought until their ammunition was exhausted, and thousands had to surrender at St Valéry-en-Caux. A granite memorial on a hillside at St Valéry commemorates the event, and the town is twinned with Inverness, the Highland capital.

The calm of Honfleur harbour belies the town's turbulent past

La-Haye-de-Routot, Normandy

6 This fascinating village lies in farmland on the edge of the Fôret de Brotonne. La Haye's **Four à Pain** is a restored 19th-century brick-built bakehouse, run as a working museum turning out mouth-watering loaves. The **Musée du Sabotier** is a workshop museum devoted to clogs (sabots).

In early summer, look for the 15m (50-foot) pyramid of wood which, on the morning of 16 July, is set alight to create the **Feu de St Clair**, an old pagan ritual taken over by the Christian church. Opposite the Four à Pain, a half-timbered cottage features a wall-niche model of the Feu de St Clair.

From the **Café des Ifs** (Yew-tree Café), marked walking routes radiate through the village and the forest.

Leave La Haye for Routot. Go left, then right, at stops signs, then continue through Bourneville as for Quillebeuf. Go left on the D95 to Ste Opportune and straight on at crossroads following the 'Réserve de Faune' sign. Hairpin right at the T-junction. Turn left at the 3.5t sign, then left at the T-junction. Follow Honfleur signs uphill to the view indicator.

Marais Vernier, Normandy

7 Bounded by an amphitheatre of wooded hills, this area was once marshland flooded by the Seine (*marais* means marsh). After vague earlier reclamation efforts, it was at the beginning of the 17th century that Dutch workers dug channels to drain the southern part of the marsh. They are still recalled in the name of the **Digue des Hollandais** (the Dutchmen's Dyke) alongside the **D103**. North of that road, the work was tackled only in 1947.

Now the Marais Vernier is mostly lush grazing land for Camargue horses and Highland cattle. Some pockets of boggy ground remain, and there are central scrubby woodlands. In spring, pink and white blossom embellishes the surrounding farmland. **La Grande Mare** is the lake to which most of the drainage water flows, on its way eventually to the Seine.

After the view indicator, go right on the D100 to St Samson then left past the church on the D39. Bear right to the give-way sign then left at the T-junction on the N178. Go first right and follow the signs to Honfleur.

Honfleur, Normandy

8 To all its other attractions, Honfleur adds the lovely old slate-roofed houses overlooking the sheltered harbour of the **Vieux Bassin** and, near by, some splendid survivals like the **Grenier à Sel** (salt stores) in the Rue de la Ville.

Erik Satie, the composer, was born in this fishing town. So was the artist Eugène Boudin, still admired for his skyscapes and his ability to 'paint the wind'. His work is featured in the **museum** which bears his name.

Another **museum** has 12 rooms richly furnished in traditional Norman style and offers visits to the old town prison. The **Musée de la Marine** is lavishly stocked with ship models and other *memorabilia* of the sea.

Honfleur commemorates Samuel de Champlain. It was from here, on eight great voyages between 1603 and 1620, that he explored Canada, claimed it for France and founded the city of Quebec.

⌐ Place Boudin

Leave Honfleur by the Rue de la République as for Pont-l'Evêque, then go left as for Tancarville on the D17. Turn right on to the N175 then left on the D534 to Cormeilles. Leave Cormeilles on the D810, continue into Lieurey and follow the D137 to Pont-Authou. Go right on the D130 then left on the D39 to Le Bec-Hellouin.

SCENIC ROUTES

Soon after Ste Opportune, a magnificent view opens up of the farms, thatched cottages and waterways of the Marais Vernier. Later, you can look back on it from a viewpoint on the circling ridge.

After Bellencombre, between Rouen and Dieppe, the **D154** runs through a classic French rural landscape with rustic buildings in a valley floor, fishponds and cattle grazing.

RECOMMENDED WALKS

8 Two walks, waymarked in green and red, head out from the centre of **St Samson** along the wooded ridgetop overlooking the Marais Vernier. For a different view, make for the **Phare de la Roque**, where an old river lighthouse provides a splendid viewpoint over the Seine.

Le Bec-Hellouin, Normandy

9 This is a lovely hillside village, massed with flowers, including rosebeds by the timbered houses on the square. Many old buildings survive here, from the tiny red-tiled wash-house by a fast-flowing stream to the stalwart ruins of what was once a powerful **abbey** going back to 1040. It has a great reputation as a centre of theological learning, and three of its 'sons' became archbishops of Canterbury – Lanfranc in 1070, Anselm in 1093 and Theobald in 1138. A **motor museum** occupies the parkland of the old abbey church. It displays luxury, sports and racing cars from 1920 onwards, including seven Bugattis.

*Continue on the **D39** then go left on the **N138**. At the stop sign, go straight ahead on the **D3** as for Rouen, through Moulineaux. Turn right at traffic lights as for Elbeuf, and right over the level crossing. Go sharp left on the **N238** and follow the signs to Rouen.*

remarkable feature of the building is the tall, slim tapering steeple added in the 19th century. Built entirely of fretted cast iron, it arrows towards the sky. There are museums here devoted to wrought ironwork (**Musée Le-Seq-des-Tournelles**), and the novelist Gustave Flaubert (in the suburb of Croisset). And there is also a **wax museum** devoted to Jeanne d'Arc (Joan of Arc). After Rouen was lost to the English in the Hundred Years' War, it was here than Joan was brought as a prisoner and subjected to a shameful trial. Its aftermath was even more despicable when, her life having been previously spared, she was burned at the stake in the old marketplace. She was canonised in 1920. The **Musée des Beaux-Arts** has a good collection of 17th- to 20th-century French paintings.

[i] Place de la Cathédrale

*Leave Rouen on the **N28** then go left on the **D928**, left on the **D151** to Bellencombre and left again on the **D154** to Dieppe.*

Rouen, Normandy

10 The glory of the historic capital of Normandy is the magnificent Gothic **Cathedral of Notre-Dame** (recently cleaned) in the midst of a splendid 'old town' carefully restored after the devastation of World War II. Rouen's tourist office, for instance, occupies a very attractive Renaissance building, once the headquarters of the tax collector.

Architects and artists of many different eras – mainly 13th- to 16th-centuries – contributed to the appearance of the cathedral in its doorways, towers, tombs, side chapels and stained-glass windows. From a distance, though, the most

The magnificence of the 15th-century Church of St-Ouen, in Rouen. The central tower of this Gothic masterpiece has often been referred to as the 'Crown of Normandy'

BACK TO NATURE

7 Where the main route turns sharp right after Ste Opportune, bear left and in about 0.8km (½-mile) watch for the 'Reserve de Faune' car park. A steeply stepped viewing tower overlooks the nature reserve around the Grande Mare. You will often see mallards, coots, grebes, teal, pochard and tufted duck on the lake itself or in the reed beds and drainage channels round it. Grey herons and Cetti's warblers are present but more secretive.

SPECIAL TO...

7 Upper Normandy is famed for apples and cider. Where the route goes straight on at Ste Opportune, turn left for the **Maison de la Pomme** ('house of the apple') at Bourneville. Displays and a video presentation illustrate the cultivation of the apple and its use in cider and the famous Calvados brandy.

10 Roadside barriers along the D132 and N238, a grandstand and a starting grid are part of the **Rouen-les-Essarts** motor racing circuit. Fangio was the French Grand Prix winner here in 1957, while the American Dan Gurney won in 1962 and 1964.

FOR CHILDREN

10 After leaving the N138 for the D3 on the way to Rouen, turn right uphill to the **Château de Robert-le-Diable**. There was no such person as Robert the Devil, but this is a genuine old stronghold of the Dukes of Normandy. In a curious mixture, as well as a Viking waxworks display, the castle also features mini-golf and children's games.

3 days – 392km (243 miles)

THE EMERALD COUNTRY

**Rennes • Vitré • Fougères • Mont St-Michel
Mont Dol • St Malo • Dinard • Cap Fréhel
Erquy • Dinan • Tinténiac • Rennes**

Starting from Rennes, the capital of Brittany, this tour is drawn briefly into Normandy to visit Mont St-Michel, the abbey and village whose setting on a fortified tidal island is one of the wonders of Europe. Along the Brittany coastline there are headlands offering walks, abundant birdlife and magnificent views – Pointeau, Grouin, Cap Fréhel, Erquy and the rest. Inland lie historic towns such as Vitré, Fougères and Dinan, while St Malo on the coast has a maritime heritage second to none. Much of the route passes sea-washed cliffs and beaches; the rest runs through eastern Brittany's peaceful rural interior.

A view of Combourg, founded in the 11th century and once home of the writer Chateaubriand

[i] Quai Chateaubriand, Rennes

Leave Rennes as for Fougères on the N12. Go right on the D528 to Liffré and in the town centre turn right for Vitré via La Bouëxière. Enter Vitré on the D857.

Vitré, Brittany

1 In the days when Brittany was separate from France, Vitré was a frontier fortress. Its triangular-plan castle, high above the River Vilaine, houses the **town museum** in three of its towers. A fourth provides an all-encompassing viewpoint. Many medieval and Renaissance buildings are still in use. The **Centre Social**, for instance, occupies a splendid 16th-century mansion with elaborate windows, doors and rooflines. Beautifully restored, the **Rue de la Beaudrairie** was the leatherworkers' quarter.

Walks lead down into the pleasant valley of the Vilaine. On the southern outskirts, in the unlikely setting of an industrial estate, look for the **Musée de l'Abeille Vivante** (Museum of the Living Bee). Here you can see, not only displays on all aspects of bee-keeping, but also five colonies working in glass-sided hives.

[i] Place St Yves

Leave Vitré for 'Fougères par Taillis' on the D179.

Fougères, Brittany

2 The most important feature of this second medieval fortress town is the huge and superb **castle** on a peninsula site all but encircled by the Nançon river. But delay going to the castle itself until you have looked at it from the attractive **Jardin Public** in the high town. Its situation and layout are seen to best effect from the gar-

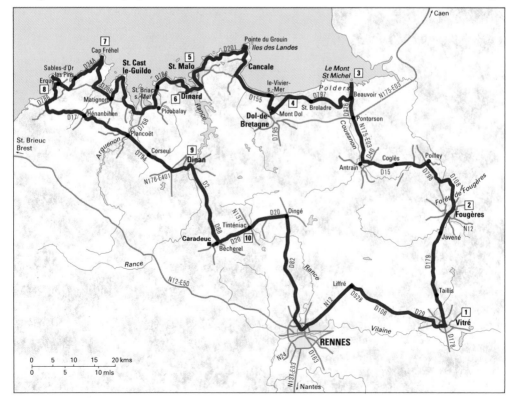

den (despite the background scar of a modern quarry). Below the castle, the low town retains many fine buildings, such as the Flamboyant Gothic **Church of St-Sulpice** and the 17th-century houses round the **Place du Marchaix**. In the high town, one 16th-century house is now the Musée Emmanuel de la Villéon, devoted to the locally-born artist who was one of the last Impressionists.

☐ Place Aristide-Briand

*Leave Fougères as for St Hilaire on the **D177**. Immediately after leaving Fougères bear right along a 'route forestière'. Go left at Carrefour du Père Tacot then straight on across the main road. At Carrefour des Serfilières bear left, taking the fourth exit. Turn right at the stop sign (this is the **D108**) to Parigné. Leave Parigné on the **D108** as for Mellé. At the crossroads go straight on, avoiding the right turn to Mellé. Go right at the stop sign along the **D798**. Turn left on the **D15** through Coglès, left briefly on the **D296** then right on the **D15** again. In Antrain, turn right at the stop sign to Pontorson and continue via Beauvoir to Mont St-Michel.*

Mont St-Michel, Normandy

3 From whatever angle, and from however far away, a first sight of this isolated tidal rock is a stunning experience. It rises from rampart walls and a clustered village to a magnificent abbey whose highest steeple spears the sky.

Reached by a causeway once served by an engaging steam tramway, Mont St-Michel lies among the mazy channels of a vast encircling bay. The lowest towers and medieval sea-wall protect a village of lanes and stairways, where the **Musée Grevin** tells the story of the abbey and the island community in a series of tableaux, and the **Archéoscope** elaborates it with the most modern sound and lighting effects. More prosaically, the **Musée de la Mer** places the island in its marine and tidal context.

Crowning the granite summit, the **abbey** dedicated to the Archangel Michael is a triumph of Romanesque and then Gothic design. Finest of all the abbey's architecture is the range of 13th-century buildings which include the refectory and the splendid cloisters.

☐ Corps de Garde des Bourgeois

*Return to Beauvoir. Turn right for Les Polders, over the bridge and immediately left. Turn left at the first stop sign and right at the second stop sign. Go right on the **D797** through St Broladre, left on the **D82** then right on the **V5** to the village of Mont Dol. Watch for a right turn before the Hôtel du Tertre up a steep and narrow road to Sommet du Mont Dol.*

Mont Dol, Brittany

4 From this hilltop with the marvellous 360-degree view, the first thing to notice is the great area of rich, reclaimed marshland of the

The Druids once worshipped here, and the quicksands of the bay were covered by forest. Mont St-Michel is steeped in magic and history

'polders' – as in the Netherlands – that you crossed after Beauvoir. Beyond them, across the bay, lies Mont St-Michel.

A good display map shows the features of Mont Dol itself – which include the scenes of the legendary struggle between St Michael and the Devil. There is also a **chapel**, an old seaward **signalling tower**, two 19th-century **windmills** and other features that add interest to a stroll among the pines, gorse and rock outcrops of a very popular excursion site.

*Return from the summit. Go right to pass the Hôtel du Tertre. Leave Mont-Dol village on the **D123**. Turn right on the **D155** and follow the signs towards Cancale on the **D76**. Go right on the **VC15** signed 'Cancale le Port'. Leave Cancale following 'St Malo par la Côte' and 'Pointe du Grouin' signs along the **D201**. Go straight on along the **C6** to Pointe du Grouin then return to the **D201** for St Malo.*

St Malo, Brittany

5 An extensive area of sheltered harbours – for fishing, freight and pleasure boats – continues the long maritime tradition of a town which was the historic base for privateers, explorers and the 16th-century Newfoundland fishing fleets.

The heart of St Malo is the granite-built district known as **Intra Muros**,

SPECIAL TO...

5 Cancale, to the east of St Malo, is famous all over France for the high-quality oysters cultivated extensively in the bay. They taste nowhere better than in the town's own seafood restaurants. Watch out for the **Oyster Museum** – everything you ever wanted to know, plus tastings.

6 After St Malo, the main road across the estuary of the Rance is an innovative hydro-electric generating station which uses tidal power in both directions – at the ebb and at the flow. The main road across the estuary runs along the dam, and you can take a guided tour of this splendid pollution-free scheme.

inside the coastal rampart walls. It is almost entirely a reconstruction from the rubble of World War II.

Look here for the historical museum (**Musée de la Ville**) in the 15th-century castle whose great keep and towers command impressive views of the harbour. **Quic-en-Groigne** is a waxwork museum recalling famous St Malo characters and events. There is a well-stocked **aquarium** as well as a **museum of dolls and old-time toys**.

Ferries sail to destinations along the coast, and there is a fast hydro-foil service to Jersey. But the **Château de Solidor** recalls much grander voyages: it houses displays on the Cape Horners.

ⓘ Esplanade St Vincent

*Leave St Malo as for Dinard. Go right on the **D114** and right on the **D266** into Dinard.*

Cap Fréhel, Brittany

7 In the 1920s a company tried to sell off building plots on this dramatic cliff-ringed headland. Fortunately, the misbegotten scheme failed. From the approach road, you may think that the cape ends at the **lighthouse** – completed in 1847, immense care having been paid to the design and the masonry work (visits can be arranged most afternoons) – and the 18th-century fortification known as the **Tour Vauban**. In fact, Fréhel extends much further out to sea. A stroll around the cape, whose majestic rock stacks are a nature reserve, opens up views into precipitous wave-lashed inlets as well as south-eastwards to the spectacularly located **Fort la Latte**, a medieval castle on a headland some 4km (2½ miles) away.

ⓘ Tour Vauban

FOR CHILDREN

4 On the way back from Mont St-Michel, call in at the **Reptilarium** in Beauvoir and let the children see the crocodiles, iguanas, lizards, pythons and boa-constrictors.

8 Sables-d'Or-les-Pins, after Cap Fréhel, caters well for children, with sandy beaches, pony rides, 'bouncy castles' and pedal cars for hire. Look for the little battery-powered electric cars. Kids love to drive these 'grown-up' vehicles on their own.

Dinard, Brittany

6 To a beautiful seafront of bays, promontories, sandy beaches and offshore rocky islets, Dinard adds hotels, restaurants, a casino, a golf club, an equestrian centre and other sporting facilities to maintain its reputation as the premier resort of Brittany's Emerald Coast. The weather is mild, some of the vegetation Mediterranean along the footpaths which wander by the coast.

Fine villas stand in lovely wooded grounds, many of them dating from the turn of the century when British high society favoured Dinard – Edward VII and George V are remembered in street names today.

Dinard attracts many musical, film and artistic events. Every summer evening at dusk there is a *son et lumière* presentation on the seafront **Promenade du Clair de Lune**.

ⓘ Boulevard Féart

*Leave Dinard on the **D786** through St Briac and continue as for St Brieuc. After Port-à-la-Duc turn right to Cap Fréhel on the **D16**.*

Fishing boats moored at Erquy, jewel on Brittany's Emerald Coast. In places along this coast the tide ebbs so far the would-be swimmer may have quite a walk to find it! So check tides first, but enjoy the superb beaches

*Return from Cap Fréhel and turn right on the **D34a** as for St Brieuc. Rejoin the **D786** for Erquy.*

Erquy, Brittany

8 Built round a west-facing bay well sheltered from the northerly wind, Erquy is a pleasant and unpretentious little resort with no trace of obtrusive modern building. The bay is busy with courses in canoeing and windsurfing, and there is a local shellfish fleet.

Take the road to the **Cap d'Erquy** and you will climb to an exhilarating headland where the heath and low-lying scrub are criss-crossed by wandering footpaths. There are cliff edges to be carefully explored, views to the broken water over dangerous offshore reefs, and a splendid if unexpected east-facing beach. You may like to ponder about the ditches and other signs of prehistoric fortifications dated as early as 4,500 years ago.

ⓘ Boulevard de la Mer

Leave Erquy on the D786 as for St Brieuc, then go left for Dinan via Plancoët. Enter Dinan on the N176.

Dinan, Brittany

9 Since its appearance in the Bayeux Tapestry, in the 11th century, Dinan has had a clear line of history, each era marked by its own architectural styles in ramparts, towers, gateways and attractive houses. Streets on the old town bear the names of medieval trade guilds. The **castle** is a fortress of mellow stonework whose unusual 14th-century oval keep houses the local **museum**.

You can admire Dinan from the upper viewing gallery of the 15th-century belfry called the **Tour de l'Horloge** (Clock Tower). Another good viewpoint, although disappointing as an actual garden, is the **Jardin Anglais** (English Garden). It overlooks the valley of the Rance, in which enticing footpaths lead under the stately viaduct over which you approached the town, towards the downstream quays from which river cruises begin.

In the **Church of St Saveur** is buried the heart of chivalrous Bertrand du Guesclin, who fought in single combat in the Place du Champ Clos in 1359 to free his brother from his English captors.

ⓘ Rue de l'Horloge

Leave Dinan for Lanvallay and turn right through Évran on the D2, which becomes the D68 as for Bécherel. In La Barre turn left for Tinténiac on the D20.

Tinténiac, Brittany

10 The church here, with its cupolas and sturdy but ornate stonework, looks slightly puzzling. In fact it is a complete turn-of-the-century rebuilding of an old ecclesiastical site, and well worth a visit.

Tinténiac lies on the Canal d'Ille et Rance. At the Quai de la Donac, a redundant grain store is now the **Musée de l'Outil et des Métiers** (Museum of Tools and Trades), displaying tools and machinery from half-forgotten rural trades.

East of Tinténiac, the **Musée International de la Faune** is a spacious zoo park which also features a scented rose garden and a well-equipped children's playground.

Continue on the D20 to Dingé. Watch for a right turn on the D82 before the Confiserie/Épicerie shop. Return to Rennes.

Rennes – Vitré 43 (27)
Vitré – Fougères 27 (17)
Fougères – Mont St-Michel 53 (33)
Mont St-Michel – Mont Dol 31 (19)
Mont Dol – St Malo 44 (27)
St Malo – Dinard 13 (8)
Dinard – Cap Fréhel 44 (27)
Cap Fréhel – Erquy 20 (12)
Erquy – Dinan 52 (32)
Dinan – Tinténiac 28 (18)
Tinténiac – Rennes 37 (23)

The original walls encircle Dinan, prettiest of medieval towns built on the River Rance, where boats depart for St Malo and Dinard

FOR HISTORY BUFFS

1 The **Musée Automobile de Bretagne** on the N12 after Rennes, tells the story of the French motor industry through such fine exhibits as a 1904 Renault with a basket-work canister for the passengers' canes and parasols. Veteran posters and accessories are also on display.

9 Before Tinténiac, turn right in La Barre, through Bécherel to the **Parc de Caradeuc** and its **château**. The 18th-century lawyer Caradeuc de la Chalotais was devoted to the independence of the Breton parliament. Louis XV imprisoned him without trial. A message he smuggled out of jail, written with a toothpick in ink made from soot, vinegar and sugar, caused a sensation.

BACK TO NATURE

5 On the breezy headland of Pointe du Grouin, telescopes are aimed at the rugged nature reserve of the Ile des Landes. It houses Brittany's biggest colony of cormorants.

7 Cap Fréhel and its offshore rock stacks are busy with gulls, fulmars, cormorants and guillemots, for whom this is France's premier nesting area. In summer the approach to the cape is purple with heather and gold with the flowers of gorse and bird's-foot trefoil.

4 days – 496km (309 miles)

THE CELTIC CONNECTION

The Boat Museum at Douarnenez will intrigue even land-lubbers with its display of craft

Quimper • Pointe du Raz • Douarnenez • Morgat
Camaret-sur-Mer • Landévennec • Brest • St Thégonnec
Ménez-Meur • Monts d'Arrée • Huelgoat • Quimper

Quimper is the capital of old Cornouaille, and the similarity of that name with Britain's Cornwall is significant. This is Celtic country, as you will see from the distinctive place-names. The Breton language is still spoken by more than half a million people, giving western Brittany the position in France which Wales occupies in the United Kingdom. In Breton, the Armor is the coastal region, where the early part of the tour follows beaches, peninsulas and unexpectedly beautiful bays and estuaries around the Rade de Brest. The Argoat lies inland – woods, moorlands and rocky hills. Many of the places visited are in the extensive and well-run Armorique Regional Nature Park.

SCENIC ROUTES

The Ménez-Hom road, **D83**, climbs to one of the finest viewpoints in Brittany.
  After Camaret, the **D355** rounds a peninsula with a beautiful outlook over the roadstead of Brest. Later, look for the view from the suspension bridge that takes the **D791** over the River Aulne.
  Around St Rivoal, the **D342** is a lane set in wooded combes.

ⓘ Place de la Résistance, Quimper

Leave Quimper on the D785 as for Pont l'Abbé, then through Pluguffan and follow the D40 through Pouldreuzic to Penhors. Bear right as for Plozévet, then left, and follow signs to Pors-Poulhan. Climb from the harbour, then turn sharp left following 'Allée Couverte' sign. Turn left at two stop signs. In Audierne, look for 'Pointe du Raz' signs and take the D784 to Pointe du Raz.

Pointe du Raz, Brittany

1 One of Brittany's classic headlands plays host to a commercial square of souvenir shops and cafés. A wasteland of bare, trodden earth and rock leads beyond the coastguard station to the actual point, and then the atmosphere changes. No careless exploitation can damage the magnificent seaward views. Pointe du Raz looks over a savage strait where jagged rocks, the last topped with a lighthouse, march towards the weird outline of the Ile de Sein – something like a Pacific atoll moved to the windswept Atlantic edge. Guides escort parties of visitors round the cliff paths, and with or without them it is easy to appreciate why the statue near the point is to *Notre-Dame des Naufragés* – Our Lady of the Shipwrecked. Knowing that Sein was once the mainland coast makes the legend of the drowned city of Ys, out in the Bay of Douarnenez, something to ponder.

Return from Pointe du Raz and turn left for Douarnenez par le CD7 on the V8 and D7. On the approach to Douarnenez, follow 'Autres Directions' and 'Toutes Directions' signs at roundabouts, then turn left on the D765 and left to Centre-Ville.

Douarnenez, Brittany

2 This town , which has no obvious centre, is the fifth busiest fishing port in France. The narrow river inlet of Port-Rhu slices deep into Douarnenez, but the main harbour of Rosmeur is on the east side of the peninsula which it helps to form. There are early morning fish auctions here, and cruise boats visit the cliffs, inlets and grottoes of the bay. Town beaches are scattered in some unexpected locations, and a good coastal

---

The Druids sent their dead for burial on a treeless isle near Pointe du Raz, noted for its wild and unforgiving seas

walk leads from Rosmeur along the Sentier des Plomarc'hs. **Le Port-Musée** opened in 1993. A tidal wall has been built to dam a basin 2km long at Port Rhu. Visitors can explore dozens of boats and admire craftsmen rebuilding a 19th-century clipper. This floating museum is unique in France.

ⓘ Rue du Docteur Mével

*Leave Douarnenez as for Brest on the **D7**, then turn left on the **D107** to Plonévez-Porzay. Watch for the left turn on to the **D63**, then take the **D47** through Plomodiern and left to Ste Marie. Turn left on the **D887**, right to the Ménez-Hom summit and return to the **D887**. Follow 'Morgat' signs through Crozon, watching for an unexpected left turn. In Morgat, follow 'Maison des Minéraux' signs towards St Hernot.*

Morgat, Brittany

3 This resort on the sheltered side of Douarnenez Bay is well equipped for watersports and enjoys good, extensive beaches with coastal promenades. There are daily summer cruises to the marine caverns of La Chambre du Diable (the Devil's Chamber), La Cheminée des Cormorans (the Cormorants' Chimney) and l'Autel (Altar Grotto).

South of Morgat, just before the village of St Hernot, the **Maison des Minéraux** houses a fascinating array of crystals, fossils and semi-precious stones such as agates and amethysts, in their natural state as well as cut and polished. Make sure you see the fluorescent cabinet where many of them gleam in exotic colours.

ⓘ Boulevard de la Plage

*After the Maison des Minéraux, bear right as for Kerdreux then almost immediately right at crossroads. Go straight on at the stop sign, follow 'Crozon' signs, then turn right at a T-junction (**D308**) into Crozon. At the roundabout, take the third exit along the **D8** to Camaret.*

Camaret-sur-Mer, Brittany

4 Set on a stunning peninsula, Camaret is a resort surrounded by beaches facing in different directions. A substantial crayfish fleet is based here, and some discarded fishing boats are beached as rotting hulks. Lobster is also fished locally, so the seafood restaurants, naturally, are well and freshly stocked.

Vauban, the great 17th-century military architect, fortified Camaret. The local history museum in the **Tour Vauban** recalls events such as the British and Dutch landing of 1694, which was furiously and famously repulsed.

The prehistoric standing stones of **Lagatjar** retain their strict straight-line alignment and, to the south, the **Pointe de Penhir** is a majestic clifftop viewpoint with dramatic natural rock formations.

ⓘ Quai Kléber

*Leave Camaret on the **D355** to Pointe des Espagnols and through Roscanvel. At a roundabout take the **D55** to Lanvéoc, then the **D63** as for Brest. At the brow of a hill at Maison Blanche, watch for a left turn at crossroads. Turn right at the crossroads at a stop sign. At the give-way sign, turn left on the **D60** to Landévennec.*

FOR HISTORY BUFFS

1 The **Alée Couverte**, at Pors-Poulhan, is a reconstructed burial chamber. Great rock slabs form the walls and others are laid across them as the roof.

On the return route to Quimper, the **Maison des Pilhaouerien** in Loqueffret recalls the 'rag and bone' families who, until the 1950s, toured the district with their donkey carts. After Châteauneuf, the rose castle in the beautiful park of **Trevarez** was one of the last built in France. During World War II it was a rest centre for the German Navy, until gutted in an RAF bombing raid. History, art and floral exhibitions are held here.

BACK TO NATURE

2 Turn left off the **D7** for the Réserve Ornithologique on the seabird cliffs of Cap Sizun. This was the first bird reserve in France with a definite educational programme. The movements and associations of whole gull colonies are followed by computer.

4 Well out of reach of any road approach, the dramatic rock stacks of the **Tas des Pois** – the Pile of Peas – can be visited on the *Sirène IV*, which sails from Camaret. Their cliffs teem with gulls, fulmars, cormorants, guillemots and storm petrels.

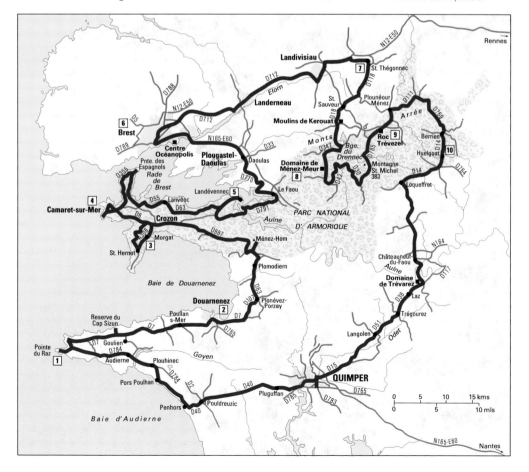

6 Océanopolis, in Brest, makes great efforts to hold children's interest. As well as the extensive aquariums there is a 'touch pool', where children can get the feel of little sea creatures, such as starfish and shellfish. The *bassin de navigation* lets them steer radio-controlled model boats, and on the bridge they are able to try out full-scale modern ship controls.

7 The **Pont Hir** walk at St Thégonnec follows a way-marked route across rural landscapes to an eerie tunnel taking the River Coatoulsac'h through a railway embankment. Another feature of the walk is a wood where you may easily surprise roe deer.

9 Ferme St-Michel is an access point to the footpaths shown in the Yeun Elez leaflet published by the Parc d'Armorique. One of them climbs the open moorland to Mont St-Michel and circles back by the lovely countryside around St Rivoal.

Landévennec, Brittany

5 Occupying an attractive peninsula where the estuaries of the Aulne and the Faou combine, Landévennec is a village in which a glance down almost any lane offers a view of the water. Brittany's oldest **abbey** was founded here in 485 by the Welsh missionary St Gwennolé. It crumbled away after the Revolution. The ruins of the final Romanesque buildings are approached by a palm-tree avenue. Exhibitions explain the history of the abbey itself, and also how Brittany rose from the wreckage of the Roman Empire, colonised in Gwennolé's time by Celts driven from Britain by the Anglo-Saxon invasions.

Return along the D60 to the D791 and turn left. In Le Faou go left as for Hanvec, over a bridge and left – at first along the riverside – through Lanvoy. Turn left at a T-junction and through Daoulas on the D770. Follow signs for Brest on the N165.

Brest, Brittany

6 For almost 2,000 years, the sea has been Brest's delight and its despair. From Roman times its great roadstead – perhaps the most beautiful in Europe, with its bays, peninsulas and feeder rivers – has been a naval base. Such places are vulnerable in time of conflict. Brest came out of World War II shattered by bombing raids. Even the street plan was redrawn, let alone the buildings. This remains the home

Left: A carved detail at Sainte-Marie-du-Ménez-Hom. Below: The unusual spire at Esquibien

of many capital ships. Only French citizens, though, may visit the base itself. Foreigners can take advantage of harbour cruises, and the **Musée de la Marine**, repository of Brest's tumultuous history, housed in the medieval **castle**, is open to all. Excellent parks include the **Vallon du Stangalard**, with its lawns, lakes, tree-shaded walks and **Conservatoire Botanique**, preserving hundreds of endangered plant species. One of Brest's newest attractions is **Océanopolis**, a complex of aquariums (the largest in Europe), marine exhibitions and pictures beamed from weather satellites in space.

ⓘ Place de la Liberté

Leave Brest for Landerneau on the D712. Follow the 'Centre Ville' sign at a roundabout in Landerneau. Continue to Landivisiau, still on the D712, then as for Morlaix on to the N12. Take the exit for St Thégonnec.

St Thégonnec, Brittany

7 In their parish closes, Breton villages vied for glory with their neighbours. At St Thégonnec, the 16th- to 18th-century masonry work of the **church** is far more elaborate than is justified by the status of the little place. The churchyard gateway and the funeral chapel are similarly ornate, and the calvary of 1610, its clustered figures telling the story of the Passion, was one of the last in the exuberant Breton style. Inside the church, look for the intricately carved pulpit of 1683.

ⓘ Rue de la Gare

Leave St Thégonnec as for Sizun on the D118, then the D18. After

St Sauveur, carry straight on at the crossroads at Croas-Cabellec, following '5 Sizun' sign. After a double-bend sign, take the first left, then go straight on at the stop sign as for Goas ar Vern. Follow the 'Barrage du Drennec' sign, then continue to St Cadou. Turn right on the **D30**, left on the **D130** as for St Eloy, and watch for a left turn to Ménez-Meur.

Ménez-Meur

8 The wooded surroundings of this estate conceal a series of open grazing areas where you can admire red, Sika and fallow deer, wild boars, several breeds of horses, and specialities such as Highland cattle and Swaledale sheep. Ménez-Meur is approached along a beautiful avenue, where interlocking trees arch over from mossy walls. There are three waymarked trails with animal, forest and general countryside themes, and the estate is famous for its displays, fairs and festivals celebrating the sturdy Breton horse.

Continue to St Rivoal on the D30, then turn left on the D785.

Monts d'Arrée, Brittany

9 After Ferme St-Michel, now a showplace for modern Breton artists and craftworkers, the **D785** runs along the upper reaches of the Monts d'Arrée, where the **Parc d'Armorique** opens out in a world of moorland summits. **Mont St-Michel** is one of the highest points, at 383m (1,256 feet). From it, a superb all-round view gives a slightly perplexing impression of a completely circular horizon. **Le Roc Trévezel**, further along the road, is a viewpoint granite tor.

Océanopolis offers children and adults alike close encounters with the mysteries of undersea life

Continue on the D785 to Plounéour-Ménez. Turn right on the D111, right on the D769 and follow signs to Huelgoat, turning right on the D14 in Berrien.

Huelgoat, Brittany

10 Built beside a peaceful lake, this is an inland resort with two contrasting characters. The town is bright and open, with lakeside walks, pedalo hire and fishing. Go to the bridge over the lake's outflow, and you look immediately into a more dramatic world. From a chaos of jumbled rocks, footpaths wander through the most beautiful forest in Brittany. Beech, oak and conifers clothe a landscape of leafy glades, tumbling streams and mysterious Celtic stones, where the legends of King Arthur, Merlin and the Druids survive.

☐ Place Aristide-Briand

Leave Huelgoat for Loqueffret on the D14. Turn sharp left on the D36 through Châteauneuf. Follow 'Domaine de Trévarez' signs, then continue on the D36 to Trégourez. Turn right on the D51 and return to Quimper.

Quimper – Pointe du Raz 60 (37)
Pointe du Raz – Douarnenez 41 (26)
Douarnenez – Morgat 53 (33)
Morgat – Camaret-sur-Mer 24 (15)
Camaret-sur-Mer – Landévennec 48 (30)
Landévennec – Brest 63 (39)
Brest – St Thégonnec 51 (32)
St Thégonnec – Ménez-Meur 28 (17)
Ménez-Meur – Monts d'Arrée 32 (20)
Monts d'Arrée – Huelgoat 29 (18)
Huelgoat – Quimper 67 (42)

SPECIAL TO...

Breton is a Celtic language, related to Cornish and Welsh, which has survived consistent attempts to crush it by French governments of the past. In the 20th century there has been a growing movement to preserve and promote its use, and secondary schools now offer Breton courses to thousands of pupils.

9 At the stop sign after Croas-Cabellec, turn left for the restored hamlet of **Les Moulins de Kerouat**, with its two antique watermills. Lessons are sometimes given on how to bake your own country-style bread. There is also the miller's home with its traditional furniture and an exhibition relating the history of the village through the lives of five generations of millers.

10 The **Moulin du Chaos**, in Huelgoat, is an old mill housing exhibits of archaeology, geology, flora and fauna.

THE LOIRE & CENTRAL FRANCE

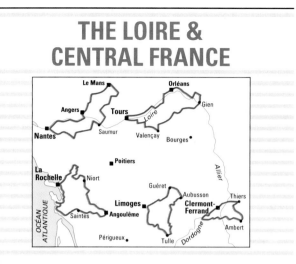

As it sweeps from the mountain country of the Central, by the Valley of the Loire and the Cognac vineyards, to the coastline and islands around La Rochelle, this area illustrates the great variety of landscape in France, even in places at identical latitudes.

Not far from the industrial city of Clermont-Ferrand you will be driving through a country of ancient volcanoes, with high cattle pastures closed till the clearance of winter snows. In the valleys of the Loire and its principal tributaries you will encounter many of France's most magnificent castles. Some rose as fortresses in medieval times. Others were built later as the lavishly furnished homes of unimaginably wealthy aristocrats.

The 'conspicuous consumption' they represented was one of the elements which helped to foment the French Revolution. Fortunately, the major castles such as Chenonceau and Blois survive as grandly restored properties of the state.

Land use here is as varied as landscape. At high levels you will find windy, upland grazings and conifer plantings, and there is a chance of snow flurries even in late spring. Lower down lie arable and pastoral farms, but the finest ground, especially near Tours and along the valley of the River Charente, is reserved for vineyards. This is the country of Vouvray, Côtes d'Auvergne, Pays Nantais, Cognac and Rosé d'Anjou wines.

The two substantial islands of Ré and Oléron are microcosmic worlds of their own. Rimmed by beautiful beaches and family holiday resorts, with fine climates tempered by the Atlantic breezes, they have a strong off-season life. Farms, vines and oyster beds all play their part, and the little towns enjoy intriguing histories. Ré, for instance, was the last place on metropolitan French soil seen by criminals shipped to Devil's Island.

As in most of France, the road network is extensive. In some places, for instance approaching Angoulême on the La Rochelle tour in the attractive valley of the Charente, you should keep a close watch on the route instructions.

Recently, ferries to the major islands have been replaced. The drive to Ré is notable for the splendidly proportioned toll bridge from the mainland. This is how an island should be approached, on a dramatic, high-level curve.

Wines are yours for the tasting in individual growers' caves. Cuisine changes with the landscape and the weather. Many regional specialities are available in the Auvergne, where meals are often of a more robust, rural style than in the resort towns of the warmer coast.

The skyline of Clermont-Ferrand, which lies beneath the volcanic region of Monts Dômes, is dominated by the magnificent Gothic cathedral which dates from 1248

Clermont-Ferrand

A great industrial centre in the heart of France, Clermont-Ferrand is the world headquarters of the Michelin tyre company. The city is dominated by its Gothic cathedral, but not far from it there stands another church of equal if not greater architectural merit, Notre-Dame-du-Port. The Musée des Beaux-Arts is housed in a wonderful old restored building. The Musée Bargoin recalls the victory of Vercingetorix and the Gauls over the legions of Julius Caesar, on the plateau of Gergovia near by.

Limoges

Limoges is the city of porcelain. Its Musée National Adrien-Dubouché shows porcelain in all its colour, elegance and stages of prepara-

The Tour St Nicolas and the Tour de la Chaîne have guarded the entrance to the harbour of La Rochelle since the 14th century

tion. Enamelware is one of the specialities of the Musée Municipal. As in Clermont-Ferrand, there are attractive individual houses, churches and public buildings in Limoges, as well as gardens around the old Roman arena and overlooking the River Vézère.

La Rochelle

La Rochelle carefully guards its waterfront. Le Gabut is an engaging modern harbourside development whose colour-washed wooden buildings, with stairs and gangways, have a maritime air. The older houses have an agreeably regular appearance, forced on the builders by strict town-planning laws.

Museums here include one of mechanical toys, another of model ships, planes and railways, a third devoted to a century and a half of yacht racing. The maritime collection occupies a sturdy harbour-entrance tower, and there is a weathership museum and a major modern aquarium.

Nantes

Very much a river city, Nantes includes two channels of the Loire, three of its tributaries and, for good measure, a canal. The city centre has just undergone a major face-lift and now has an efficient modern tram newtork. Look for the moated castle of the dukes of Brittany, the cathedral, begun in 1434, the old quarters and the half-dozen parks, including a riverside Japanese garden. A planetarium complements the nearby museum devoted to the life and works of the science fiction pioneer Jules Verne.

Tours

If you want to hear perfect spoken French, go to Tours. The capital of Touraine is spacious and unhurried, with elegant public buildings and a beautiful cathedral. There are promenades on rivers – the Loire and the Cher. The Château-Royal houses historical museums. The Musée des Beaux-Arts is in archbishops' old palace. Archaeology, and medieval and Renaissance art are the concern of the Musée Archéologique in the superb 16th-century mansion called the Hôtel Gouin. Other museums and studios cover the wines of Touraine, dolls, gemstones and enamelwork, military transport, the story of journeymen-craftsmen and the handloom weaving of silk.

LAND OF QUIET VOLCANOES

**Clermont-Ferrand • Royat • Puy de Dôme • Col de Guéry
La Bourboule • Le Mont-Dore • Besse-en-Chandesse
St-Nectaire • Ambert • Moulin Richard-de-Bas
Thiers • Clermont-Ferrand**

Unlike many industrial cities, Clermont-Ferrand has the advantage of backing immediately on to hill country, and these are no ordinary hills. They are the relics of huge volcanic convulsions thousands of years ago. Now green and wooded, they provide space in the valleys for holiday resorts, including spas whose thermal waters were famous in Roman times. The area's 20 mineral springs supply the nation with bottled water. Look for energetic walks with all-encompassing hilltop views, for the only ski museum in France, for the home of French cutlery and for a majestic papermill where the techniques of the 14th century are still applied today.

SPECIAL TO...

1 Turn left off the **D941c** to follow the **D5** to the motor racing circuit of Charade. It hosts important national races, but lost Grand Prix status some years ago. Jim Clark won the first French Grand Prix run on the circuit in 1965.

2 Just before the junction with the **D941a**, the **Village Auvergnat** is a recently-built centre where many of the specialities of the region are on sale, including honey, jams, liqueurs, the well-known local cheese and Côtes d'Auvergne wines.

BACK TO NATURE

2 At 1,465m (4,085 feet) the Puy de Dôme is the highest of 80 extinct volcanoes in the district. It dominates a characteristic volcanic landscape. Some hills retain their hollow crater shapes; others are the old volcanic cores. Flowers and butterflies are abundant, and look for red kites and honey buzzards in the skies above.

The Château Meillant near Clermont-Ferrand displays an individuality characteristic of the region

[i] Boulevard Gergovia, Clermont-Ferrand

Leave Clermont-Ferrand on the N89 as for Tulle. Go right on the D767 then right on the D941c to Royat.

Royat, Auvergne

1 Not in the least overshadowed by its great industrial neighbour Clermont-Ferrand, Royat is a perfect example of a French spa which has moved with the times. Starting with the Romans, people have been coming to drink the mineral waters and relax in thermal baths here for 2,000 years, but its development as a fashionable spa dates from the 19th century. Today everything is up to date, with attractive modern buildings. To the traditional 'cures' Royat has added keep-fit regimes and courses for anyone who wants to give up smoking.

Its central area is crammed into a narrow river valley where there is still room for parks and open spaces as well as for the **Etablissement Thermal** (Thermal Establishment) and the inevitable casino. Among the alleyways of the upper town, look for the **Maison du Passé** (House of the Past), the **museum** of old Royat, and for the **Taillerie**, where rock crystals and gemstones are cut and polished.

[i] Place Allard

Leave Royat on the D68. Go left on the D941a and immediately right on the D68. Go straight on to join the toll road to the summit of Puy de Dôme. Check for 'ouvert' sign.

Vieux Brioude in summer foliage

Puy de Dôme, Auvergne

2 The toll road to this volcanic summit spirals upwards at an average gradient of 12 per cent (1 in 8.3). It reaches a high-level world apart – Puy de Dôme is a glorious viewpoint, a spectacular hang-gliders' launch area, the site of a Roman temple, dedicated to Mercury and an exhilarating walkers' hill. You may be lucky enough to see colourful hot-air balloons wafting across the lovely Auvergne countryside. The modern world, in the form of an observatory, television mast and souvenir shop, is also present on top. Access to the Puy de Dôme is a fascinating story and many old illustrations are displayed locally. The first car reached the summit in 1913, but in those days the usual way up was by a steam train. The toll road opened only in 1926. On the summit look for the statue of Eugène Renaux. In 1911 his biplane landed safely on the plateau at the end of a prize-winning flight from Paris. The elegant lava and wood buildings covered with copper roofs house a reception and information centre.

Return to the D941a and turn right. Go straight ahead on the D216 then on the D27 and on the D983. Stop at a major car park immediately before the junction with the D80.

Le Mont-Dore has been a favourite spa since Roman times

Col de Guéry, Auvergne

3 This is one of the most dramatic viewpoints in the Auvergne, looking down the precipitous valley between **La Roche Tuilière** and **La Roche Sanadoire**. These two huge rock towers rise from a wooded crater and are the remains of a volcanic eruption something like two millions years ago. Like the Puy de Dôme, they are included in the biggest regional nature park in France, the **Parc des Volcans d'Auvergne** (Regional Nature Park of Auvergne Volcanoes).

Tuilière, as you will see close up later from the **D80**, was the vent of the volcano, whose lava spewed out from the earth's molten core and cooled into the tall, brittle columns exposed today. Sanadoire was part of the cone. But the landscape was shaped by more than just volcanic activity: the valley between the rock towers was ground out by a retreating Ice Age glacier.

Turn right on the D80 to Rochefort-Montagne, then turn left and follow the N89 and D922 to la Bourboule.

RECOMMENDED WALKS

4 Many people visit **Orcival**, to the north of La Bourboule, for its beautiful pilgrimage church. This village in the deep wooded valley of the Sioulot is also an excellent walking centre. Waymarked paths climb through forests, to the crater-lake of Servière, and to the dizzily-balanced Roche Branlante (the Rocking Stone).

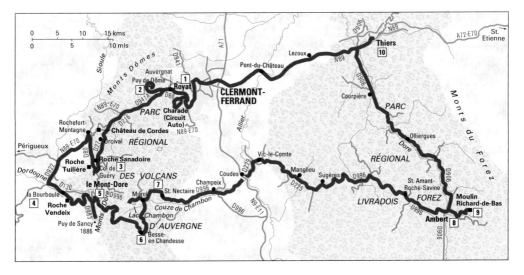

FOR CHILDREN

2 Before the Puy de Dôme toll road, the **Zoo des Dômes** includes an imaginative children's playground. The 'mini-plane' roundabout introduces youngsters to the thrills of hang-gliding without actually launching them into the air.

5 At Le Mont-Dore, the **Parc des Loisirs** offers an exhilarating summer toboggan ride, and boats rush down a series of cascades. A carousel and an Apache fort add to the fun.

BACK TO NATURE

6 On the **Col de la Croix St Robert** look for the roadside wildflowers – violas, vetches, trefoils and many other. The sound of cowbells is a sign that these grassy uplands provide rich summer pasture.

SCENIC ROUTES

The **D27** is a high road through typical Auvergne countryside of cattle farms, woodlands, attractive villages and little valleys. Then the tour enters the magnificent volcanic landscapes around the Roche Sanadoire. The Col de la Croix St Robert road, brightened by splashes of hillside broom, looks to deep valleys and wooded summits. Beyond St Nectaire, the D996 goes through a narrow glen with thickly wooded sides and exposed rock faces. After Vic-le-Comte, it wanders past farms and broadleaved woodlands, conifer plantations and little river valleys, then swoops down to Ambert on the plain.

The pretty spa of La Bourboule is also a thriving winter resort

La Bourboule, Auvergne

4 Two thermal establishments continue the spa traditions of this little valley town where tree-lined streets follow the banks of the upper Dordogne. The mineral waters here contain arsenic – in medicinal, not murderous proportions. La Bourboule is very well supplied with sports facilities, and has many attractions for children, including a model train museum and another devoted to fairytales.

The **Parc Fenestre** is a pleasant wooded area with pathways, a lake and a narrow-gauge railway. It also houses the town station for the cable-car system to the Plateau de Charlannes. At 1,250m (4,100 feet), Charlannes is a place of wide-ranging views, and a ski resort in winter. For a more intimate view of La Bourboule itself, walk up to the granite boulder called **Le Rocher des Fées** (the Fairies' Rock) which overlooks the town from the northwest.

i Place de l'Hôtel de Ville

> *Leave La Bourboule on the D130 to Le Mont-Dore.*

Le Mont-Dore, Auvergne

5 Upstream from La Bourboule, here is another spa resort. Le Mont-Dore is well known for activities as diverse as fishing, mountaineering and amateur classical music. Instrumentalists and singers from all over France gather here to practise, rehearse and perform in concert. The **Promenade des Artistes** is a pleasant walk on the woodland ridge overlooking the town. There are higher attractions here, too: the **Salon du Capuchin** for instance, is not some elegant town-centre hall, but a forest clearing reached by a funicular railway (built in 1898 and now a historic monument) and then a final climb on foot. The superlative high-spot of Le Mont-Dore is up the **D983** as it climbs a steeply wooded valley to the ski runs and chairlifts on the alpine meadows

below the Puy de Sancy. Be ready for a drop in temperature. Take a cable-car and then walk to the summit at 1,885m (6,180 feet), to admire the colossal views from the highest point in the Auvergne.

i Place de l'Hôtel de Ville

> *Return on the D983 from the Puy de Sancy, then right on the road signed 'Besse par Col-Croix St Robert'. Check 'ouvert' sign. Follow the D36 to Besse.*

Besse-en-Chandesse, Auvergne

6 This is an engaging little town which has preserved, in narrow streets and tiny squares, many old houses from the 15th and 16th centuries. Some have connecting doors which allow the townspeople – walking through their neighbours' homes – to reach the church in winter while avoiding the chill open air. The Auvergne has snowy winters, and Besse has created a satellite ski resort called **Super-Besse**. One fascinating place to visit in the old town is a **ski museum**, the first in France. Here, Pierre-André Chauvet has assembled a remarkable collection of skiing *memorabilia*. There are skis and bindings ancient and modern, of many different styles, from France, Switzerland, Norway, Sweden and the Austro-Hungarian empire. Illustrations cover curiosities such as historic Russian army snowploughs, and early events of the pioneering ski club of Besse, founded in 1902.

i Place Docteur-Piper

> *Leave Besse on the D5 to Murol then go right on the D996 to St-Nectaire.*

St-Nectaire, Auvergne

7 One of the most exuberant of the typical Romanesque churches of the Auvergne is the one in this village split into upper and lower parts in the winding and wooded valley of the Courançon. A hundred and more ornamented pillars surround the nave and the choir.

The **Maison du St-Nectaire** allows you the chance to sample the local cheese – St-Nectaire gave its name to a round, nutty-flavoured cheese made in many parts of the Auvergne – as well as the wines and bayberry liqueur special to the district.

St-Nectaire is another spa. There are modern thermal baths, but at the **Cornadore grotto** you can see the naturally warm water welling up. Try the mineral waters at a little pavilion in the parkland at **Les Thermes**.

i Les Thermes

Continue on the D996 to Champeix. Follow signs to Coudes and Vic-le-Comte, then continue on the D225 and D996 (sometimes signed N496) to Ambert.

Ambert, Auvergne

8 Two notable buildings here are the granite church of St John and the curious town hall. Begun in 1471 in Flamboyant Gothic style, and decorated by a master mason obviously enjoying himself, **St-Jean Church** has later additions such as a frisky little Renaissance belfry. Look for the carved coat of arms of Ambert's old trade guilds – saddlers, shoemakers and the rest – and for the optical illusion which makes the interior seem longer than it really is.

The **Hôtel de Ville** (town hall) is entirely circular and arcaded all the way round. It was built in 1820 as the grain market.

In the industrial area, a splendid museum of steam and traction engines, road rollers, tractors and mobile distillation plants is known, thanks to the French passion for acronyms, as **AGRIVAP**. In the centre of town a **museum** of a different kind is devoted to the 'divine cheese' Fourme d'Ambert. Tasting sessions follow the guided tour.

i Place de l'Hôtel de Ville

Leave Ambert on the D57 for Moulin Richard-de-Bas.

Moulin Richard-de-Bas, Auvergne

9 Traditional papermaking is one of the most fascinating industrial processes. This restored 14th-century mill in the valley of the River Laga, which still turns its waterwheel, tells the story of papermaking from ancient Egyptian papyrus via the strict rules of the craft laid down by the Chinese in about AD105, to the Arabs' discovery of its secrets from Chinese soldiers captures in the defence of Samarkand in 751, and on beyond the invention of mechanical printing.

All the traditional processes of crushing linen into the basic pulp, the smoothing, drying and pressing are displayed. There are early manuscripts on show, a gorgeous 18th-century atlas, a mid-19th-century printing press, parchments, vellums and thousands of watermarks.

Richard-de-Bas also produces papers of the highest quality. One speciality, made when the petals of

cornflowers and marigolds from the mill's own gardens are mixed with the pulp, is flowered paper where each sheet is individually patterned.

Return to Ambert and take the D906 then the N89 to Thiers.

Thiers, Auvergne

10 France's 'capital of cutlery' is an attractive town with its red roofs rising on a hillside from a bend on the River Durolle. Many fine medieval and later half-timbered houses survive along the steep streets of the old quarter.

The museum and workshop of **La Maison de Couteliers** display an astonishing variety of knives, scissors, table settings and hallmarks. There are workshops all over the town where modern craftsmen and designers keep up the ancient tradition. Down on the Durolle, several little waterfalls used to provide power for the cutlery factories. Look for the **Creux d'Enfer**, much less forbidding than its name – the 'Drop to Hell' – suggests.

i Place du Pirou

Return from Thiers on the N89 and continue to Clermont-Ferrand.

Clermont-Ferrand – Royat 18 (11)
Royat – Puy de Dôme 11 (7)
Puy de Dôme – Col de Guéry 30 (19)
Col de Guéry – La Bourboule 28 (19)
La Bourboule – Le Mont-Dore 13 (8)
Le Mont-Dore – Besse 26 (16)
Besse – St-Nectaire 17 (11)
St-Nectaire – Ambert 83 (52)
Ambert – Moulin Richard-de-Bas 5 (3)
Moulin Richard-de-Bas – Thiers 57 (35)
Thiers – Clermont-Ferrand 46 (29)

FOR HISTORY BUFFS

8 A Scottish-Auvergne connection exists in the 16th-century **Sainte-Chapelle** at Vic-le-Comte, built for Jean (or John) Stuart, a descendant of the Scottish royal family and regent of Scotland during James V's minority. He was Duke of Albany and Comte d'Auvergne. The chapel features an unexpectedly light interior and a splendid balustraded gallery with statues of the Apostles. There are also remains of the castle of the Comtes d'Auvergne.

RECOMMENDED WALKS

10 Much of this tour is in the Livradois-Forez regional nature park. There are dozens of official footpaths here, one starting from the Salle Polyvalente in Olliergues on the D906 between Ambert and Thiers. Taking about three hours, it explores the farmlands, woods, old village churches and rural lanes above the valley of the Dore.

A papermaker at work in Moulin Richard-de-Bas where thousands of visitors a year can see how this simple necessity is produced

3/4 days – 411km (255 miles)

LIMOUSIN: HEARTLAND OF FRANCE

Limoges • Ségur-le-Château • Pompadour • Uzerche
Tulle • Gimel-les-Cascades • Les Monédières • Treignac
Lac de Vassivière • Aubusson • Guéret • Limoges

Porcelain from Limoges and tapestries from Aubusson are two of the main features of a tour which also includes a district enraptured with the horse; its breeding, its training and its performance in all kinds of competitions. Historic towns are matched by fine recreational facilities, especially on and around two beautiful wooded reservoirs. Limoges, the starting-point, has been an industrial centre for centuries and is still expanding.

St Yrieix, where the discovery of kaolin in the 1760s transformed the region's fortunes

[i] Boulevard Fleurus, Limoges

Leave Limoges on the D704 to St Yrieix, then take the D18, which becomes the D6, to Ségur-le-Château.

Ségur-le-Château, Limousin

1 You may be mystified by the number of rivers at Ségur. In fact, they are all the Auvézère, which double loops through a narrow, winding valley. The tiny medieval town has long since lost its influential position, but once-aristocratic **mansions** still fight off the years. Riverside **mills** remain in place, the ruined 12th-century **castle** broods absent-mindedly on its hilltop, and in summer the 15th-century **Tour St Laurent** shows off embroidery, lace, dolls and other souvenirs of days gone by.

Continue on the D6, then take the D7 to Pompadour.

Pompadour, Limousin

2 In the 18th century this was the estate of the Marquise de Pompadour, favourite of Louis XV. Since 1872 it has been the home of the **French National Stud Farm**, devoted principally to the breeding of Anglo-Arab horses. The stallions are stabled in the Puy Marmont; **La Jumenterie de la Rivière** is the home of the mares and their foals. Flat and cross-country races, show-jumping and carriage-driving events are held regularly.

[i] Château de Pompadour

FOR HISTORY BUFFS

1 Turn right at the entrance to St Yrieix on the way from Limoges to Ségur-le-Château, for the unobtrusive but well-stocked **Musée de la Porcelaine** at the Les Palloux china factory. Limoges, Meissen, Delft, Chinese and Japanese figures, vases and dinner services are all on display. It was the kaolin deposits of St Yrieix which launched the porcelain industry at Limoges.
On the return route to Limoges, **La Tour de Zizim** in **Bourganeuf** was the home (or, in some versions of the story, the prison) of an exiled 15th-century Ottoman prince who equipped it with Turkish baths and even a harem. It is now a museum with less glamorous exhibits.

SPECIAL TO...

1 Ségur-le-Château is noted for the craft of working with chestnut wood. By the riverside here look for the little hut with a display illustrating the work of the feuillardiers – the woodcutters who supplied the chestnut stakes for the plants in the Périgord vineyards. Dozens of craftsmen in the district still work with chestnut wood.

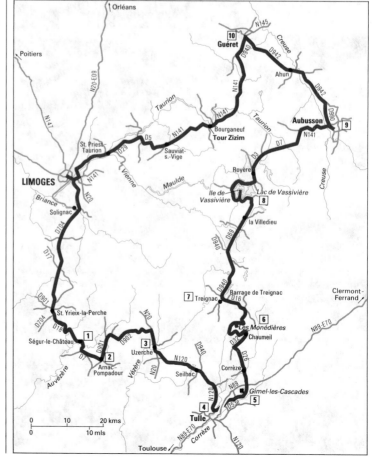

Leave Pompadour on the D901 to Lubersac, then follow the D902 and turn right on the N20 to Uzerche.

Uzerche, Limousin

3 Historic gateways and fine old houses with towers, turrets, carved lintels, ornamented windows and heraldic designs are all preserved here. Uzerche stands on a peninsula ridge bounded on three sides by the River Vézère, and there are attractive views from the high-set **Esplanade de la Lunade**. Behind the esplanade, the Romanesque **Church of St-Pierre** features an eerily impressive crypt built around 1030.

ⓘ Place de la Lunarde

Leave Uzerche on the N20, then immediately take the N120 to Tulle.

Tulle, Limousin

4 You may find this a place of odd contrasts. The pleasant approach road swinging down wooded valleys arrives at a town whose modern parts are dull; but it has a fascinating old quarter crossed by lanes and stairways, and there is a bustle around its riverside quays. Tulle gave its name to a fine-woven silk, but one of its main industries now is armaments.

There is some fine modern stained glass in the 12th-century **cathedral**, and the extensive **Musée de la Cloître**, built round the arcades and gardens of a dignified old Benedictine monastery, illustrates local history in a quiet and peaceful setting. Paintings, sculptures, porcelain and archaeological finds share a building with historic firearms.

You will need a strong stomach to look over some of the illustrations in the **Musée de la Résistance et de la Déportation**, which recalls the grim days of World War II when many local men were deported, never to be heard of again.

ⓘ Quai Baluze

Leave Tulle as for Clermont-Ferrand. After a hairpin climb out of the built-up area, go straight on under a bridge, following the D9 then the D53e to Gimel.

Gimel-les-Cascades, Limousin

5 On the approach to Gimel, try to catch a glimpse of the dashing waterfalls which gave the village its name. From Gimel itself there is a dramatic outlook down a steeply wooded ravine. Footpaths wander past the spray-soaked triple falls. Although nowadays it is off the main roads, a hint of Gimel's previous religious importance is given by the great treasure of its **parish church** – a 12th-century gold and bejewelled reliquary of St Stephen. The saint's stoning to death is one of the scenes picked out in fine enamel and precious stones.

Leave Gimel following the 'Tulle 13' sign. Turn right following the 'Etang de Ruffaud' signs, then follow 'Gare de Corrèze' and 'vers RN 89' signs. Cross the N89 and continue on the D26 through Corrèze. Go right on the D32 to Chaumeil, left on the

This château, together with the title Marquise de Pompadour, was given to a Parisian girl named Jeanne Antoinette Poisson when she became Louis XV's mistress and the power behind the throne

D121, right on the D128 as for Lestards, then take a side road right to Les Monédières.

Les Monédières, Limousin

6 At about 911m (2,990 feet) above sea-level, the summit here is a magnificent all-round viewpoint. Many of the faraway hills are *puys* – the remains of extinct volcanoes. The hilltop is a favourite launching-place for hang-gliders.

Return to the D128 and turn right following 'Chaumeil' sign. Go left on the D32 to Lestards then left on the D16 to Treignac.

Treignac, Limousin

7 Roofs are slaty-grey here, a sign that this is a different part of the country from the warmer villages visited before Les Monédières. There is a fine view of the town from a **viewpoint tower** in the centre, but Treignac demands closer investigation before it reveals its old buildings in medieval and Renaissance styles. They descend to the Vézère river, which is crossed by a 15th-century bridge. A **museum** exhibits historic furnishings, craft and farm tools, weaving equipment and local ironwork. The restored **parish church** displays locally-worked stained glass and there is a simple little chapel, reached by a walk past the Stations of the Cross, which offers a good view westwards through a woodland clearing.

RECOMMENDED WALKS

1 Clearly waymarked from the D6 through Ségur-le-Château, four numbered pathways explore a beautiful countryside of modest hills and woodlands. The 'rivers and streams' walk wanders along the banks of the Auvézère, and there are fine views down to the river from the low ridges which follow its winding course.

7 Treignac offers high- and low-level paths, some to hilltop viewpoints. Best of these is the walk past the local hospital, by wooded lanes and an open hillside, to the poised granite boulder called **La Pierre des Druides** (the Druids' Stone).

BACK TO NATURE

6 On the **Monédières hills**, conifer plantations rise above the lower deciduous woodland. The original forest was deliberately set on fire, once by Julius Caesar and again during the 16th-century religious wars. *Myrtilles*, or blueberries, grow in profusion and are sold locally. Wild boar are occasionally seen in autumn and fungi grow in profusion.

7 In the winding gorge of the Vézère just below Treignac, the **Rocher des Folles** is a series of granite pillars on the edge of a weathered cliff.

8 There are sandy beaches at the wooded **Barrage de Treignac** reservoir, formed by a dam on the Vézère. It is ideal for fishing, swimming and sunbathing parties. Swimming from the main beach, beside the **D940**, is supervised in summer.

Further on, the **Lac de Vassivière** offers tuition in sailing, windsurfing and horse and pony rides. This beautiful reservoir is a noted recreational area, and there are easy walks, suitable for children, in the forest which surrounds it.

*Leave Treignac on the **D940** as for Eymoutiers. Turn right on the **D132e** which becomes the **D69**, signed 'Lac de Vassivière'. Go right on the **D992** to La Villedieu, where you should watch for a left turn on the **D34**. Go straight on avoiding a '19t' sign, left at a Stop sign as for Beaumont, then follow signs 'Ile de Vassivière'.*

Lac de Vassivière, Limousin

8 The route here stops before a bridge across to the main island in an extensive and well-wooded reservoir. The lake offers sports and leisure activities of many kinds. It has a 45km (28-mile) shoreline. Visitors are welcome to walk to the island, where there are woodland paths, outdoor sculpture displays and a castle.

*Retrace your route and turn right on the **D222** as for Peyrat. Turn right at the stop sign to Royère. Go left on the **D3**, watch for a right turn signed 'Aubusson 24' and continue to Aubusson.*

*Leave Aubusson on the **D990** and turn left on to the **D942** to Guéret.*

Guéret, Limousin

10 You may be tempted to skip through Guéret, but its **museum** deserves a visit. Occupying an 18th-century mansion surrounded by pleasant formal gardens, it has valuable collections of Aubusson and other tapestries; ceramics from France, the Netherlands and Ming dynasty china; and a wonderful display of religious art, especially in enamel-work, dating from the 12th century.

ⓘ Avenue Charles de Gaulle

*Leave Guéret on the **D940** then follow 'Limoges' signs through Pontarion and take the **N141**. Go through Bourganeuf and continue before turning right on the **D5** as for Ambazac then watch for a junction where you should bear left uphill on the **D29** at the 'Limoges 27' sign. Return to Limoges.*

From St Yrieix to Ségur-le-Château the **D18** and **D6** run through pleasant undulating country of low hills and little valleys, and woodlands interspersed with grazing land. The **N120** sweeps down wooded valleys to Tulle, the **D9** to Gimel is a fine winding road with views to the tumbling waterfalls, and after Gimel there are attractive roadside fishing lakes. West of **Chameil**, alpine-like country rises to conifer-clad summits.

Aubusson, Limousin

9 At heart Aubusson is a dignified old town with many discreetly restored buildings. Most of all, though, it is the capital of French tapestry, introduced here in the 14th century by Flemish weavers. **La Maison du Vieux Tapissier** displays hundreds of examples of tapestry work, from classical works of the 17th century to dazzling ultra-modern abstracts. Several tapestry workshops and studios are open to visitors. They work on a full range of designs, from copies of the style of Louis XIV's reign to something suitable for France's TGV super-express trains.

ⓘ Rue Vieille

For 500 years, Aubusson has been synonymous with exquisite tapestry, and remains so today. But be sure and make time to climb up to the ruins of the castle for a view over this pretty town and the River Creuse winding below

Limoges – Ségur-le-Château 58 (36)
Ségur-le-Château – Pompadour 10 (6)
Pompadour – Uzerche 25 (15)
Uzerche – Tulle 31 (19)
Tulle – Gimel-les-Cascades 11 (7)
Gimel-les-Cascades – Les Monédières 40 (25)
Les Monédières – Treignac 20 (12)
Treignac – Lac de Vassivière 40 (25)
Lac de Vassivière – Aubusson 49 (30)
Aubusson – Guéret 41 (26)
Guéret – Limoges 86 (54)

Unique Marais Poitevin is a network of canals and islands

ℹ️ Place de la Petite Sirène, La Rochelle

Leave La Rochelle over the toll bridge to Île de Ré. Take the 'Itineraire Nord', visiting La Flotte and St Martin-de-Ré on the way to Phare des Baleines. Return by the D201 via Le Bois-Plage, then right on the D735 back over the toll bridge.

Île de Ré, Poitou-Charente

1 Linked to the mainland by a modern bridge, here is an island – 28km (17 miles) long and 3–5km (2–3 miles) wide – of holiday beaches. The old fishing and trading port of **La Flotte** once shipped salt and brandy to America. **St Martin-de-Ré**, the principal town, has unexpected rampart walls, a town centre virtually on an island, a local museum (**Musée Naval et E-Cognac**) and a citadel where visitors are welcome to admire the outer defences and the old quay. The inner part is a state prison. At the northern point of the island you can visit the **Phare des Baleines**, a lighthouse named after the whales that used to be seen offshore. A little **marine museum** stands near by.

ℹ️ Quai de Sénac in La Flotte and Avenue Victor Bouthillier in St Martin-de-Ré

Follow the D735 as for La Rochelle, on to the dual-carriageway numbered N237 then N137, and continue to Rochefort.

Rochefort, Poitou-Charente

2 You may wonder, entering it through unremarkable suburbs, if

OF RIVERS & ISLANDS

La Rochelle • Île de Ré • Rochefort • Brouage
Ile d'Oléron • Saintes • Angoulême • Niort • Coulon
Fontenay-le-Comte • La Rochelle

The arms of La Rochelle feature a full-rigged ship with cannons at the ports. That mixture of war and sea dominates the history of the coast and islands here. You will see famous old harbours, citadels and the roadstead where Napoleon surrendered to the British ship Bellerophon. Inland, this is the country of the Cognac vineyards, and in the gentle Marais Poitevin you will be tempted to explore the canals of what was once the Gulf of Poitou.

Rochefort is worth a visit, but this is a special town. In 1666 thousands of workers, under the orders of Louis XIV's chief minister Jean Baptiste Colbert, built a huge arsenal and naval shipyard here. There are guided tours of the beautiful mansard-roofed **Corderie Royale**, with its 372m (1,220-foot) hall where the ropes were twisted. Museums in Rochefort cover art and

FOR HISTORY BUFFS

1 Until 1938, prisoners shipped to Devil's Island, the infamous penal colony in French Guinea, left from the citadel at **St Martin-de-Ré**. There is still a prison here.

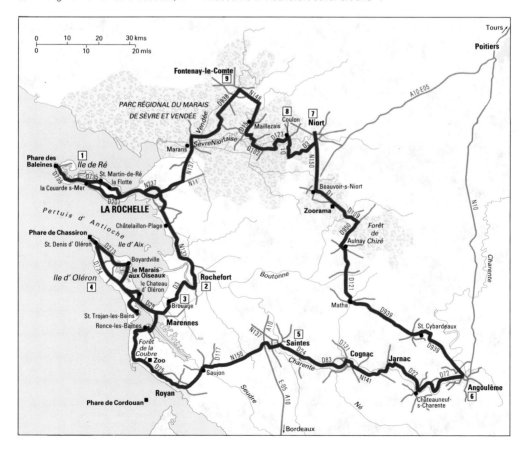

FOR CHILDREN

1 There is plenty for children at L'Arche de Noé (Noah's Ark) before the Phare des Baleines on Île de Ré.

4 Before you leave Île d'Oléron, turn right for St Trojan-les-Bains and the narrow-gauge railway which potters for 6km (3½ miles) through pinewoods.

SPECIAL TO...

At Ré and Oléron are the oysterbeds which cover great areas and are a vital part of the local economy. You can join a tour of the beds from La Flotte on Ré, and there is an oyster museum at St Trojan on Oléron.

5 At Cognac and Jarnac on the route between Saintes and Angoulême, are world-famous cognac houses such as Hennessy, Martell, Rémy Martin, Courvoisier and Hine.

FOR HISTORY BUFFS

4 Reached by ferry from Boyardville on the Île d'Oléron, the Napoleonic museum on the little island of Aix, Maison de l'Empereur, recalls how Napoleon spent his last night on French soil before surrendering to the British ship *Bellerophon*.

history, and its background as a military port. The unobtrusive but exotically furnished **Maison de Loti**, house of Pierre Loti (1850–1923), who mixed two careers, as a marine officer and a novelist of the sea, stands in a quiet side street.

ⓘ Avenue Sadi Carnot

Leave Rochefort on the D733 as for Royan, then go right on the D238e to Soubise and left on the D3 signed 'Hiers-Brouage'.

Brouage, Poitou-Charente

3 Away from main roads, this fine little fortified town is now also away from the sea and it now stands half deserted among the salt marshes. The retreat of the waters ruined its position as a busy trading port. From the ramparts, the French tricolour and the maple leaf of Canada fly side by side. Samuel de Champlain, the founder of Quebec, was born here in 1567. There is a comprehensive exhibition in the church on the founding of what was at first 'New France'.

ⓘ Porte Royale

Continue on the D3, turn right at the traffic lights over the toll bridge on to Île d'Oléron. Bear right on the D734 through Château d'Oléron. Go right in Dolus on to the D126 through Les Allards and Boyardville, then via Foulerot, Port du Douhet, La Brée and St Denis to the Phare de Chassiron. Return to St Denis, then take the D734 to Dolus and follow 'Le Viaduc' signs back over the toll bridge.

Île d'Oléron, Poitou-Charente

4 Larger than Ré (30km/18 miles long and 6km/3½ miles wide), this is another holiday island of villages, picturesque harbours, vineyards, woodlands and fine sandy beaches. Look for the grassy site of the 12th-

century fortress which gave the town of **Le Château d'Oléron** its names, the river resort of **Boyardville** with its pinewood dunes and beach, and the lighthouse tower of the **Phare de Chassiron**, where the waves are seen breaking over offshore reefs and shallows.

ⓘ Place de la République in Château d'Oléron

Follow the D26 off the island then turn right at the 'La Tremblade' sign. Go right opposite Camping les Pins, and right at the T-junction over another toll bridge. Go right on the D25 to Royan, then take the N150 to Saintes.

Saintes, Poitou-Charente

5 Back from the resorts and islands of the coast, this is a handsome district capital. There is a good **regional museum** here, others concentrating on fine arts, folklore and archaeology. Roman remains include a triumphal arch. Saintes lies astride the River Charente, and cruise-boats sail from its garden-backed quays.

ⓘ Cours National

Leave Saintes on the D24, which becomes the D83. Go right on the N141 and right on the D83 to Cognac. Take the N141 through Jarnac, then turn right on the D22. After Vibrac watch for a left turn – away from Châteauneuf – to St Simieux. Go right through Sireuil, left on the D53, right on the D84, left on the D41 and right on the D72 to Angoulême.

Angoulême, Poitou-Charente

6 This is a busy industrial town, but its old upper town is worth a visit. The chief glories of the old town are its imposing hilltop location, the views from the wooded paths round its ramparts, and the glorious façade of its subtly-lit **cathedral** (much restored in the 19th century). There are museums, exuberant Renaissance buildings, and rare active survivors of the papermills which once made Angoulême's fortune.

ⓘ Place St-Pierre

Leave Angoulême on the D939 to Matha. In the town centre, turn right to Aulnay, following the D121. After Aulnay, go right on the D950 left on the D109 and join the D1 through Chizé. Turn right on the N150 to Niort.

Niort, Poitou-Charente

7 Niort, on the River Sèvres, is a working town with various industries. The riverside here has walks and footbridges, gardens and vestiges of old mill streams. Past and present town halls (Hôtels de Ville) are richly ornamented, and there is a great deal of fine Renaissance design. Customers bustle around the glass-and-wrought-ironwork **market hall**. The multi-towered **castle** or **Donjon** may have been built by the 12th-century English Kings Henry II and Richard the Lionheart.

ⓘ Rue Ernest-Pérochon

The Château de Terre-Neuve at Fontenay-le-Comte is full of fascinating architectural detail

Leave Niort on the N11. Turn right on the D3, then right on the D1 to Coulon.

Coulon, Poitou

8 In the heart of one of the most appealing landscapes in France – the farms, market gardens, woodlands and waterway maze of the long-drained **Marais Poitevin** – Coulon is an attractive village where punts are available for hire, and escorted cruises also start, on some of the 40,000km (25,000 miles) of water channels. Not all, of course, are navigable, but they are an enchanting haven. Some picnic sites, reachable by water, are remote from any road. Coulon's **museum** tells the story of the marshes, and the aquarium displays all the fish species of this 'Green Venice'.

ⓘ Place Église

Leave Coulon on the D123 as for Le Vanneau, then go right on the D102, which becomes the D104 through Damvix. Go straight on at the give way sign, then right on the D15 through Maillezais. Go left on the N148 to Fontenay-le-Comte.

Fontenay-le-Comte, Loire Valley West

9 There are no fishing-smacks now, sailing under the **Pont des Sardines** (Sardine Bridge) at Fontenay, but the riverside is a pleasant recreational area with footpaths and little gardens. Fontenay preserves its historic buildings – even the tourist office was once a toll-house for the port. The **Église Notre-Dame** is an impressive Gothic church with a beautiful walnut pulpit and, high on an outer wall, a gilded Madonna. Beside it there is a regional **museum**. The **Château de Terre-Neuve** is a splendid 16th-century castle whose richly ornamented fireplaces feature alchemists' symbols and griffins.

During the Renaissance, the town became the home of poets and writers, including Rabelais, who was educated in a convent here.

ⓘ Quay Poëy d'Avant

Leave Fontenay on the D938ter for La Rochelle.

La Rochelle – Île de Ré 11 (7)
Île de Ré – Rochefort 109 (68)
Rochefort – Brouage 19 (12)
Brouage – Île d'Oléron 15 (9)
Île d'Oléron – Saintes 154 (96)
Saintes – Angoulême 76 (47)
Angoulême – Niort 113 (70)
Niort – Coulon 20 (12)
Coulon – Fontenay-le-Comte 40 (25)
Fontenay-le-Comte – La Rochelle 50 (31)

5 days – 512km (319 miles)

THE WESTERN LOIRE VALLEY

**Nantes • Clisson • Cholet • Doué-la-Fontaine
St Hilaire • Saumur • Baugé • Le Lude
Le Mans Circuit • Le Mans • Angers • Nantes**

Although it starts in Nantes, the largest town in Brittany, this tour soon leaves all Breton influences behind as it heads for the inland valleys of the Loire and the Sarthe. There are many memories of the Vendée Wars, started when the country people of that region took arms against the excesses of the Revolution. You will find some of France's finest *son et lumière* presentations here. One of the world's most famous motor-racing circuits is part of the ordinary road network. The Pays Nantais and Anjou are packed with vineyards. Many superb French biscuits originated in the Loire. And one of the many links between France and England is that this was the heartland of the Plantagenet kings.

Cholet's elegant theatre in a town rebuilt after the events of the 1790s when it was razed three times

FOR HISTORY BUFFS

3 In a forest clearing beside the **D196** after Maulévrier (on the way from Cholet to Doué-la-Fontaine), the chapel at the **Cimetière des Martyrs** commemorates victims of the Revolutionary fury in the Vendée Wars. Virtually alone in France, the Vendée region saw little to celebrate at the bicentennary of the Revolution in 1989.

4 After Doué-la-Fontaine, turn left off the **D69** for **Rochemenier** and its strange troglodytic farms. You can visit furnished underground dwelling houses – with their cowsheds, barns, wine-cellars and even a chapel – still inhabited early this century.

Angers, home of the Counts of Anjou, from whom England's powerful Plantagenet dynasty descended after a royal marriage in 1129

ⓘ Place du Commerce, Nantes

Leave Nantes for Clisson on the D59 through St Fiacre. In Gorges go left of the D113 then take the D59 again into Clisson.

Clisson, Loire Valley West

1 The Vendée Wars and the savage reprisals of the Revolutionary government army all but obliterated this little riverside town. Then it was completely rebuilt, but not as it had been before. Present-day Clisson is mostly a tribute to Palladian Italy, with colonnades, loggias and belltowers of a style seen nowhere else in western France.

Look for the stabilised but unfurnished ruin of the 13th- to 15th-century **castle**, the 15th-century **market hall**, the two **medieval bridges** contrasting with the soaring 19th-century road viaduct, and Italianate creations such as the **Temple d'Amitié** and the **Church of Notre-Dame**.

There are beautiful walks in the valleys of the Sèvre Nantaise and the Moine. Local wines may be tasted. But Clisson itself is the great attraction, especially as an Italianate skyline to a leafy riverside view.

ⓘ Place de la Trinité

Leave Clisson on the N149. Turn left as for Beaupréau on the D762 then go along the N249 and follow signs to Cholet.

Cholet, Loire Valley West

2 The **Musée des Guerres de Vendée**, here in a town where only 20 buildings were left standing in their brutal aftermath, is the place to learn about the Vendée Wars of

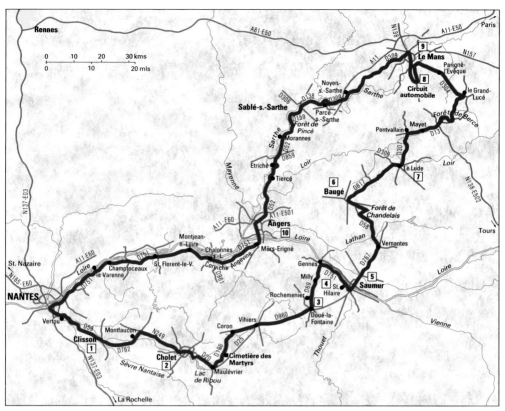

1793–96. It explains how the Vendée rising against the Revolutionary government's policies of mass conscription and the overthrow of all previous loyalties, was at first successful, then viciously crushed.

Other exhibitions are at the Musée des Arts, the Musée Paysan with its old-style dairy and country house interiors in the leisure park by the Ribou lake, and the Maison des Sciences, Lettres et Arts whose attractions include a planetarium.

This is a famous textile town with many splendid modern buildings. Its trademark is the red-and-white handkerchief – the *mouchoir de Cholet* – whose design, as you will learn locally, is rooted in another incident of the Vendée Wars.

[i] Place de Rougé

Leave Cholet on the D20 as for Poitiers. In Maulévrier turn left and right as for Vihiers, then left on the D196 through Chanteloup to Coron. Go right on the D960 to Doué-la-Fontaine.

Doué-la-Fontaine, Loire Valley West

3 If you arrived in the middle of Doué without paying attention to its outskirts, you might shrug it off as an ordinary little town. It is far from that. The zoo, adapted from the cliffs, caverns and ditches of an old quarry site, houses lions, tigers, lemurs, birds or prey, deer, emus, rarities such as snow panthers, and 15 separate monkey enclosures. Its Naturoscope explains the problems of threatened species and the destruction of their habitats.

The **Musée des Vieux Commerces** features seven old-style shops and a rose-water distillery, in part-restored 18th-century stables. The **Maison Carolingienne** is the substantial ruin of a fortress built before 1050.

Nobody is certain about the origins of Doué's arena, Roman in style but much later in date. However, there is no doubt about the **Moulin Cartier**. Built in 1910, it was the last windmill raised in Anjou.

[i] Place du Champ de Foire

Leave Doué on the D69 to Gennes. Go right as for Saumur on the D751 through La Mimerolle and into St Hilaire.

St Hilaire, Loire Valley West

4 Just before this village suburb of Saumur, the **Musée du Champignon**, in a cave system cut into the roadside cliffs, is more than simply an exhibition about mushrooms and how they are grown. The underground galleries were dug in medieval times, part of a network of more than 480km (300 miles) throughout the district, which produces 75 per cent of France's cultivated mushrooms. Turn right in St Hilaire for the **École National d'Équitation**. This is France's national riding academy, excellently housed and staffed. In the practice arena, in front of high wall mirrors, you may see members of the acadamy's Cadre Noire put their horses through the intricate, disciplined and stylish movements for which they are famous all over Europe. They also perform summer season shows.

Continue on the D751 into Saumur.

Saumur, Loire Valley West

5 Straddling the Loire, this very appealing town is passionate about horses and the cavalry, wines, museums and exuberant outdoor displays. The **Château de Saumur**, overlooking the river, houses three separate collections. The **Musée des Arts Décoratifs** concentrates on the decorative arts – ceramics, enamel-

The Château at Saumur was thought so beautiful by one Duke of Anjou, the poet René the Good, that he dubbed it 'the castle of love'

ware, carvings in wood and alabaster. Another, **Musée du Cheval**, celebrates centuries of horsemanship; the third, **Musée de la Figurine-Jouet** has more than 20,000 models and figurines.

The cavalry has two separate exhibitions, one recalling its mounted days, the other taking the story to more recent times with a comprehensive display of tanks and armoured cars.

Second only to Champagne, Saumur is famous for its sparkling wines. Several firms welcome visitors to their cellars. **Notre-Dame de Nantilly**, dating from the 12th-century, houses a valuable collection of medieval and Renaissance tapestries. And the old quarter of Saumur with its restored 17th-century houses adds to the attractions of a justifiably self-confident town.

ⓘ Place de la Bilange

*Leave Saumur on the **N147** as for Le Mans. At the roundabout take the second exit to Vernantes on the **D767**. In Vernantes, turn sharp left at the traffic lights as for Baugé, then right on the **D58** as for Baugé through Mouliherne. In Le Guédéniau go right in the **D186** as for Lasse. Turn left following 'Les Caves de Chanzelles' sign. At the roundabout in the forest take the fifth exit for Baugé. Rejoin the **D58** and continue to Baugé.*

Baugé, Loire Valley West

6 Plenty of space has been left around Baugé's 15th-century castle, originally a hunting lodge of

Good King René, Duke of Anjou. Holding displays of weapons, coins and ceramics, it stands before public gardens dipping to an attractive riverside. The **Convent of La Girouardière** houses a venerated relic – a jewelled cross believed to contain a piece of the True Cross brought to France by a crusader knight. Its unusual design was adopted as the Cross of Lorraine. Look also for Baugé's charming 17th-century **Hospice-St-Joseph** (pharmacy) with its beautiful array of apothecaries' jars.

Sometimes an unfamiliar language may be seen or spoken here, describing Baugé, for instance, as 'bela kaj malmova urbeto': the **Château de Grésillon**, on your exit route from 'this fine old town', is an international Esperanto centre.

ⓘ Place de l'Europe

*Leave Baugé on the **D817**, which becomes the **D305**, then go right on the **D306** to Le Lude.*

Le Lude, Loire Valley West

7 Pride of this little town is the richly furnished **château**, rebuilt in Renaissance style after an English garrison was driven out – with heavy damage to the fabric – in 1427. Its situation is most attractive, above balustraded gardens rising from the River Loir, whose waters eventually feed the larger Loire. One of France's most dramatic *son et lumière* presentations takes place here. It recalls five centuries of events and personalities, from the English occupation to the Second Empire. This outstanding show is enhanced by fountains and a lively firework display reflected in the river.

In the town itself, **La Sentinelle** is an unusual museum with a huge collection of military uniforms and flags from all over the world.

ℹ Place Nicolay

Leave Le Lude on the D307 to Pontvallain. Go right on the D13 through Mayet and across the N138 to Le Grand-Lucé. Turn left at the give way sign and left on the D304 as for Le Mans. Go under the bridge, then left following the 'Angers' sign, under another bridge and follow the 'Tours' signs along the N138. Go right at the roundabout on the D140 as for Arnage, then right on the D139 to the grandstands of the racing circuit.

Le Mans Circuit, Loire Valley West

8 Prosaically, they may be the N138, D140 and D139, but these roads are also part of the great motor-racing circuit where the Le Mans 24-Hour Race is held every June. The N138 is the **Mulsanne Straight**, along which Jaguars, Porsches and Mercedes howl at over 320kph (200mph).

There is a smaller but linked **Bugatti Circuit**. The two tracks play host to five major car and motorcycle races, plus a 24-hour truck race! You can watch test sessions from the main grandstands, which are informally open on non-competition days. An excellent **motor museum** also recalls that this was where Wilbur Wright, over from the United States, made the first powered flight in Europe in 1908.

ℹ Acceuil Reception

Continue on the D139 into Le Mans.

Le Mans, Loire Valley West

9 Apart from some handsome churches, the busy, modern town offers little to the visitor, but Le Mans has strong links with the Plantagenets. Henry II of England, for instance, was born here. Long before his time there was a Gallo-Roman settlement on the great rock-ridge in the heart of the modern sprawl. The old walled town – **Vieux Mans** – retains its high-level medieval street plan. Split by the rue Wilbur Wright, which lies at the foot of a ravine cut through the heart of the rock, it features finely detailed Renaissance houses and later town mansions, leading to the majestic **Cathédrale St Julien**.

ℹ Rue de l'Étoile

Leave Le Mans on the D309 as for Sablé. In Parcé cross the river then go first right at the crossroads, left to Solesmes then continue to Sablé. Go straight across the D306 for Centre-Ville. At the roundabout take the last exit, then a side road right for Pincé. This is the D159. Bear right on the C15 for 'Pincé par la Forêt'. Rejoin the D159 then follow the D18 and D52 through Morannes. Continue through Etriché and Tiercé. Go straight on along the N160 then right on the N23 to Angers.

Le Mans is synonymous the world over with the speed and glamour of motor racing. There is not an oil-rag to be seen, however, in this tranquil corner of old Le Mans, dominated by its exquisite cathedral

Angers, Loire Valley West

10 Here in the heart of Anjou lies a university town of parks, gardens and colourful floral decorations, with a grand Plantagenet **castle** rising in towers of banded stonework, and a cathedral, **Cathédrale Saint Maurice**, best approached by the Montée St-Maurice, a stairway climbing from the River Maine.

The longest tapestry in France, completed in the late 14th century to show the Apocalypse, is on display in the castle. Angers is a tapestry town. Many others, ancient and modern, are on show in the castle itself and in individual museums and galleries.

Fine Renaissance buildings survive, both around the cathedral and elsewhere. River cruises follow the Maine, and for the adventurous there are hot-air balloon flights to waft you high above the castles, vineyards and villages of Anjou.

ℹ Place Kennedy

Leave Angers through Les-Ponts-de-Cé on the N160. In Mûrs-Érigné, turn right to go through Chalonnes and Champtoceaux on the D751 and return on the N249 to Nantes.

Nantes – Clisson 27 (17)
Clisson – Cholet 36 (22.5)
Cholet – Doué-la-Fontaine 58 (36)
Doué-la-Fontaine – St Hilaire 29 (18)
St Hilaire – Saumur 4 (2.5)
Saumur – Baugé 44 (27)
Baugé – Le Lude 24 (15)
Le Lude – Le Mans (circuit auto) 75 (47)
Le Mans (circuit auto) – Le Mans 10 (6)
Le Mans – Angers 106 (66)
Angers – Nantes 99 (62)

3/4 days – 428km (267 miles)

THROUGH CHÂTEAU COUNTRY

**Tours • Amboise • Chenonceau • Valençay
Romorantin-Lanthenay • La Sologne • Gien
Orléans • Chambord • Blois • Vouvray • Tours**

S ome of the most elegant castles in Europe are within easy reach of Tours, in and around the valley of the Loire. Vineyards abound in Touraine, 'the garden of France'. Although this route starts and finishes beside the Loire, it also goes into the lonely area of pools, farms and woodlands known as the Sologne. You can visit one of the most beautiful flower-filled parks in France, a top-class racing car museum in an unobtrusive country town, and the house where Leonardo da Vinci – friend, guest and pensioner of François I – painted and dreamed of inventions which became reality only in our time.

SCENIC ROUTES

Towards Amboise, the D751 is an attractive riverside road beside the Loire, though very dry years such as 1990 exposed great areas of sandbanks.
There is a pleasant run on the D81 from Amboise towards Chenonceau, and fine rural countryside beyond that to Valençay.

[i] Boulevard Heurteloup, Tours
Leave Tours on the D751 to Amboise.

Amboise, Loire Valley Central

1 You will enter Amboise along a classic plane-tree avenue, with the Loire out of sight beyond the riverside embankment. The **château**'s massive walls tower over the town-centre streets. This impressive building is only a fifth of the size it was during its 16th-century heyday. A son et lumière presentation brings to life

The Château Sully, restored to its rightful beauty after wartime damage

François I's glittering court of those days. In the **Musée de la Poste**, model coaches, postilions' liveries, records, engravings and other relics tell the story of the mail service by land, sea and air.
On the climb out of Amboise, pause at the exotic 18th-century **pagoda of Chanteloup** (all that remains of a château there). The topmost gallery of this 44m (144-foot) hillside tower is a splendid viewpoint over the Loire.

[i] Quai Géneral de Gaulle

After the pagoda turn left then right as for Chenonceaux on the D81. Go left on the D40 then right to Château de Chenonceau.

Chenonceau, Loire Valley Central

2 Lacking the final 'x' of the similarly named little town near by, with its ivied houses and old coaching inns, this 16th-century riverside **castle** was one of the most striking architectural exercises of its day. The bridge which linked it to the south bank of the Cher was adapted as a gallery of two storeys and attic-level rooms, with the River Cher flowing through the arches underneath. Extending for almost 61m (200 feet) across the river, this is still the most noteworthy feature of a richly furnished castle. Chenonceau stands surrounded by water channels. The woodland grounds include formal riverside gardens, and a waxworks museum recalls the personalities involved in its lively story. There are excellent *son et lumière* shows.

Continue on the D40. In Chisseaux, go straight on the D80 to Francueil, take the D81 to Céré-la-Ronde, then the C5 and D90 to St Aignan. Go left on the D675, right on the D17, right for Valençay on the D33, left on the D37 in Villentrois and right on the D956 into Valençay.

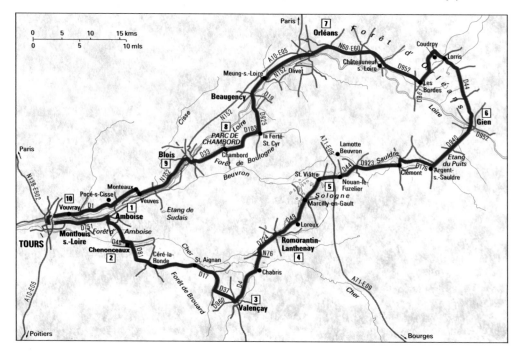

Valençay, Loire Valley Central

3 The great 16th-century **castle** here was owned by several famous financiers. A half-interest in the vast 19,000-hectare (47,000-acre) estate was briefly held by the Scotsman John Law, who introduced the system of credit. In 1719–20 he dominated the French banking system, until his enterprises collapsed in insolvencies and rancour.

Later, Valençay became the residence of Talleyrand, Napoleon's foreign minister, whose diplomats and dignitaries were extravagantly entertained. From 1808 to 1813 Ferdinand VII of Spain was held in virtual house arrest here, which is why the town's Hôtel d'Espagne is so named. A *son et lumière* show brings these varied characters back to life.

The castle is still lavishly furnished. Fallow deer graze in a sunken park, and you will hear peacocks' screams echoing through the grounds. Do not be put off by the ramshackle appearance of the separate **motor museum**, whose exhibits include a spidery Bedelia cycle-car of 1914, a lovely little 1930 Amilcar sports model and an Alpine-Renault of 1971.

i Avenue de la Résistance

*Leave Valençay on the **D4** through Chabris, then continue straight ahead on the **D128**. Cross the **N76** and follow the signs to Romorantin.*

Romorantin-Lanthenay, Loire Valley Central

4 In this 'capital' of the Sologne district, the River Sauldre splits into several channels. From the main-road bridge there is a most beautiful view downstream to the ivy-covered walls and colourful flower boxes of the restored watermills.

The town centre includes several attractive buildings, notably the ancient-timbered **Carroir d'Orée** which houses an **archaeological museum**. In the elegant **Hôtel de Ville** (town hall), the second floor is devoted to a **museum** about the rural life and traditions of the Sologne.

Matra, the aerospace company, has a factory here. The town's **Musée de la Course Automobile** is of far higher quality than you might expect, because it houses historic Matra competition cars, such as a Le Mans 24-Hour Race winner and Jackie Stewart's Formula One Matra-Ford V8.

i Place de la Paix

*Leave Romorantin for Loreux on the **D49** and continue to Marcilly. Turn left at the T-junction there and first right for St Viâtre, still on the **D49**.*

La Sologne, Loire Valley Central

5 At St Viâtre you are well into the Sologne, a huge tract of more than half a million hectares (nearly 2,000 square miles). It is an all but level countryside of heath and woodland, widely separated arable and livestock farms, red-tiled brick houses and hundreds of lonely pools. In this slightly mysterious landscape, whose people are regarded in other parts of France as clannish and self-contained, only the trees create any kind of horizon.

The Sologne is also a land of hunters, wild-fowlers and fishermen. Until the second half of the

The ancient cloth-working town of Romorantin-Lanthenay is built across the River Sauldre and retains many fine medieval buildings. The great French king François I spent part of his youth here

FOR CHILDREN

6 The kids will have plenty of opportunity to work off some energy at the Étang du Puits, before you reach Gien. This wooded recreational lake offers sandy beaches, rowing boat and pedalo hire, pony rides and a little children's playground. Sailing dinghies and windsurfers hurtle around.

BACK TO NATURE

7 In Orléans, the magnificent floral park called La Source takes it name from a curious natural feature. Officially, the River Loiret rises here. In fact, its waters are diverted from the Loire almost 30km (19 miles) upstream. They disappear underground for all that distance before welling up again in the park.

8 Turn left off the D33 in the Parc de Chambord for a high-level 'hide', from which you can watch a herd of red deer in a grazing enclosure in the forest.

FOR HISTORY BUFFS

7 In Lorris, after leaving Gien, turn left on the D961 to find the Musée de la Résistance et de la Déportation. Set in well-tended gardens, it tells the story of the Resistance movement in World War II through displays of documents, photographs, maps and weapons, and newspapers of the clandestine press.

8 On the way from Orléans to Chambord, turn left in Meung-sur-Loire for the château and its grim medieval dungeons. They feature a torture chamber and a hideous underground oubliette where prisoners generally died in an agony of starvation or disease. One famous prisoner in the 15th century was the vagabond poet François Villon.

19th century much of it was unhealthily covered by even greater areas of stagnant water. Extensive drainage schemes and tree-planting created the landscape of today.

Leave St Viâtre on the D49, then avoid the left turn for Lamotte Beuvron and go straight ahead on the D93 to Nouan-le-Fuzelier. Go left as for Orléans, then right as for Chaon on the D122 and left on the D44. Go right on the D923 as for Aubigny to Clémont. Turn left at the crossroads on the D7, then follow signs to Étang du Puits. Continue to the D948, turn right for Argent then left on the D940 to Gien.

Gien, Loire Valley Central

6 From a leafy promenade by the Loire, the hillside in this town, famous for its faïenceware, rises to a little plateau shared by the 15th-century castle and the modern church, both of brick rather than stone. The castle houses the Musée International de la Chasse, with displays on every imaginable aspect of hunting.

Replacing a building wrecked in World War II, the church shows inside and out, what decorative effects can be achieved in brickwork. Its dedication to St Joan is appropriate. It was here in 1429 that she first made contact with the Dauphin's army and began her mission to liberate France.

i Rue Anne de Beaujeu

Left: The Château at Blois, where the French kings held court for 200 years. Below: Gien, badly bombed during the war but since meticulously restored

Leave Gien for Lorris on the D44. Continue as for Bellegarde. Immediately after the 'La Chaussée' sign take the first left. Go right on the V3 into Coudroy. Turn left at the stop sign, through Vieilles-Maisons and left on the D88. Bend right then left, and watch for a right turn at the crossroads along a gravel forest road, passing the '3t' sign. Bear left at a junction of forest roads, left after a 50m warning sign for give way ahead, and turn right along the tarred road (this is the D961). Turn right on the D952 and follow the N60 and the N152 to Orléans.

Orléans, Loire Valley Central

7 Every spring, Orléans organises a festival celebrating Joan of Arc's intervention – not at all appreciated by the French official army commanders – which raised the English siege of the city in 1429. Visit the Maison Jeanne d'Arc for the whole dramatic story. Her equestrian statue stands in the Place du Martroi.

The Musée des Beaux-Arts houses a valuable collection of French and Italian paintings. Now used for civic receptions, the luxuriously furnished 16th-century Hôtel Groslot is open to visitors. The Musée Historique et Archéologique (local history and archaeology) is housed in the Renaissance surroundings of the Hôtel Cabu.

Cathédrale Sainte-Croix dominates the townscape above the Loire. Look for its stained-glass windows telling the story of Joan of Arc, its beautifully carved choir stalls and its 32 18th-century medallions illustrating the life of Christ.

i Place Albert 1er

Leave Orléans on the N152 as for Blois, avoiding the autoroute. Continue through Meung-sur-Loire to Beaugency. Go left on the D925 as for Limoges, crossing the river bridge. Continue straight over the D951 and on to La Ferté-St-Cyr. Go right on the D103 to Crouy, left on the D33 and continue through the Parc de Chambord to Chambord.

Chambord, Loire Valley Central

8 The Renaissance **château** of **Chambord** is the biggest of all the castles of the Loire. Begun as the favourite hunting lodge of François I, it has no fewer than 440 rooms, and stands in the midst of a 5,443-hectare (13,450-acre) estate circled by a 32km (20-mile) wall!

Most of the forested estate is a hunting reserve, but parts of it are open to visitors. Chambord is beautifully furnished, with fine paintings and tapestries. It houses an exhibition on hunting, and another on its own history. A viewing terrace stands high among the intricate rooftop decorations.

Continue on the D33. After Nanteuil go under the bridge through St Gervais-la-Forêt and right on the D956 to Blois.

Blois, Loire Valley Central

9 A gorgeous open-air staircase built for François I (and possibly designed by Leonardo da Vinci) is only one of the architectural delights of the hilltop **castle** here. The same king commissioned the decorated façade which overlooks the lovely little garden in the Place Victor-Hugo. Archaeological and fine arts museums are housed in the **castle** and there is a gallery devoted to Robert Houdin, the great 19th-century conjuror from whom the escapologist Houdini took his stage name. In the town, a street, a stairway and a statue commemorate Denis Papin, an early steam-engine pioneer. Attractive old buildings include the half-timbered **Maison**

Louis XIV often brought his court to Chambord, one of the loveliest of the French châteaux

des Acrobates with its carvings of jugglers and tumblers. Tours can be arranged of the famous **Chocolaterie Poulain**, the chocolate factory founded in Blois in 1848. Bicycles can be hired from the railway station and several shops in town.

[i] Avenue Laigret

Leave Blois on the N152 as for Tours. In Veuves, turn right on the D65 to Monteaux. Bear left for Cangey along the D58 which becomes the D1. Continue through Limeray. Keep left in Pocé as for Amboise then go right following the 'Vouvray' sign. Turn left on the D46 and continue to Vouvray.

Vouvray, Loire Valley Central

10 There hardly seem to be enough vineyards around Vouvray to justify its reputation as a white wine village. In fact, most are on the upland plateau hidden by limestone cliffs. You can buy wine at several caves, some of them dug into the limestone.

The **Écomusée** explains the cultivation of vines, illustrates old-style crafts including the sewing of the characteristic local embroidered bonnets, and describes the impact on the countryside of the TGV super-express railway lines.

[i] Rue Gambetta

Leave Vouvray on the N152 and return to Tours.

Tours – Amboise 24 (15)
Amboise – Chenonceau 13 (8)
Chenonceau – Valençay 51 (32)
Valençay – Romorantin-Lanthenay 29 (18)
Romorantin-Lanthenay – La Sologne 18 (11)
La Sologne – Gien 74 (46)
Gien – Orléans 89 (55)
Orléans – Chambord 54 (34)
Chambord – Blois 17 (11)
Blois – Vouvray 50 (31)
Vouvray – Tours 9 (6)

SCENIC ROUTES

The **Parc de Chambord** is beautiful forest country. After Monteaux, the **D1** runs parallel with the limestone cliffs which rise to the vineyard plateau.

SPECIAL TO...

8 At Beaugency, between Orléans and Chambord, follow signs to the **Musée Dunois**. In a 15th-century castle, the arts and traditions of the district round Orléans are preserved. Each of its rooms has a special theme such as furniture, toys or costumes.

RECOMMENDED WALKS

7 Pause for a few minutes at Coudroy, after leaving Gien. Here, there is a short footpath, which follows the bank of the Orléans Canal. Only fishermen now come to this 300-year-old waterway, long since closed to navigation.

10 Ask at one of the tourist offices about walks around the **Val de Cisse**. Monteaux, between Blois and Vouvray, is a good centre for them. Using minor road and field tracks, you can wander through farms, woods and vineyards on a fresh, airy plateau above the valley of the Loire.

46

DORDOGNE & SOUTHWEST FRANCE

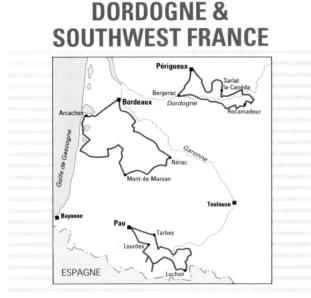

West to east, plains to mountains, sandy shores to towering river cliffs, here is another region which shows the remarkable variety of France. On the coast there are uninterrupted expanses of surf-washed beaches. Behind them stretch vast areas planted with pines.

The Pyrenean foothills offer bracing spa resorts where walks by mountain streams and wildflower meadows are the order of the day. In the valleys of the Dordogne and the Vézère you will find the greatest cluster of prehistoric sites in Europe, many of them troglodytic dwellings quarried thousands of years ago.

Lourdes attracts millions of pilgrims and visitors every year. Smaller numbers make the journey to the glorious hilltop church in St-Bertrand-de-Comminges. You can visit weird underground caverns, one group bizarrely reached, not by going deep into the bowels of the earth, but by heading uphill in a cable car, and you can find out about traditional rural crafts and ways of life in display areas large and small, some conveniently placed, others deliberately very much off the beaten track.

Oysters are a major crop where the Bordeaux route reaches the coast. Inland, connoisseurs of wine and brandy can lose themselves among the vineyards of Armagnac, Bergerac, Barsac, Graves and Sauternes.

The driving is very varied. West and south of Bordeaux there are few natural obstacles to divert the roads from long, flat straights through the forests. Winding river valleys are the norm for Périgueux. The Pau tour, as it climbs into the Pyrenees, is for pass-stormers.

Some of France's most glorious towns and villages are here. Rocamadour is one of the most stunningly located places in Europe, but there are also Domme and Sarlat and La Bastide d'Armagnac to cherish.

Wildlife parks include bird reserves, zoos for endangered species and an atmospheric place devoted to the ancient worship of the bear. You can find out, in museums and exhibitions of many different types and sizes, about tobacco, seaplanes, prehistoric art, clockwork figures, hussars and the red-hot prominences arcing from the surface of the sun.

In the Dordogne you will find regional delicacies such as *foie gras* from both ducks and geese, and the rare elusive truffles. Around Bordeaux, much of the cooking is done with wine. At Arcachon, ask for oysters and the other 'fruits of the sea'.

Bordeaux
Bordeaux is the capital of Aquitaine and of wine, the heart of a region of world-renowned vineyards. It was one of the first cities in France to pedestrianise its shopping streets, and a pioneer in computerised traffic management. Among its elegant public buildings, look for the river façade of the 18th-century Place de la Bourse and the sumptuous Grand-Théâtre of the same era. There are bustling covered markets, craft shops and studios of every kind. Museums and galleries take in painting and decorative arts, the history of the region of Aquitaine, vintage printing presses, natural history collections with magnificent crystal displays, the customs service, military history and the Resistance movement. Cruise boats sail down the Garonne and their joint estuary, the Gironde. A recently introduced touring opportunity is a helicopter jaunt over your own selection of Bordeaux vineyards.

Périgueux
Périgueux is a handsome town whose beautiful old quarter, where the merchants and craftsmen used to live, includes many fine Renaissance and medieval buildings. The perhaps over-restored cathedral, Saint-Front, is a fascinating sight, all domes and cupolas, giving Périgueux an almost Ottoman-Empire skyline.

The Musée du Périgord in Cours Tourny has expanded well beyond its original brief to exhibit the results of excavated Roman sites. The Musée Militaire shows uniforms and weapons from several centuries, and tells the story of the

district's war-ravaged past. There are pleasant gardens, and squares with pollarded trees. You can stroll along the rue des Gladiateurs to the site of the Roman arena. This is a cool place in summer, planted with shrubs and trees, its fragmentary Roman archways within sight and sound of a modern mosaic-tiled fountain.

Pau

In the 19th century, the British invaded Pau, but not with any martial intent. Three Scots laid out a golf course for the British colony. At the turn of the century and through the 1920s, Pau was one of the great British resorts of Europe. There was American influence, too. Orville and Wilbur Wright set up the world's first aviation school here. The town has lovely parks and gardens. Find the boulevard des Pyrénées and you will see not only a fine promenade, but also a glorious southern mountain horizon. A rebuilt funicular railway climbs from a lower avenue. Some of the finest state rooms in France are in the majestic, if much restored, château, which houses a rich collection of tapestries. On one weekend in June, Pau echoes to the scream of high-pitched engines. There is a famous racing circuit here, including public roads and driveways to the leafy Parc Beaumont.

Right: The opulent, fertile Valley of the Dordogne at Périgueux
Below: The sun sets over Bordeaux

4 days – 486km (301 miles)

LES LANDES: COAST, DUNES & FOREST

Bordeaux • Gujan-Mestras • Arcachon • Biscarrosse
Mimizan • Sabres • Mont-de-Marsan • Labastide d'Armagnac
Barbotan-les-Thermes • Nérac • Sauternes • Bordeaux

South of Bordeaux the essential flatness of the Landes is disguised by two notable features. Along the coast there are long fine-sand beaches backed by substantial dunes. Inland lies a huge forest area with carefully watered croplands in extensive clearings. You will find lively seaside resorts, a settlement of oyster-farmers, a revitalised spa and a beautifully situated rural church dedicated to Our Lady of the Cyclists. The Médoc vineyards lie north of this tour, but amateurs of wine may appreciate passing from Sauternes to Barsac and from Barsac to Graves.

BACK TO NATURE

1 Turn right in Le Teich, on the way to Gujan-Mestras, at the 'Parc Ornitholigique' sign. The **bird reserve** here in the scrubland delta by the Bassin d'Arcachon is especially strong in wildfowl, but you should also look for whiskered terns, black-winged stilts, herons, storks and little egrets, as well as numerous dragon flies.

FOR CHILDREN

1 Street signs in Gujan-Mestras are decorated with ladybirds – *coccinelles*. This is a link with **La Coccinelle animal park** at La Hume. Here, children are offered 'a nothing like and surprising walk' among domestic and farm animals, with pony rides, trampolines, swings and toboggans as a bonus.

i Cours du XXX Juillet, Bordeaux

Leave Bordeaux on the N250. Go straight ahead on the D650 through Le Teich to Gujan-Mestras.

Gujan-Mestras, Aquitaine

2 The two parts of this strung-out cluster of villages on the southern side of the great Bassin d'Arcachon could hardly be more oddly matched. Take any of the streets with 'port'

Rolling countryside near Mézin, in this fine farmland region

The highest sand dune in France being put to good use at Pilat

signs, to the right of the main road, and you enter the almost timeless world of the oyster farmer. The ports are seven rectangular inlets of the bay, lined by identical wooden workshop cabins. Outside lies the paraphernalia of oyster cultivation – boat tackle, mounds of emptied shells and piles of sharpened wooden stakes to be driven into the bed of the bay where the oysters grow.

Elsewhere, Gujan-Mestras is a modern holiday resort. Turn left for the 'Parc Aquatique' (water park) called Aquacity. The pools, slides, wave machine and water chutes of **Aquacity** share the large leisure area at **La Hume** with a flimsy-looking 'rustic' village where some 50 serious craftworkers settle every summer. There is also a well-stocked **museum of ship models and ship design**.

i Avenue de Lattre de Tassigny

Continue on the D650 to Arcachon.

Arcachon, Aquitaine

2 Although the oysters of the Bassin d'Arcachon have been celebrated since the 16th century, the town itself is a resort created in the railway age. Arcachon has a well-equipped yacht haven and fishing port. A high-set figure of Christ blesses the harbour. Walk to the end of the breakwater and you will see not only the far-out oyster beds but also a stone anchor sailors' memorial. The **aquarium** and **museum** specialise in the creatures of the bay and the open sea. You can sail to the oyster beds, to the **Île aux Oiseaux** (Bird's Island) in the bay, and across the mouth of the bay to the peninsula resort of **Cap Ferret**. Back from the waterfront the town have lively shopping and café areas, and it is generously supplied with woods and parkland. Arcachon's status as the most stylish resort on the Côte d'Argent ('silver coast') is well deserved.

i Place Roosevelt

Leave Arcachon on the D218 into Pyla-sur-Mer and past the Dune de Pyla. Continue to Biscarrosse.

Biscarrosse, Aquitaine

3 A pinewood resort with bungalows, hotels and a few colour-washed apartment blocks, Biscarrosse-Plage has a not-yet-finished air, added to by the fact that sand blows around its streets. But there is a splendid beach here, backed by dunes, with white-topped breakers creaming in.

The older part of the settlement, Biscarrosse-Bourg or Biscarrosse-Ville, is separated from the beach resort by a full 9.6km (6 miles) of open road. This is a handsome place. Its church stands among bright and well-watered gardens dotted with birch trees.

On the southwestern edge of town lies an attractive lake rimmed by low wooded hills. This is a good sailing and angling centre, and it was briefly, between the wars, the French base of a flying-boat service from New York. The Musée de l'Hydraviation, on the road to the lake, recalls those flying-boat days, and there is a Musée de la Nature near by.

i Avenue Plage

Leave Biscarrosse on the D652 through Parentis-en-Born to Ste Eulalie, then take the D87 to Mimizan.

Mimizan, Aquitaine

4 This is another split-personality town, approached along the shore of the Étang d'Aureilhan, where Winston Churchill was often a guest of the Duke of Westminster on an estate there. He left several paintings of local scenes.

Mimizan divides at the Papeteries de Gascogne, a huge papermill which

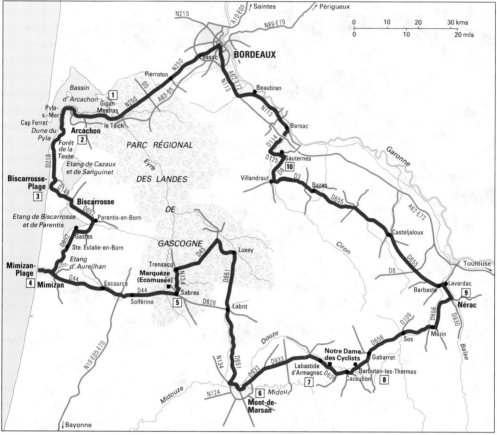

The colourful flower festival at Fourcès is a local source of pride

wafts an unmistakable smell along the prevailing wind. The holiday resort is very modern, with fine beaches ideal for surfing. You can explore the forest to the south, on foot or along the cycle tracks.

The inland part of Mimizan is built round a largely derelict 11th-century Benedictine **abbey**. The little town **museum** faces it.

In summer the riverside bull-ring promotes *courses landaises*, acrobatic affairs, similar to the Provençal form of bullfighting in which the bulls are unharmed. Stilt-walking is another speciality!

i Avenue Martin

Leave Mimizan on the D44 to Sabres.

FOR HISTORY BUFFS

5 On the **D44** before Sabres, the village of Solférino recalls a battlefield in Italy. The estate here, owned by Napoleon III, was given the name after his successful part in the battle against Austria in 1859. A **museum** holds mementoes of his Second Empire.

FOR CHILDREN

5 On the way to Mont-de-Marsan, to keep the children occupied on the drive across the flat forest and farmland after Trensacq, ask them to count how many bends there are in the 18km (11 miles) of the **D45**.

RECOMMENDED WALKS

3 After the Dune du Pilat south of Arcachon, the D218 runs through the pinewoods, scrub and sand-hills of the **Forêt de la Teste**. Park here, and you will find many informal footpaths off to the right, leading to beaches lapped by the Atlantic breakers.

7 Ask at the tourist office in Labastide d'Armagnac for the map of the waymarked walks southwest of the little town. They climb gently into a lush landscape of woodlands, farms and Armagnac vineyards.

Sabres, Aquitaine

5 A pleasant if unremarkable road-junction village, Sabres still has a station on the railway built in 1890 to link it with Mimizan. The line is now used to take visitors to the remotely located Écomusée at Marquèze, 5km (3 miles) to the northwest.

This splendid place is part of the **Parc Régional des Landes de Gascogne**. Displays make it clear how the great forests used to support little local industries such as iron and glass works, brick and tile kilns. Then, in the second half of the 19th century, the government decided to manage the pine forests on a virtually industrial scale.

Marquèze, based on a large forest clearing, shows you both how the timber resources have been exploited and what kinds of activity were discarded – charcoal-burning, water-mills, sheep-farming and the cultivation of fruit trees.

*Leave Sabres on the **N134** as for Bordeaux. In Trensacq turn right on the **D45**. Turn right on the **D651** through Luxey, then continue to Mont-de-Marsan.*

Mont-de-Marsan, Aquitaine

6 You will not be long in Mont-de-Marsan before realising that this is a place of some consequence. Its elegant 19th-century public buildings, immaculately kept, stand among modern equivalents, which are imaginative in design, but do not clash. In fact, Mont-de-Marsan is an important government centre.

It stands where the Rivers Midou and Douze merge into the waggishly named Midouze. The **Parc Jean Rameau** is an attractive woodland area, with many flowering shrubs, overlooking the Douze.

A pair of restored 14th-century buildings house the **museum and the art gallery**. The **Church of Ste Madeleine** is worth visiting for its marblework and elegant ornamented ceiling.

Like Mimizan, Mont-de-Marsan is a centre for *courses landaises*, but the great sporting enthusiasm is for horse-racing. The impressive race-course

plays host to a dozen meetings every year.

[i] Place Leclerc

*Leave Mont-de-Marsan on the **D932** as for Roquefort. Bear right on the **D933** to St Justin, then right on the **D626** to Labastide d'Armagnac.*

Labastide d'Armagnac, Aquitaine

7 Almost miraculously, the arcaded square here, **Place Royale**, has survived with little alteration since 1291. Three sides are still taken up by arches and cool, covered walkways. The fourth features the 15th-century church. Some guidebooks give Labastide a cursory mention, but go to the flowery Place Royale and you will find an architectural gem of effortless charm.

The tourist office, in one of the arcades, leads to a little **costume museum**. There is also a display of Armagnac brandy. Away from the square, a 17th-century **chapel** houses an exhibition of the *bastides*, the historic fortified villages.

Beyond Labastide, turn right on the **C1** for **Château Garreau**. At the end of a dusty gravel road between its ridgetop vineyards, the estate's **Musée du Vigneron** has exhibits on old distillery techniques and equipment, and on the rural life of Armagnac.

[i] Place Royal

*Continue on the **D626** to Cazaubon and turn left on the **D656** to Barbotan-les-Thermes.*

Barbotan-les-Thermes, Aquitaine

8 Unlike the spa towns of some other countries, those in France have not mouldered away. Barbotan, whose thermal baths were probably known to the Romans, has been completely refurbished. Brightly decorated hotels, shops, cafés and restaurants line the busy and effectively pedestrianised main street. Sparkling new buildings house the **baths** which attract an increasing number of curistes (cure-seekers) – more than 20,000 of them every year.

There are attractive gardens, pleasant walks and an opportunity to admire relics of the past, such as the 12th-century **church** whose clocktower is built above one of the medieval town gateways.

Just outside Barbotan is the **Lac de l'Uby**. This well-equipped leisure area offers sailing, tennis and mini-golf facilities as well as a sandy beach, pony rides, pedalo hire and a children's play park.

[i] Maison du Curiste

*Continue on the **D656** through Gabarret to Nérac.*

Nérac, Aquitaine

9 Only one wing remains, high above the River Baïse, of Nérac's lovely Renaissance **château**. Climb the stairs to the elegant, open, first-floor gallery, and you will find a **museum of archaeology and history**. Close by, the **Church of St Nicholas**

has a severe frontage but some good 18th-century stained glass. There are grand views across the river to **Petit Nérac**, a hillside quarter of fine old buildings with dark red roofs. Its church spire soars in glorious silhouette against the sky.

River boats run cruises on the Baïse. Upstream, the **Promenade de la Garenne** offers you a stroll through a pleasant woodland park with fountains and an open-air theatre.

Leave Nérac on the D930 to Lavardac, then go left to Casteljaloux and follow signs to Bazas. Continue to Villandraut. Turn right on the D8 through Nouillan and Brouquet, then left on the D125 to Sauternes.

Sauternes, Aquitaine

10 Arriving at Sauternes, the centre of one of the most famous white wine districts, you will come to the **Place de l'Église**, which would be the heart of the village if there were a village for it to be the heart of. Only a handful of buildings surround the square, one of them where the local wine producers offer their wares. There is also a map showing the locations of the eight vineyards which regularly welcome visitors.

Not included in this display is the aristocratic 16th- and 17th-century **Château Yquem**. Its Château Yquem wine, with the superlative classification of *Premier Grand Cru Classé*, was the first to be produced from grapes affected with the 'noble rot' provoked by the misty mornings and warm afternoons of autumn.

Continue on the D125 as for Budos, then go right on the D114. Follow this road over the autoroute to the N113. Turn left there through Barsac and return to Bordeaux, avoiding the autoroute.

Bordeaux – Gujan-Mestras 47 (29)
Gujan-Mestras – Arcachon 13 (8)
Arcachon – Biscarrosse 42 (26)
Biscarrosse – Mimizan 38 (24)
Mimizan – Sabres 47 (29)
Sabres – Mont-de-Marsan 81 (50)
Mont-de-Marsan – Labastide d'Armagnac 29 (18)
Labastide d'Armagnac – Barbotan-les-Thermes 16 (10)
Barbotan-les-Thermes – Nérac 42 (26)
Nérac – Sauternes 82 (51)
Sauternes – Bordeaux 49 (30)

Below: The Church of St Nicholas at Nérac. Right: The crest at Château Yquem, which has given its name to one of the world's most celebrated wines

4 days – 383km (238 miles)

THE DORDOGNE: JOURNEY INTO PREHISTORY

Périgueux • Grotte du Grand Roc • Les Eyzies • Lascaux II Sarlat • Souillac • Gouffre de Padirac • Rocamadour Domme • Les Milandes • Bergerac • Périgueux

Although there are remains of old Roman buildings in the heart of the town of Périgueux, our starting-point, this tour featuring two of France's loveliest rivers, the Dordogne and the Vézère, will take you much further back into the history of man, tens and even hundreds of thousands of years ago. Limestone is the key to the appeal of these districts, providing the huge cliffs, the amazing caves and underground rivers, and the golden building stone of beautiful towns like Sarlat and Domme.

☐ Place Francheville, Périgueux

Leave Périgueux on the N89 as for Brive. Go right on the D710, left on the D45 then right on the D47 to Grotte du Grand Roc.

SCENIC ROUTES

1 The approach to the Grotto du Grand Roc on the D47 introduces the stunning limestone cliffs which characterise this tour.

Grotte du Grand Roc, Aquitaine

1 The great natural limestone wall here, facing the Vézère, with its overhangs forming the pitched roof lines of some bizarrely located houses, is honeycombed with ancient dwellings and caverns. In the Grotte du Grand Roc you will find an underground wonderland whose cave floors and hanging gardens of fretted limestone look like a spiky coral

Singer Josephine Baker lived at the Château at Les Milandes with her brood of adopted children

reef (wire grills protect some of the formations). In the same magnificent cliff, the prehistoric rock shelters of **Laugerie Haute** and **Laugerie Basse**, which yielded countless objects left behind by their Ice Age inhabitants, are open to visitors.

Less forbidding than its name, the **Gorge d'Enfer** (Gorge of Hell) is set in a little wooded, grassy side valley whose caves display 25,000-year-old wall carvings. There is also an animal reserve, a fishing lake and a picnic site. Further on, the **Musée de Spéléologie**, entered by a stairway up a colossal overhanging cliff, illustrates the daring work of the modern cave explorers.

Continue on the D47 into Les Eyzies.

Les Eyzies, Aquitaine

2 If the Vézère is the 'valley of mankind', the village of Les Eyzies, spectacularly located between a northern limestone cliff and the river, is at the heart of the greatest concentration of prehistoric sites. The **Musée National de la Préhistoire**, built into the cliff face, is devoted in particular to the palaeolithic era, starting perhaps 2½–3 million years ago with the first traces of primitive man. Near by the **Abri Pataud** is a cliff shelter of more than 20,000 years ago. As a complete contrast, Les Eyzies also offers a **botanical garden** of medicinal plants; other displays here explain the culture of the crayfish and the bee.

☐ Place de la Mairie

Leave Les Eyzies on the D706 to Montignac. Turn right on the D704, then right again for Lascaux II.

Lascaux II, Aquitaine

3 Discovered in 1940, the caves at Lascaux are decorated with the most celebrated prehistoric paintings in the world – lively representations of bulls, deer and horses created nearly 18,000 years ago.

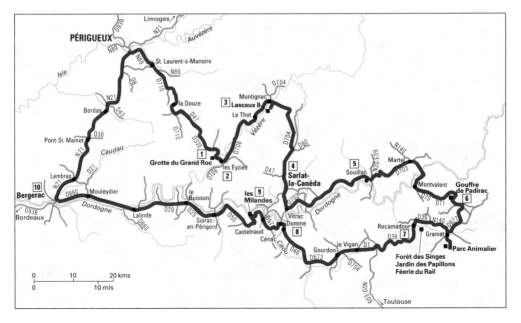

3 Off the **D706**, after Les Eyzies, several sites illustrate the everyday life of our very remote ancestors. **Préhisto-Parc** features outdoor tableaux of Neanderthal and Cro-Magnon (a type of 'modern' man), hunting expeditions and household scenes of 15,000 years ago. **La Roque St Christophe** is an amazing troglodytic fortress town, lived in from prehistoric days to the 18th century, with five great terraces overlooking the River Vézère. At Le Thot, a modern museum and gallery explain the environment and art of prehistoric times. In the parkland, present-day animals such as red and fallow deer, bison, tarpan and Przewalkski's horses can be compared with life-size replicas of mammoths and aurochs (an extinct type of ox).

4 The first ridge-top road on the tour is the **D704** to Sarlat, giving wide-ranging views over rolling wooded hills.

5 After Montvalent, on the way from Souillac to Padirac, there is a landscape change as the **D70** and **D11** run through the parcels of sheep-grazed land on the limestone plateau known as the causse.

The caves have had to be closed to the public to prevent deterioration of the original paintings, but painstakingly exact replicas are on display at the neighbouring site called Lascaux II. A visit here cures visitors of any notion that our ancestors of 800 generations ago were nothing more than primitive louts. Much older than Lascaux, the nearby cave site of **Régourdou** is also open to visitors. The brown bears in its park match displays in the museum there about the prehistoric cult of the bear.

i Place Léo-Magne, Montignac

*Return to Montignac and turn right on the **D704** to Sarlat.*

Sarlat, Aquitaine

4 The golden stone of Sarlat and the effortless grace of its Gothic and Renaissance buildings make this one of the loveliest towns in the Dordogne region. Even the tourist information office is housed in a 15th-century mansion near the handsome **cathedral** of the 16th and 17th centuries. Shaded alleys and courtyards in the old town are busy with a craftsmen's market and shops at which every third or fourth seems to specialise in *foie gras*. **L'Homo Sapiens** is a little museum of archaeological discoveries, prehistoric art forms, stone and flint tools. There is an imaginative **Aquarium** concentrating on the 30 or more species of fish found in the River Dordogne. On a wooded hillside above the square, pleasant public gardens can be found.

i Place de la Liberté

The honey stone and grey roofs of old Sarlat – a maze of medieval streets – contrast with newer parts of this busy market town. The Saturday market is a sight to see, and the Theatre Festival in late July to early August is popular with leading Parisian companies

*Leave Sarlat on the **D46** for Vitrac. In Vitrac-Port watch for a left turn on to the **D703** to Carsac and Souillac. Turn left on to the **N20** in Souillac.*

Souillac, Midi-Pyrénées

5 The glory of this busy centre in the Dordogne valley is the restored 12th-century Romanesque church called **Abbatiale Sainte Marie**, whose red-and-white tiled roofs culminate in a series of cupolas, as in the cathedral at Périgueux. The carvings in the church are particularly fine. Behind the church you may hear the incongruous music of a 1920s jazz band. This is just one of the lifelike exhibits in the **Musée de l'Automate**. Tableaux of moving life-size figures also include a glamorous lady snake-charmer and a clown and a splendid animated 19th-century Passion Play.

i Boulevard Louis-Jean Malvy

*Leave Souillac on the **D703** to Martel. Turn right on the **N140**, left on the **D70** then right on the **D11** to Miers and left on the **D91**. Go left on the **D60**, right at the Y-junction at the stone cross, then right at the T-junction to Gouffre de Padirac.*

Two great gourmet specialities of the Dordogne are truffles and *foie gras*. Truffles are rare edible fungi which grow underground, often in oak woods, and are dug out by truffle-hunting dogs – and even pigs. These trained animals are weaned on truffles from an early age and are trusted not to eat the precious quarry. The production of *foie gras* – goose or sometimes duck-liver pâté – involves grotesque force-feeding of the birds with huge quantities of maize. The pâté is preserved, often with a minute portion of truffle included, and sold at a luxury price.

5 Quercyland is a fun park on the outskirts of Souillac, where children subdued by all the prehistory can work off some energy.

7 Just after the **Jardin des Papillons** on the D36 before Rocamadour, **La Féerie du Rail** (The Enchanted Railway) is a huge model layout with 60 trains hauling coaches and freight wagons past mountain villages, farms, a castle, a fairground and a windmill, and over a viaduct menaced by the ice cliffs of a glacier.

7 Turn left in Gramat, then take the **D677** and the **D14** to the Parc Animalier. This zoo houses more than 300 species including bear, chamois, lynx, yak, moufflon, birds of prey and breeds of farm animals 'in peril of extinction', such as Limousin, Gascon and Normandy pigs. To find the park, turn left on the N140, then take the D677 and the D14.

On the D36 approaching Rocamadour there is an impressive **Forêt des Singes** (Monkey Forest), where macaques (similar to the Barbary apes of Gibraltar) roam freely. You can buy and distribute popcorn, one of the monkeys' favourite snacks. Alongside, the **Jardin des Papillons** houses free-flying exotic butterflies of many colourful species from Europe, Asia, Africa and the Americas.

There are falconry displays at the **Rocher des Aigles** in Rocamadour.

7 At busy times, you may appreciate leaving the narrow streets of Rocamadour for a walk, steep in places, based on old sheep tracks in the **Alzou Valley**. It starts from the bridge on the D32 below the town and heads up-river.

8 A leaflet you can collect at Domme shows three way-marked walks, starting from the walled gateway of the Porte des Tours. They descend by shady paths to the River Dordogne and wander through higher farmland.

Gouffre de Padirac, Midi-Pyrénées

6 Open since the late 19th century when it was discovered, the Padirac chasm is one of the greatest underground sights in Europe. Lifts and stairways descend to the otherworldly cavern of a subterranean river where, by boat and pathway, you can visit glorious floodlit limestone chambers like the Great Dome Gallery, walls of stalagmites and a petrified waterfall. Cafés and restaurants, a picnic area and a small zoo are clustered above ground.

Continue on the D90 to Padirac, turn left and follow signs to Gramat. Leave Gramat on the N140 northwards, then turn left on the D36. Turn left on the D32 into Rocamadour.

Rocamadour, Midi-Pyrénées

7 Words and pictures rarely do justice to the reality of Rocamadour, the magnificent fortified pilgrimage town whose historic houses, sanctuary churches, bishops' palace, museums and – at the highest level – skyline castle cascade down a ter-

Legends of miracles abound in Rocamadour, but for today's visitors the reality is equally magical

raced limestone cliff. It became a place of pilgrimage in the 12th century, visited by the great and the good of Christendom. Lifts and staircases, including the long and tiring pilgrims' Holy Way, are threaded through the town. Once you have turned on to the D32 you should pause to admire the stunning situation of the place, from the viewpoint beside the Hotel Belvedere. In Rocamadour itself, the finest view is from the castle ramparts. The D32 road avoids the town centre often crammed with visitors. There are parking places in the valley.

Continue on the D32 to Couzou, go right on the D39 through St Projet, right on the D1 then join the D673 to Gourdon. Turn left as for Sarlat then left as for Salviac, leaving Gourdon on the D763. Go right on the D6, which becomes the D46 to Cénac. Go right on the D49 to Domme.

Domme, Aquitaine

8 This lovely, mellow hilltop town, founded with defensive ramparts and gateways around 1280, provides one of the finest viewpoints in France. The River Dordogne curves below the town, giving way to fields,

farmhouses and lines of poplars on the riverside plain. Limestone cliffs, woods and hill villages march to the horizon. In Domme itself there are beautiful townscape views round every corner. A good **museum** illustrates local domestic life in the past. Shops sell local honey, jams, truffles and *foie gras*. In the central square, an old covered market hall is now the entrance to a marvellous series of **underground caverns** with mirror lakes and floodlit limestone columns.

i Place de la Halle

Return to Cénac and go straight on along the D50, through St Cybranet, then continue as for Siorac. In Pont-de-Cause bear right for Castelnaud. In Castelnaud, go straight ahead for Fayrac and Les Milandes. Turn left on the D53 as for Siorac then after a 'virages' sign watch for a sharp right uphill signed 'Château des Milandes'.

Les Milandes, Aquitaine

9 Perched on a terrace giving spreading views over the Dordogne valley, the restored 15th-century castle in the attractive and tucked-away hamlet of Les Milandes was owned from 1949 to 1969 by the American singer Josephine Baker, star of the Paris cabarets between the wars. It was here that she founded a philanthropic foundation to look after children from all over the world. Beyond the castle, the white courtyard of the farm which was also part of Josephine Baker's estate houses a rural **museum** explaining the improvements in agricultural techniques through the years.

Continue from the farm museum and bear left as for Veyrines. Turn right on the D53 then take the D50 to Siorac and the D25 to le Buisson. Follow signs to Lalinde, then Bergerac.

Its spectacular hilltop position has made Domme a coveted prize throughout France's turbulent history – Edward III's English army once occupied it for 22 years!

Bergerac, Aquitaine

10 A cobbled car park which slopes down towards the River Dordogne is a convenient base for a stroll round the restored old town at the heart of present-day Bergerac. There are narrow lanes of part-timbered houses, and tiny squares, one of them shaded by chestnut trees where a statue of Cyrano de Bergerac, the 17th-century nobleman and soldier famous for his large nose, stands, nobly cloaked. The impressive **Musée du Tabac** in the town hall (Maison Peyrarède) illustrates the discovery of tobacco, its sources, and the local tobacco trade, as well as displaying beautifully worked pipes, cigarette holders, snuffboxes and tobacco jars. Its curious second-floor exit leads back down to street level through the **town museum** (history and regional ethnography). Near by, the **Musée du Vin et de la Batellerie** combines several long-standing Bergerac interests – wine, barrel-making and river traffic. There are also guided visits to the old **monastery** housing the wine council on which all the Bergerac growers are represented.

i Rue Neuve d'Argenson

Leave Bergerac on the N21 and return to Périgueux.

Périgueux – Grotte du Grand Roc 44 (27)
Grotte du Grand Roc – Les Eyzies 3 (2)
Les Eyzies – Lascaux II 30 (19)
Lascaux II – Sarlat 27 (17)
Sarlat – Souillac 34 (21)
Souillac – Gouffre de Padirac 38 (24)
Gouffre de Padirac – Rocamadour 29 (18)
Rocamadour – Domme 52 (32)
Domme – Les Milandes 15 (9)
Les Milandes – Bergerac 62 (39)
Bergerac – Périgueux 49 (30)

SCENIC ROUTES

7 After Rocamadour, the D32 climbs above a deep canyon with tiers of limestone cliffs. The riverside road from Castelnaud beyond Fayrac open up a tremendous view to the castle of Beynac, and the D29 runs past rapids and wooded islets in the Dordogne on the way to Lalinde.

FOR HISTORY BUFFS

9 On the way from Domme to Les Milandes, on a glorious viewpoint site above the village of the same name, **Castelnaud** is a restored medieval castle which houses displays on artillery and siege warfare. During much of the Hundred Years' War, the castle was held by the English.

4 days – 392km (243 miles)

THROUGH THE HIGH PYRENEES

Pau • Tarbes • Bagnères-de-Bigorre
St Bertrand-de-Comminges • Bagnères-de-Luchon
Col du Tourmalet • Gavarnie • Cauterets • Lourdes
Grottes de Bétharram • Pau

This is a summer tour, exploring some of the highest roads in the Pyrenees mountains. The Col du Tourmalet usually opens only after the snows clear in June. It is hardly worth tackling this tour when the mountain skyline south of Pau is wreathed in clouds; the spectacular scenery along the southern part of the route would be lost to view. In any case, you might not enjoy driving over the high passes in bad visibility. The mountain roads are exhilarating in fine weather, hairpinning to great summit viewpoints. There are pleasant resorts in the foothills; you can visit some majestic underground caverns; and Lourdes is the greatest religious pilgrimage town in Europe.

The Château overlooking the Foix, survivor of innumerable armed assaults in medieval times, commands an unforgettable view of the Pyrenees

ⓘ Place Royale, Pau

Leave Pau on the N117 to Tarbes, avoiding the autoroute.

Tarbes, Midi-Pyrénées

1 With centuries of history as a regional capital behind it, Tarbes is a busy, prosperous, confident and go-ahead city. There is a strong summer programme of musical, theatrical, artistic, floral and sporting events.

Just off the town centre, the **Jardin Massey** is an attractive woodland park with pools, statues, a bandstand, an open-air theatre and peacocks' outlandish cries echoing over the lawns. Be prepared to give way to families of mallards waddling between the ponds and streams. In the heart of the park, the **Musée Massey** is an elegant 19th-century mansion with a fine collection of French, Flemish and Italian paintings, and a superb display on the hussars, the élite cavalry corps not only of France, but also of countries all over the world.

Although the present-day hussars stationed at Tarbes are mechanised units, the **national stud** of Anglo-Arab horses founded in 1806 continues to flourish. The **stables** are regularly open to visitors, and Tarbes hosts several show-jumping and dressage events during the year.

ⓘ Place de Verdun

Leaves Tarbes on the D935 to Bagnères-de-Bigorre.

The Musée Massey at Tarbes houses a collection of France's élite cavalry corps, the hussars

Bagnères-de-Bigorre, Midi-Pyrénées

2 Offering thermal baths, a casino, sports facilities and healthy walks, with industry kept discreetly in the outskirts, Bagnères is a typical southern spa nestling in the forested foothills of the Pyrenees. Occupied in prehistoric times, it was taken over by the Romans, who were the first to build bath-houses over its warm-water springs. Its reputation as a spa increased through the years and came to a peak in the 19th century, as the architecture of the thermal establishments shows. The **Musée Bigourdan** has local displays, while the **Musée Salies** is given over mostly to paintings.

Bagnères is well-known for its authentic folk-singing concerts. Tennis and the hiring of horses, ponies or all-terrain bicycles can be arranged. As well as fishing, often for rainbow trout, the River Adour running through the town is used for lively white-water canoeing.

ⓘ Allées Tournefort

*Leave Bagnères on the **D938** as for Toulouse. Turn right on the **D26**, then right on the **D929** through Hèches. Watch for a left turn, just as you see the 'Rebouc' sign, down over a level crossing and immediately left, following the **D26** again. In St Bertrand-de-Comminges, go right at the crossroads, uphill on the **D26**.*

St Bertrand-de-Comminges, Midi-Pyrénées

3 Here is a most attractively located village whose red-roofed houses climb a modest ridge between the farmlands of the plain and the wooded Pyrenean foothills. The village and its unexpectedly majestic **cathedral** both take their name from a 12th-century bishop buried here. Pilgrims

have been coming in great numbers since the Middle Ages.

In the 16th century the cathedral interior was remodelled with stunning carved-wood screens around the choir. The splendid organ also dates from that time, and is played at many recitals. Outside, the beautiful arcaded cloisters look incongruously across to the wooded hillsides, which were a refuge for Resistance fighters in World War II.

The village preserves several fine old buildings, such as the 15th-century **Maison Bridaut** with its stone tower and timber-framed upper storeys. The tourist office gives access to a **museum** of sculptures and local archaeological finds.

Below the village stands an isolated 12th-century **basilica** in Italianate surroundings with tall cypress trees. Much of its masonry was taken from the ruins of a Roman settlement.

ⓘ Les Olivetains

*Return downhill then go straight ahead on the **D26** through Valcabrère. Turn right on the **N125** and follow signs to Luchon.*

Bagnères-de-Luchon, Midi-Pyrénées

4 Most elegant and luxurious of the Pyrenean spas, Luchon (as it is generally known) is centred on a lively tree-lined avenue, with pavement cafés leading to the gardens of the thermal establishment. There is a stylish atmosphere both about the town itself and about the way it conducts its business. Walking, rock-climbing, fishing, clay-pigeon shooting, canoeing and rafting, tennis, hang-gliding and horse-riding, archery and golf are all catered for here. Many visitors come to the spa (the largest and most fashionable Pyrenean spa) not because they are unwell, but because they want a 'toning-up'.

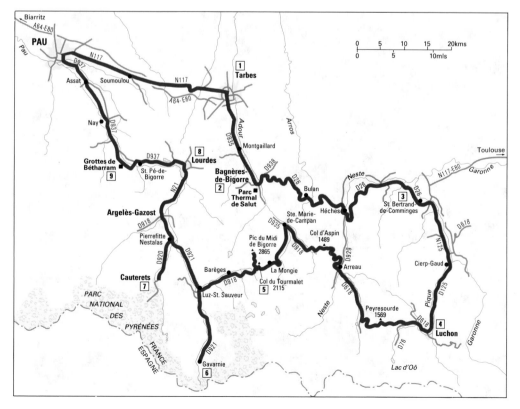

BACK TO NATURE

5 From July till September, when the toll road is open, visitors are welcome to find out about extra-terrestrial affairs at the dramatically located **Observatoire et Institut de Physique du Globe** on the Pic du Midi. It has done pioneering work on cosmic rays and the huge, arching solar protuberances, and produced some of the finest-quality photographs ever taken from Earth.

SPECIAL TO...

5 The passes of Aspin and Tourmalet are classic stretches of the famous **Tour de France** cycle race. If you are here on the day of the Tour, forget about driving. Park among the thousands of spectators and watch the battle for the coveted 'King of the Mountains' title.

RECOMMENDED WALKS

5 After Luchon, turn left on the D76 towards the **Lac d'Oô**. From a car park in this green steep-sided Pyrenean glen, it is a straightforward walk up to the lake, fed by a 275m (900-foot) cascade from Lac d'Espigno higher still.

Biblical Herod was exiled here in Roman times; centuries later, St Bertrand-de-Comminges built his cathedral in this serene place

The history of the town and district is well illustrated in the **Musée du Pays de Luchon**. This 18th-century mansion has a dozen exhibition rooms also devoted to the wildlife of the Pyrenees, the development of mountaineering and 2,000 years of curistes from the time of notable Romans such as Pompey and Tiberius, who sojourned at the even-then handsomely equipped resort they knew as *Ilixion*.

i Allées d'Étigny

> *Leave Luchon on the D618 over the Col de Peyresourde. In Arreau go right on the D929 then, opposite the Esso station and not before, bear left uphill over the Col d'Aspin on the D918. Turn left in Ste-Marie-de-Campan to follow the D918 to the Col du Tourmalet.*

Col du Tourmalet, Midi-Pyrénées

5 At an altitude of 2,114m (6,936 feet), this is the highest through-road summit in the French Pyrenees. The road climbs relentlessly under five avalanche shelters to the ski resort – almost a ghost village at the height of summer – of La Mongie. Hairpin bends then take it up the final stretch, overlooked by colossal granite peaks and pinnacles, to the Col. From the top, the view ahead is magnificent, over peaks and ridges ranged to the horizon.

At a neck-craning angle to the

north you will see the still higher observatory buildings and soaring television mast on the 2,865m (9,400-foot) summit of the Pic du Midi. A right turn just after the actual Col leads along the steep and twisting toll road – to be driven cautiously – which climbs towards the summit and its astounding viewpoint.

> *Immediately after the summit of the Col du Tourmalet, bear left through Barèges to Luz-St-Sauveur. Turn left on to the D921 to Gavarnie.*

Gavarnie, Midi-Pyrénées

6 The narrow road to Gavarnie can be a trial in summer, because it is the busy dead-end approach to one of the most dramatic landscapes in Europe. South of the village lies the sublime **Cirque de Gavarnie**, a mountain amphitheatre piled with snow, whose rim at over 3,000m (10,000 feet) marks the boundary between France and Spain. Of its many waterfalls, the **Grande Cascade**, one of Europe's biggest, drops 442m (1,450 feet).

You can get really close to the Cirque only on foot or on horseback. A spectacular winding road does, however, climb through wild country from Gavarnie to finish at a border col further west.

Gavarnie itself lies in a fine location with a river crashing through. It has an information centre for the **Parc National des Pyrénées** (Pyrenees National Park) and, in the heart of a famous climbing area, several monuments to the pioneering mountaineers. Try to be here in the evening after the press of day visitors has eased. In the mountains, dusk brings a special magic.

i Maison du Parc National

Return to Luz-St-Sauveur and take the D921 as for Lourdes. Immediately after leaving Soulom, turn left on to the D920 to Cauterets.

Cauterets, Midi-Pyrénées

7 Situated in a narrow river valley, Cauterets is the remotest of the Pyrenean spas. In medieval times it was believed the waters cured sterility. It has sulphur waters, thermal baths, a casino, unexpectedly handsome town houses and hotels, and well developed winter sports facilities. Victor Hugo and George Sand were among the famous literary figures who came this way and helped to spread its reputation.

There is another information centre here for the Pyrenees National Park, which you can enter by various roads and footpaths. There is also a small museum with seasonal film shows. Waterfalls tumble down near by, especially alongside the road to the Pont d'Espagne.

One of the most engaging features of Cauterets is that, although the railway which used to serve it has long since gone, the glorious rustic **station**, all varnished ornamental woodwork, has been lovingly preserved. Looking at it, you are not quite literally transported back to the 19th century.

i Maison de la Montagne
place Clemenceau

Return to the D921. Turn left and continue to Lourdes.

Lourdes, Midi-Pyrénées

8 In 1858, a 14-year-old girl called Bernadette Soubirous, walking by the rocky banks of the river at Lourdes, experienced the first of a long series of visions of the Virgin Mary. During her lifetime, pilgrims in increasing numbers, having heard of these wonders, journeyed to Lourdes. Two splendid basilicas were built beside the original grotto. In 1958, a third underground basilica was opened.

The beautiful riverside parkland where this complex is located attracts millions of visitors every year, many of them seeking cures for ailments or disabilities. The **Pavilion Notre-Dame** tells the story of St Bernadette and the pilgrimages (**Musée Bernadette**) and there is also a museum of sacred art (**Musée d'Art Sacré du Gemmail**). Climbing through woodland, the **Chemin du Calvaire** passes the 14 Stations of the Cross.

Lourdes itself is often crammed with people and their cars. Overlooking the town from a rocky bluff, the medieval château-fort houses the **Musée Pyrénéen**, a museum of the arts and traditions of the folk of the foothills. One-tenth scale models show off typical Pyrenean architecture.

Take the funicular railway to the **Pic du Jer**. It opens up elevated views of the town, the valleys and the mountains.

i Place du Champ Commun

Leave Lourdes on the D937, following 'Bétharram' signs. Go through St Pé, then turn left off the D937 and left again to the Grottes de Bétharram.

Grottes de Bétharram, Midi-Pyrénées

9 These underground caverns are explored by remarkably varied forms of transport – cable cars, boats and a little 'train' of towed wagons. There are five different levels of caves and stalagmites, stalactites and curious limestone formations such as the Sphinx Window. You are shown old river levels, and taken for a cruise on a subterranean lake in a cavern 50m (165 feet) high. The fourth and fifth levels are linked by the present river dashing over a series of 80m (260-foot) falls.

Return to the D937, turn left and continue to Pau.

Pau – Tarbes 38 (24)
Tarbes – Bagnères-de-Bigorre 20 (12)
Bagnères-de-Bigorre – St Bertrand-de-Comminges 65 (40)
St Bertrand-de-Comminges – Bagnères-de-Luchon 35 (22)
Bagnères-de-Luchon – Col du Tourmalet 87 (54)
Col du Tourmalet – Gavarnie 37 (23)
Gavarnie – Cauterets 40 (25)
Cauterets – Lourdes 29 (18)
Lourdes – Grottes de Bétharram 13 (8)
Grottes de Bétharram – Pau 28 (17)

The grandeur and the opulence of Lourdes, where nearly three million pilgrims come each year, many praying for a cure from illness

FOR HISTORY BUFFS

8 Away from the sanctuary area, Lourdes has two museums devoted to showing how it looked in 1858, the year of Bernadette's first vision. The **Musée de Lourdes** features shops and street scenes, while the **Musée du Petit Lourdes** is a miniature stonework reproduction of the original simple village, towered over by its château-fort.

FOR CHILDREN

5 The Col de Peyresourde near Luchon is an area where the children can play place-name games. Ask them to find the villages with no consonants in their names, and the one which sounds singularly unhealthy.

8 Check at the tourist office in Lourdes if there is a meeting at the Model Racing Club 3 Vallées. If you are lucky, the children can watch radio-controlled scale-model cars – competition models, not toys – race on its miniature outdoor circuit.

THE SOUTH OF FRANCE

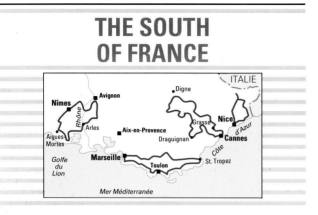

There is no single theme along the littoral of the south of France, nor even a single name for it. West of Marseille lie the flamingo lagoons, the pools, the rice fields and the baking hot summer pastures of the Camargue. East of the city stretches a sublime coast of capes and rocky inlets – the beautiful *calanques*.

Beyond the great roadstead of Toulon are the islands off Hyères, wonderful cruising grounds including, at Port Cros, an entire island nature reserve.

St Tropez is...quintessentially St Tropez, and you can have a great deal of innocent enjoyment simply watching people whose aim in life is to induce you to do just that. On a grander scale, the great resorts of the Côte d'Azur – Cannes, Nice, the immensely wealthy and independent principality of Monaco, and Menton – are all to be seen.

Behind Nice and Monaco is the *arrière-pays*, the 'back country', the mountain country of the great escape from summer crowds. Europe's answer to the Grand Canyon lies there. You can drive to a high and lonely pilgrimage church, imagine yourself on the Monte Carlo Rally, take a ride on the last of the country railways, or wander over a summer plateau of lavender fields and beehives.

Back from the Camargue lie Avignon and the haunting remains of the troubadours' court at Les Baux; Arles and St Rémy with their memories of the mind-racked artist Vincent van Gogh; and the landscapes made famous in the gentle and gently mocking takes of Alphonse Daudet.

On the Cannes and Nice routes, be ready for hair-pinned mountain roads, although most have been improved for tourist traffic. Watch for forest fires. Sadly, these are annual events. In 1990 they devastated huge areas of pine and oak and chestnut trees as far inland as Collobrières and Draguignan.

On the coast, try the seafood restaurants serving Mediterranean mullet, bass and cod, and the great bouillabaisse. Be ready for lots of garlic, and enthusiastic use of olive oil. In Nice, the cuisine reflects the Italian past.

Vines were planted here by Greek colonists 2,500 years ago. Most of the modern wines are classified as Côtes de Provence, and the most attractive vineyard country is perhaps around Gassin and Ramatuelle on the St Tropez peninsula. There is also intense cultivation behind the little resort of Cassis.

The South of France, the Côte d'Azur, the Riviera – under whatever name, should the coast become too crowded and stylish for you, half an hour inland, you will find yourself in a dramatically different world of hills and mountains, forests and river valleys, where time slows down in delightful hilltop villages drowsing beneath a dazzling southern sky. This is the true enchantment of the South.

Marseille

Marseille is the greatest port in France, extending west to the far-away oil refineries of the Golfe de Fos. The yacht harbour, right in the heart of the city, makes a pleasant area for a stroll. The story of Marseille from the days of the Ligurians, Greeks and Romans, by way of the Revolution and the patriotic song which came to be called La Marseillaise, is told in four separate museums. Other museums cover art, pottery, furniture, tapestries, marine life etc. There are many substantial churches, parks, gardens and, at La Canebière, a renowned avenue of shops, hotels, restaurants and pavement cafés. A magnificent view opens up from the hilltop Church of Notre-Dame-de-la-Garde. Offshore lies the sea-bound rock of the Château d'If. You can sail here and recall the story of Dumas' Count of Monte Cristo.

Cannes

In Cannes, the great boulevard de la Croisette stretches eastwards from the casino and the Palais des Festivals. Every May, during the

The lively and cosmopolitan waterfront of Marseille

world-famous Cannes Film Festival, the Palais steps are staked out by twitchy television crews. The finest viewpoint is the observatory at Super-Cannes, at 325m (1,065 feet) above sea-level and 2km (1 mile) to the northeast, from which the town is seen in its wider landscape context between the Alps and the sea. Sail to the Îles des Lérins: St-Honorat is a monastery island and on Ste-Marguerite, which offers scented forest walks, was the prison of the real-life Man in the Iron Mask,

Nice
Nice is the capital of the Côte d'Azur. Its Promenade des Anglais recalls the 19th-century British visitors who made its name. The Russian royal family also favoured Nice, and you will see the green and gilded towers of the Orthodox cathedral where they and their court, which transferred here *en masse* every year, used to worship. There are fine shops, markets (notably the flower market), squares and gardens. Corsica ferries leave from the port. Eastwards, by the Cap de Nice, expensive vil-

las hide above flowery balustrades. In addition to churches, palaces, museums and galleries, there is the Parc des Miniatures, enjoyed by children, which tells the story of Nice itself. The Musée Terra Amata is an imaginative exhibition based on a prehistoric site, whose story starts 400,000 years ago.

Nîmes
Nîmes found favour with the Romans. Their arena, with space for 21,000 spectators, plays host to concerts and bullfights today. The Maison Carrée is a pillared 1st-century BC temple (one of the best preserved in existence) housing a little museum. Archaeology, history, the planets, fine arts and the story of Nîmes are topics covered in other exhibitions. Below a hillside park lies the grand if somewhat faded Jardin de la Fontaine. Its 18th-century masonry and water channels were built on the site of the Roman baths, providing a cool retreat from the harshness of the Provençal summer sun.

4 days – 352km (221 miles)

EAST FROM MARSEILLE

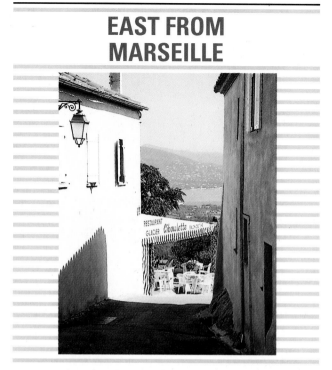

Marseille • Cassis • Cap Canaille • Bandol • Toulon
Hyères • Gassin • St Tropez • Port Grimaud
Grimaud • Chartreuse de la Verne • Aubagné • Marseille

Starting from Marseille, France's second biggest city and the main seaport in the Mediterranean coast, this tour visits fishing villages which now have their own substantial holiday clientele, and larger resorts as different in style as Hyères and St Tropez. All these places have grown up over the centuries, but Port Grimaud is an all-of-a-piece modern development, almost literally an architect's dream. Inland, the tour follows the high wooded ridges of the Massif des Maures as well as going to an awesomely remote monastic house and the country of a film-maker who captured the soul of Provence.

Painters like Matisse and Dufy enjoyed the Provençal charm of Cassis – and probably its famous local wine too

In Gassin, one begins to taste the Mediterranean life – food and drink enjoyed outdoors under a blue sky and a hot sun

[i] La Canebière, Marseille

Leave Marseille on the D559 to Cassis.

Cassis, Provence-Alpes

1 With cream and ochre-washed buildings overlooking the harbour, any number of bars, cafés and seafood restaurants to choose from, and convenient beaches, Cassis has the obvious look of a holiday resort. But it is a fishing port too, and boats take visitors to the beautiful *calanques*, the rocky inlets in the roadless coastline to the west.

Cassis has a life and history independent of the summer tourist crush. A ruined castle (not accessible to the public) on a cypress-clad hill watches over it. A modest but informative local **museum** shows how the settlement dates back to Roman times and before. The **town hall** is also worth a visit; illustrations show how it was rebuilt from a shambolic ruin in the 1980s.

[i] Place Baragnon

Head out of Cassis on the D559 then right following 'Route des Crêtes' signs on to the D41a and the D141 to Cap Canaille.

Cap Canaille, Provence-Alpes

2 Less a conventional cape than a wall of towering sea-cliffs – at 395m (1,300 feet) Europe's highest cliff, this is one of the most superb viewpoints in France. It looks west to the mazy coastline of the *calanques*, with offshore islands and rock pinnacles seeming to float in the air, like dreamy hills in old Chinese paintings.

Continue into La Ciotat. Go right at the T-junction on to Avenue Victor Hugo, then left and left

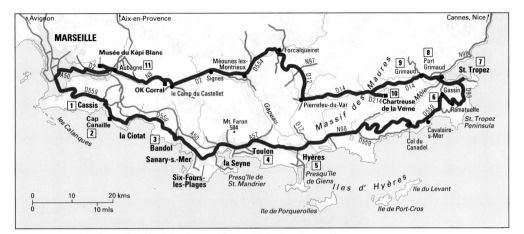

again along the seafront, following signs for Bandol.

Bandol, Provence-Alpes

3 This is Cassis writ large, a resort with a marina, a fishing port and even more seafood restaurants. Boats sail from Bandol on cruises along the coast, but the most popular trip is to Bendor, a rocky island crammed with hotels and restaurants, beaches, sailing, diving and tennis clubs, an art gallery and an exhibition on wines and spirits from nearly 50 countries. It also has a **maritime museum**, an open-air **theatre** and a **zoo**.

i Allées Vivien

Continue on the D559 through Sanary, then go left on the D63 and follow signs to Toulon.

Toulon, Provence-Alpes

4 With its interlocking harbours and a busy dockyard, Toulon is a famous and historic naval port. In World War II, in 1942, much of the French fleet was scuttled here, so that it would not come under German control. There is a great deal of civilian activity too. Ferries sail to Corsica and Sardinia, cargo ships use the freight quays, and smaller boats run scheduled services to the offshore islands as well as making shorter trips round the harbour. There is a well-stocked naval museum, the **Musée Naval**, with many detailed ship models.

Bandol offers all that the sophisticated traveller expects from the south of France. Katherine Mansfield wrote her story Prelude *here in 1916*

Toulon has perhaps the most amazing suburban background of any city in Europe. The hillside districts behind the town centre suddenly rear up in the colossal limestone cliffs of Mont Faron. A one-way road system reaches the summit, the climb being up a steep incline with forbidding drops. As an option, a cablecar runs from Super Toulon. There are wonderful views from Mont Faron, pinewood picnic sites, a children's playground, a **zoo** and a comprehensive memorial exhibition on the 1944 liberation of Provence.

i Avenue Colbert

Leave Toulon on the N98 to Hyères.

Hyères, Provence-Alpes

5 This is the oldest of all the modern Riviera resorts, although standing back more than most of them from the sea. Hyères is a town of colourful gardens. The old quarter, reached through its original medieval gateways, is a place of cool narrow streets, historic buildings and an authentic atmosphere of people going about their daily business. Hyères is mature enough not to be any kind of tourist trap.

SPECIAL TO...

1 Cassis is noted for the highly regarded white wines which the sheltered climate and fine soil of the hillsides behind the town allow more than a dozen vineyards to produce. The vines here were wiped out by disease in the 19th century, but the growers have revived the trade by using grafting techniques brought from Texas.

FOR CHILDREN

1 In Cassis, a pleasant little park by the post office includes a pond with goldfish, mallards and terrapins. There is a scrambling frame which takes the shape of jocular-looking fish with gaping mouths.

RECOMMENDED WALKS

2 The three magnificent rocky inlets west of Cassis – the *calanques* – and the wooded peninsulas which border them are easily reached by a network of footpaths. Park your car at the far end of the Avenue des Calanques and follow the marked paths to sheltered Port-Miou, the limpid waters and Aleppo pines of Port-Pin and the wild, needle-like rocks of En Vau.

SCENIC ROUTES

The D559 leaves Marseille by the winding climb, under wooded cliffs and banks of valerian and broom, to the Col de la Gineste.

The climb to Cap Canaille – as well as the summit view – is one of the most spectacular on the coast.

Look for the views to the island of Bendor from the bay after Bandol.

FOR HISTORY BUFFS

4 As Captain Bonaparte, Napoleon first made a name for himself at the age of 24, when the Republican army attacked British-held Toulon in 1793. Under withering enemy fire, his artillery battery bombarded a British strong-point at the fort now named after him, forcing the British ships to withdraw.

7 Two processions, called *Bravades*, are held every year in St Tropez. The first, in May, honours St Torpes, the town's patron saint. A month later, the second Bravade celebrates the defeat of a strong Spanish fleet which tried to capture the town in 1637. Fierce resistance by the local militia drove it away. Participants wear splendid uniforms and carry blunderbusses – which are fired (blanks only) at all opportunities.

SCENIC ROUTES

Where clear of woodland, the **RF32** on the way to the Col de Canadel has a glorious outlook to the sea.

The high road from Gassin to Ramatuelle looks over a beautiful settled landscape of woodlands, farms and farmyards.

The **D14** to Collobrières gives a fine impression of the wooded ridges and deep lonely valleys of the Massif des Maures. Then from Pierrefeu towards Rocbaron, the **D12** climbs sharply as it overlooks the vineyard plain it is leaving behind.

BACK TO NATURE

5 From Hyères-Plage, on the **D97** south of town, ferries run to the beautiful nature reserve island of **Port Cros**. Footpaths explore its bays and forests, and a summer exhibition in the **Fort de l'Estissac** uses audio-visual programmes and aquariums to explain the sea life of the Mediterranean. There is even an underwater offshore nature trail for swimmers with flippers and masks.

7 On the left after Gassin, the **Chemin du Radio Phare** passes three old stone windmills on the way to a short circular walk outside the perimeter fence of a radio beacon. This is a splendid viewpoint, but the great attraction is the number and variety of brightly-coloured butterflies which flit around.

Napoleon and Queen Victoria, among others, enjoyed the climate of Hyères

The museum takes the town's history back to the times of the Greeks and Romans – as *Olbia* it was a Greek colony, established by settlers from Marseille. There are some handsome old churches (**St Louis** associated with King Louis IX who landed at Hyères after crusading and **St Paul** with a Romanesque front), and from the **castle ruins** in a hilltop park a panoramic view is revealed of the inland hills and the sea.

i Rotonde Jean-Salusse

Leave Hyères on the N98 as for Le Canadel. Watch for a left turn following the N98 signed 'La Môle'. Turn right on the D41 as for Bormes then, at a blind bend on a brow, left on the RF32, the Routes des Crêtes. Go straight on along this road, always on a tarred surface. Turn right at the Col de Canadel, away from La Môle, then left on the D559 through La Croix-Valmer. Watch for 'Auberge les Sarments' sign, then immediately bear right off the D559 to Gassin.

Gassin, Provence-Alpes

6 Sensitively restored in recent years, this hilltop village often attracts cooling breezes on hot summer days. There are lanes and stairways, houses with potted flowers and pocket-handkerchief gardens, a **parish church** barely illuminated by the modern abstract stained glass in its three tiny original windows, restaurants on a shaded terrace and, above all, views to the delicious miniature landscapes of the St Tropez peninsula.

Leave Gassin for Ramatuelle, where you should turn left at a stop sign, right at a second stop sign, then left towards the N98a. At traffic lights, turn right on that road into St Tropez.

St Tropez, Provence-Alpes

7 Publicity about the personalities – from the writers Guy de Maupassant and Colette to artists Henri Matisse, controversial writer, designer and film director Jean Cocteau and 'sex kitten' actress Brigitte Bardot – who have settled here, has always tended to hide the fact that this red-roofed town clustered beside a bay is an interesting place in its own right. St Tropez shops ask high prices, and the resort is full of deeply tanned characters in high summer fashion, who may be wealthy residents or simply mere day-trippers putting on an act – it can be fun to try to classify them. Needless to say, café and nightlife is abundant if you can afford the price and keep the pace.

An old chapel has been turned into a museum – **Musée de l'Annonciade** – featuring paintings and sculptures by some of the notable artists who have lived here including Bonnard, Braque, Dufy and Utrillo, while lesser lights try to sell their canvases in an unofficial gallery by the harbour rails. The hexagonal 16th-century citadel is now a naval museum (**Musée de la Marine**) on several floors, where you can peruse the exhibits (which include a reconstructed Greek galley) to the accompaniment of unearthly cries from the local peacocks.

The fine sandy beaches are 4 to 5km (2½–3 miles) from St Tropez town, on the far side of the headland on which it stands. They are varied and very popular. Parking can be difficult.

i Quai Jean-Jaurès

Return along the N98a. At a roundabout join the N98 as for Fréjus, then under the bridge take the right lane for Port Grimaud and left at the roundabout to the 'Visiteurs' car park.

Port Grimaud, Provence-Alpes

8 In the 1960s this was simply a wasteland of marsh and gravel pits. Then the architect François Spoerry created a brand-new village on a lagoon by the sea – a kind of Provençal Venice with canals and peninsulas, bridges and water-buses, shops, cafés, restaurants and colour-washed houses, each with its own boat mooring right outside the door. Everything was to be a modern expression of traditional Provençal design. In the wrong hands, Port Grimaud could have been a tacky disaster. Instead, it is a triumph.

Return to the roundabout, go over the bridge then right at the T-junction. Straight on at the next junction then left on the D14 to Grimaud.

Grimaud, Provence-Alpes

9 Further inland, the medieval hillside town which gave Port Grimaud its name retains many old buildings, notably houses in the arcaded street of the Knights Templar, and the massive Romanesque church. Above all Grimaud, which takes its name from the powerful Genoese Grimaldi family (now rulers of Monaco), is dominated by the hilltop ruins of an 11th-century castle. It provides a wonderful viewpoint.

i Boulevard des Aliziers

Leave Grimaud on the D558 then turn left on the D14. Turn left on the mostly unsurfaced D214 signed 'La Verne'.

Chartreuse de la Verne, Provence-Alpes

10 The road is lonely, slow and dusty to this remote and impressive monastery established by the Carthusians as long ago as 1170. At the time of the French Revolution it was deprived of its revenues, and the monks left secretly, disguised as peasants. The buildings then passed through several hands, and are now owned by a trust and are being renovated. In 1983 another order of monks – the Order of St Bruno – moved in. There are guided tours (for visitors discreetly dressed) showing the historic buildings and the breathtaking view of high ridges

and deep valleys, covered by the forest of the Massif des Maures.

Rejoin the D14 and follow it through Collobrières to Pierrefeu. Turn right on the D12 through Puget-Ville and Rocbaron to Forcalqueiret. Go left on the D554 and continue to Méounes, then right on the D2 via Signes, and right at Le Camp on the N8 to Aubagné.

Aubagné, Provence-Alpes

11 At the heart of this town, surrounded by a cat's-cradle of motorway bypasses, there are public gardens and cool tree-shaded squares. In one of them the tourist office pavilion houses a colourful display – using the painted clay-model figures called **santons** which are made in great numbers by craftsmen in the town – of scenes from the films of the writer and director Marcel Pagnol, a native of Aubagné. After the world-wide screening in the 1980s of new versions of his stories Jean de Florette and Manon des Sources, interest in Pagnol, who died in 1974, spread widely. Guided tours are organised round the real-life locations he used in the countryside near Aubagné. In the western outskirts of the town, the **Musée de la Légion Etrangère** (Foreign Legion Museum) has displays on its years of service in the baking Sahara sands.

i Avenue du 8 Mai

Leave Aubagné on the D2 and return to Marseille.

Marseille – Cassis 23 (14)
Cassis – Cap Canaille 7 (4)
Cap Canaille – Bandol 25 (16.5)
Bandol – Toulon 35 (22)
Toulon – Hyères 25 (16.5)
Hyères – Gassin 69 (43)
Gassin – St Tropez 18 (11)
St Tropez – Port Grimaud 8 (5)
Port Grimaud – Grimaud 6 (4)
Grimaud – Chartreuse de la Verne 24 (15)
Chartreuse de la Verne – Aubagné 93 (58)
Aubagné – Marseille 19 (12)

An experiment in Provençal lifestyle design that worked triumphantly at Port Grimaud. Cars are forbidden here, but there is mooring for up to 2,000 sailing craft

RECOMMENDED WALKS

11 There is access at Collobrières to the long-distance footpaths which explore the deep wooded valleys and ridgetops of the **Massif des Maures**. For instance, GR90, offers a strenuous half-day hike out and back to the hermitage of **Notre-Dame-des-Anges**. Further on, Signes on the D2 is the starting point of forest and hill walks on the **Massif de la Sainte Baume**.

FOR CHILDREN

11 On the **N98** before Aubagné, the **OK Corral** has far more attractions than simply the Wild West elements its name suggests. As well as a 'western' street and railway, pony rides, cowboys and Indians, there are swooping roller-coasters which produce a total white-knuckle experience.

SPECIAL TO...

11 Collobrières, near Chartreuse de la Verne in the Maures massif, has many varieties of the chestnut candies called *marrons glacés*. Two major producers in the village sell chestnut-based sweets, syrups and creams.

4/5 days – 440km (273 miles)

THE RIVIERA & ITS HINTERLAND

Cannes • Cap d'Antibes • Antibes • Biot • Grasse
Gourdon • Plateau de Caussols • Castellane
St André-les-Alpes • Riez • Moustiers-Ste-Marie
Gorges du Verdon • Draguignan • Fayence
Mons • Cannes

From Cannes and other coastal resorts, and millionaires' Riviera villas, by way of artists' and craftworkers' villages and the perfume capital of the world, this tour climbs into the glorious mountain scenery that forms the backdrop to the Côte d'Azur. Limestone cliffs and ridges, spectacular valleys and range upon range of faraway mountains reach a landscape climax in the magnificent Gorges du Verdon. There is a great deal of mountain-road motoring, and an optional route at one point if you do not relish the thrill of driving on an exposed road above the gorges with steep, unguarded drops.

RECOMMENDED WALKS

2 On the south side of the Cap d'Antibes, turn off the Boulevard J F Kennedy for the Sentiers des Douaniers – the Excisemen's Path. Starting alongside the wall of a private estate, it leads to a beautiful little park set among rocks above the sea, with a lovely bay stretching to the west.

Nothing quite prepares the visitor for the extraordinary location of Moustiers-Ste-Marie, where a star on a chain spans a huge chasm

i Boulevard de la Croisette, Cannes

Leave Cannes on the N7 towards Golfe-Juan, then bear right on the N98 signed 'Antibes par Bord de Mer'. In Juan-les-Pins watch carefully for all the 'Cap d'Antibes' signs and join the Cap d'Antibes coast road, D2559.

Cap d'Antibes, Côte d'Azur

1 There are tiny family-style beaches and boat moorings on the east side of the Cape, which also includes security-guarded millionaires' retreats and, at the Hôtel du Cap and the Eden Roc restaurant, two of the most exclusive establishments of their kind on the coast. A fine museum devoted to Napoleonic and naval history – **Musée Naval et Napoléonien** – occupies an old gun battery, perhaps surprising visitors from the United Kingdom with contemporary cartoons showing the British as the enemy. Around the Villa Thuret there is a botanical garden, and right on the summit of the Cape the Sanctuaire de la Garoupe, a seafarers' chapel beside the lighthouse tower, which is a marvellous viewpoint, houses a collection of simple but affecting thanks-offerings, often for a safe return from a voyage.

American writers and artists were attracted to the Cape from the 1920s onwards. Scott Fitzgerald's novel *Tender is the Night* had its real-life setting here. It is possible to trace

As a young general, Napoleon commanded the coast at Antibes, important in French history for 1,000 years

the exact course of the disastrous car journey described in James Thurber's *A Ride with Olympy*. And Orson Welles once arrived in a hurry for a cash-raising meeting in the Hôtel du Cap, having come by taxi all the way from Rome!

*Continue on the **D2559** into Antibes.*

Antibes, Côte d'Azur

2 The old town here, with its narrow streets, cafés and restaurants, is one of the most attractive and least pretentious on the coast. Antibes' connection with the ancient Greeks – it was founded as *Antipolis* by Greek colonists from Marseille in the 4th century BC – attracted the Cretan writer Nikos Kazantzakis, author of *Zorba the Greek*, to settle here, as did the British novelist Graham Greene. While the **archaeological museum** in the old fortification of the Bastion St André may look gloomy from the outside, it has a wonderful collection of thousands of exhibits going back to Etruscan, Greek and Roman times, many recovered from the sea. The old **castle** was a stronghold of the powerful Genoese Grimaldi family. With the little 'cathedral', it watches over the bustling market place, and was long since turned into the **Musée Picasso**. The artist used part of it as a studio for six amazingly fruitful months in 1946, and now it contains many of his – and other artists' – paintings and ceramics, making it one of the most important Picasso collections anywhere. The so-called cathedral is, in fact, a church, with Romanesque tower and east end and 17th-century façade.

☐ Place de Gaulle

*Leave Antibes on the **N98** as for 'Nice par Bord de Mer'. Take the left-hand lane, turn left at the*

*traffic lights for Biot, then right and left on the **D4** to Biot.*

Biot, Côte d'Azur

3 On the approach road to Biot, a road to the right leads to the **Musée National Fernand Léger**, unmistakable thanks to the huge abstract in multi-coloured tiling which decorates its frontage. With more than 300 works on display, it celebrates the life of one of France's major 20th-century artists, and was opened in 1960 with fellow-artists Picasso, Braque and Chagall as its honorary presidents. The charming little town of Biot is largely given over to the shops and studios of painters, potters, woodworkers, embroiderers and craftworkers of many other kinds. Even the town maps are on painted ceramic tiles. Glassmaking is important here nowadays and it can be observed at the **Verrerie de Biot** near the southeast exit from the town. Gates and ramparts of the medieval town survive, and away from the tourist bustle there is a pleasant arcaded square beside a 15th-century **parish church**. The museum features mementoes of the days when the Romans and, later, the Knights Templar, were estab-

Biot is the stop to make when looking for distinctive purchases for house and garden

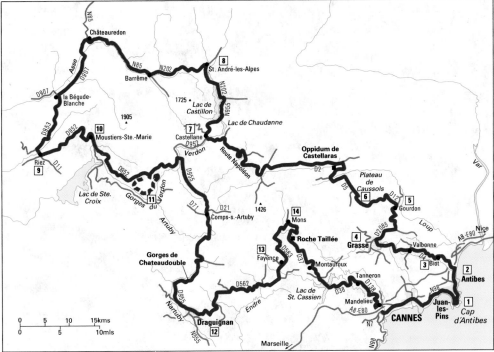

4 In Grasse, the **Musée des Trains Miniatures** on the Routes de Cannes has a fascinating model railway collection. The layout includes locomotives and rolling stock from many European countries and from many different eras, right up to the TGV – France's high-speed Train de Grande Vitesse.

SCENIC ROUTES

Approaching Gourdon, the **D3** looks deep into the valley of the Loup, then reveals a stunning view of the village in the eagle's-eyrie location on the summit of a plummeting cliff.

West of Gourdon, look for the dramatic bending of the bare limestone cliffs to the right of the **D12**.

Running at first under tiers of limestone cliffs, the **D5** dives into the wooded upper valley of the Loup, with marvellous views to the hillside, which it then climbs diagonally to the viewpoint summit of the Col de Castellaras. Later, there is a spectacular approach to Castellane.

Above: The bare simplicity of the fortress at Gourdon. Right: The perfume industry came to Grasse from Italy in the 16th century and now provides France with one of its chief exports, and its loveliest

lished here, and has a dazzling pottery display.

ⓘ Place de la Chapelle

> *Continue on the D4 via Valbonne to Grasse, turning right at a T-junction on the outskirts to follow the D4 towards the town centre.*

Grasse, Côte d'Azur

4 Spread over a south-facing hillside so that it basks in the sunshine and has splendid views over a lovely plain towards the sea, Grasse enjoys a year-long calendar of concerts, drama, dance and exhibitions of every kind. The old town, crammed with 14th- to 18th-century buildings, is Italian in appearance and atmosphere. Around it, Grasse expanded with exuberant 19th-century architecture in typical French Riviera style.

Grasse has the most famous perfume industry in the world, and one museum, **Musée International de la Parfumerie**, traces its history as well as the processes by which huge amounts of flower petals are distilled down to tiny volumes of the ultimate essence. The **Maison Fragonard**, named after the rococo painter who was born in the town, is a perfume factory open to the public. The **Musée d'Art et d'Histoire de Provence**, housed in an 18th-century mansion, celebrates the art and history of Provence.

Another museum, the **Musée de la Marine**, has gathered an intriguing collection of ship models to illustrate the career of the 18th-century Admiral de Grasse, an ally of George Washington in the American War of Independence. A statue on one of

the town's outlook terraces recalls Washington's gratitude to him.

ⓘ Place de la Foux

> *Leave Grasse on the D2085 as for Nice. At Pré du Lac turn left at the roundabout and immediately bear left on the D3 to Gourdon. Turn right for the car park at the entrance to the village.*

Gourdon, Côte d'Azur

5 Some writers sneer at Gourdon for being a tourist trap. You will probably disagree, because this old Saracen stronghold, set on the edge of a cliff which gives it tremendous views down into the valley of the Loup, goes about its business quietly. In the narrow lanes of restored and impeccably kept buildings, shops sell lavender, honey, herbs, perfumes, pottery, wines, basketwork and glassware, many of these goods being produced in the district.

The historic **Château de Gourdon**, with terraced gardens on the edge of the cliff, has architectural details from the 12th century onwards. Here you will see valuable furnishings, as well as collections of arms and armour, and 'naive' paintings by European and American artists.

Leave Gourdon on the D12 as for Caussols. In about 8km (5 miles) watch for a junction sign and then go sharp left under a sign giving advice to 'Visiteurs'.

Plateau de Caussols, Côte d'Azur

6 A notice at the turn-off of the D12 warns that gathering stones, mushrooms and snails is forbidden. Do not worry about the mild potholes on the early stretch of the road. The surface never deteriorates too badly.

Here on the high limestone plain is a countryside not many casual tourists know: clumps of pines and rock outcrops, occasional sheep farms, isolated holiday homes, groups of beehives and, here and there, a survivor from the days of the *bories*, the stone-built shepherds' huts. There are mountain ridges to north and south, with the remote white buildings of the CERGA observatory high on the northern rim. The scenery may be faintly familiar to film buffs: this was the setting of the Charles Bronson thriller *Cold Sweat*.

Turn right at a T-junction beside a postbox, following an old sign 'St Lambert'. This is the D12 again. Turn sharp left as for Thorenc on the D112, then follow 'Thorenc' signs on the D5. Go left on the D2, left on the D2211, then right on the N85 to Castellane.

Castellane, Côte d'Azur

7 A modest little town on the Route Napoléon, Castellane lies in a constricted location where the River Verdon elbows its way through the hills. Directly overlooking the square is a massive cliff, 184m (604 feet) high, on which the original settlement, dating from Gallo-Roman times, was built. When the population decided, eventually, to settle in the valley, plague, floods and occupation in the time of the religious wars in the 16th century was their reward. Now the classic outing at Castellane is a walk up the steep and occasionally rough pathway to the 18th-century **Chapel of Notre Dame du Roc**, a magnificent clifftop viewpoint.

i Boulevard St Michel

Continue on the N85, go right on the D955. Then left on the N202 to St-André-les-Alpes.

St-André-les-Alpes, Côte d'Azur

8 This is a quiet little inland resort a world away from the hustle of the coast. But St André was once a busy enough place. The village had four cloth mills, but all that remains of the industry is the canal which supplied their water-power. In the latter part of the 19th century it became the railhead of a line from Nice, and the place from which stagecoaches took passengers further on. This railway, now extended to Digne, is the last survivor of the old inland lines. St André station is a halt on the year-round railcar service, and there are summer excursions

Just the thing to work off that fine French meal is a brisk walk up the cliff at Castellane, all 184m (604 feet) of it!

BACK TO NATURE

6 On the Plateau de Caussols, the rich limestone soil allows the growth of a riot of wildflowers. They flourish all over the natural pastureland, and colour the crevices of the hundreds of rock outcrops which are characteristic of the plateau. Orchids are particularly abundant from April to June.

FOR HISTORY BUFFS

7 From near a car park on the D5 just before the summit of the Col de Castellaras, a steep footpath climbs to the hilltop ruins of **Castellaras** itself, a magnificently sited medieval fortress town. You will be able to make out the old castle, the barracks and the humble quarter where the peasants and their flocks took refuge in times of war. The whole town dominated the upper valley of the Loup.

RECOMMENDED WALKS

8 One walk from the centre of St André-les-Alpes heads briefly south on the N202 before turning right for the steep climb to the 'lost' village of Courchons. Orange markers show where the footpath cuts out the hairpin bends of the Courchons road. Another route heads south-east up to the **chapel of Méouilles** overlooking the mountain-ridged reservoir of the Lac de Castillon.

SCENIC ROUTES

After St-André-les-Alpes there is a beautiful run to Barrême. Then the **N85** squeezes through a narrow ravine at the tortured rock scenery of the Clue de Chabrières. The scenery changes completely with a lovely climb from La-Bégude-Blanche to a panoramic plateau viewpoint. The **D952** to Moustiers-Ste-Marie gives an introduction to the dizzying cliffs and clefts of the Gorge du Verdon.

The **D955** approaches Draguignan down a winding and thickly wooded gorge.

All the way to Mons, and beyond it, the route winds over hills covered with pine and oakwoods, with deep roadless valleys often in view.

BACK TO NATURE

10 After Riez, the **Lapidaire Pierres de Provence** on the D952 displays beautiful examples of rose quartz, agates, amethysts and other semi-precious stones. This is a fine area for minerals and gemstones, but much of it is protected as a geological reserve.

on the steam-hauled **Train des Pignes** (the Pine Cone Train).

St André lies in an attractive valley that has helped it achieve its present-day renown as a centre for hang-gliding and free-fall parachuting.

ⓘ Place Paslorelli

Continue on the N202 to Barrême, then turn right on to the N85 and left on the D907, then in La Bégude-Blanche take the D953 to Riez.

Riez, Provence-Alpes

9 Two structures show how old the settlement of Riez is. A group of columns now standing isolated at the edge of the field was once part of a 1st-century **Roman temple**; and there is an early **Christian baptistery** (dating from some time in the 4th to 7th centuries), complete with the original font, inside a 19th-century building set up to preserve it.

The old town may have a faded look, but its streets contain medieval doorways and Renaissance frontages, some in the course of restoration. In pre-Roman times, the settlement stood on the summit of the **St Maxime** hill overlooking the present-day town in the valley below. St Maxime, which is the site of an attractive chapel, is a pleasant place for a stroll. A popular Riez industry is the production of santons, characteristic Provençal painted clay figurines, originally made for the

Surely one of nature's most delightful harvests – fields of perfumed lavender at Riez

traditional Christmas crib, but now sold as souvenirs.

ⓘ Allées Louis Gadiol

Leave on the D952 to Moustiers-Ste-Marie.

Moustiers-Ste-Marie, Provence-Alpes

10 Any history of Moustiers pales before its amazing situation, clustered round the banks of a tumbling mountain stream at the foot of a huge gash in towering limestone cliffs. Footpaths climb to a spectacularly located church, **Notre Dame de Beauvoir**, set on a high rocky terrace. Across the break in the cliffs, and silhouetted against the sky, a chain supporting a gilded star was, according to tradition, first placed there by a crusader knight, who had sworn to do it when released from weary years of imprisonment. The town is famous for its glazed pottery, or faienceware. The industry established in the 17th century died out for a generation or two, and restarted in the 1920s, but without equalling the delicacy of the early designs, many of which are on show in the local museum, **Musée des Faïences**.

ⓘ Rue du Seigneur de la Clue

Continue on the D952 to La Palud. Go straight on through La Palud, then bear right on the D23, the Route des Crêtes. You have a choice here. If you enjoy exposed and narrow roads with steep, unguarded drops, follow the D23 all the way back to La Palud and

turn right to rejoin the **D952**. *If you do not enjoy this kind of road, go along the* **D23** *to the first two or three belvederes, then retrace your route and turn right again on to the* **D952**. *Only the later part of the* **D23** *is difficult.*

Gorges du Verdon, Provence-Alpes

11 Landscape superlatives are needed here, because this is France's equivalent, on a smaller scale, to the Grand Canyon in Colorado. The River Verdon, on its way to Castellane, runs through a huge ravine in the limestone mountains, with colossal drops, vertigo-inducing views, exciting low-level footpaths and the possibility of organised expeditions on foot and by canoe, raft or rubber dinghy, right through the heart of the gorge. There are magnificent, high-level roadside views from railed-off belvederes (look-out points), some of which, on the Routes des Crêtes, have warnings not to throw stones off the edge – they might fall on walkers 715m (2,350 feet) below!

Continue eastwards on the **D952**. *After a stretch of overhanging cliffs, turn right on the* **D955** *to Comps and Draguignan.*

Draguignan, Provence-Alpes

12 Down from the mountains, and the vast military training area of Canjeurs which occupies the scrubland plateau south of the River Verdon, Draguignan marks a return to the milder landscapes of mid-Provence. There is a dignified old town here, and a fine **museum**, housed in the one-time palace of the Bishop of Fréjus, with thousands of exhibits connected with local industries, including a reconstructed olive oil mill. Shaded squares and gardens fend off the sun. On the Boulevard John Kennedy, the **American military cemetery** commemorates the mostly Franco-American Provençal landings of August 1944. In front of the memorial there is an imaginative tribute in the form of a massive relief map, in bronze and copper, illustrating the campaign.

i Boulevard Clemenceau

Leave Draguignan on the **D562** *as for Grasse. Go left on the* **D563** *to Fayence.*

Fayence, Provence-Alpes

13 Here is a classic back-from-the-coast village, facing southwards into the sun as its red-roofed houses climb a hillside from the plain. Fayence has a very well-cared-for 18th-century **church**, a good selection of craft studios and galleries, and terraces which act as splendid viewpoints. You may find it pleasant to laze around them, look out over the plain and watch the gliders soaring from one of France's most important launching fields far below.

i Place Léon Roux

Continue on the **D563** *to Mons.*

Mons, Provence-Alpes

14 The colonists from Ventimiglia in what is now Italy, who founded this little hilltop village in the 13th century, picked the location well. The spacious square, in fact a semi-circle,

A rooftop view over Moustiers-Ste-Marie, prettiest of Riviera towns

looks out over an extensive view from the islands off Cannes to the Italian Alps, with suggestions that, on a really clear day, Corsica appears as a smudge on the horizon. Mons survived two outbreaks of plague and the desertion of all its citizens after a brigands' raid in 1468, to doze in the sun for centuries before it recently decided to emphasise its situation as one of the 'belvederes of the Côte d'Azur'. There is a maze of cool, narrow alleyways. The historic ramparts are still partly in place. Local arts and crafts are displayed in a **gallery**. And the streets usually bear two names – one in French and one in Provençal.

i Centre Culturel

Leave Mons on the **D56** *as for Callian, then go left on the* **D37**. *Follow the* **D37** *to the left for Montauroux at a T-junction where the right turn is signed 'Callian 0.5km'. Follow the 'Grasse' sign in Montauroux, still on the* **D37**, *cross the* **D562**, *then go left on the* **D38** *through Tanneron. At a five-road junction after Tanneron bear right for Mandelieu, then watch for an abrupt left turn avoiding a road straight ahead signed 'Poney Club'. Take the* **D92** *to Mandelieu. Turn right on the* **N7** *then take the fourth exit at a roundabout signed 'Les Plages'. Go right at the T-junction as for Napoule, then keep in the right lane and return to Cannes.*

SPECIAL TO...

9 On the way to Riez you will pass through one of France's biggest lavender-growing areas. Naturally, this is fine country for bees, and a great deal of honey is also produced here. **Maison de l'Abeille**, on the approach to the town, houses a fascinating exhibition, explained by an enthusiastic owner, of modern and historic bee-keeping and honey-making.

14 From the Lac de St Cassein to Mandelieu, the beautiful **Tanneron massif** is planted out with mimosa. In summer there is no trace of the brilliant yellow blooms which light up the winter hillsides.

FOR CHILDREN

14 In Mons, ask them to find the electricity meter for the house at 22 Su Lou Coustihoun.

FOR HISTORY BUFFS

14 After Mons, **Roche Taillée** to the left of the D56 is a fine example of Roman civil engineering, a deep cutting in a limestone outcrop to take part of the 40km (25-mile) aqueduct which supplied the town of Fréjus near the coast. The aqueduct is still in use today, and it is possible to walk alongside it as it contours the hillside. Roche Taillée is also a glorious viewpoint over the wooded limestone gorge of the Siagne.

3 days – 232km (145 miles)

EXPLORING THE CÔTE D'AZUR

Nice • Cap Ferrat • Monaco • Menton Castillon • Sospel • Col de Turini Vallon de la Gordolasque • Madone d'Utelle • Nice

In the early stages, this tour visits world-famous resorts – Nice and Monaco – where the characteristic 'wedding cake' architecture of the Côte d'Azur now stands side by side with ultra-modern designs; but later it turns north into an entirely different scene. Often using steep and hairpinned roads, the route climbs spectacular valleys and wooded mountain ridges. Far from the hustle and bustle of holiday crowds, the valley of the Gordolasque is a cleft in the wildest part of the Maritime Alps, and the pilgrimage church of Madone d'Utelle crowns a remote and atmospheric hilltop.

FOR CHILDREN

1 Cap Ferrat Zoo, in a former estate of King Leopold II of the Belgians, raises many young animals, including llamas, kangaroos, gazelles and monkeys. Children enjoy its daily 'chimpanzee school'.

RECOMMENDED WALKS

1 On Cap Ferrat, the **Maurice Rouvier walk** is a promenade from the harbour to Beaulieu, while the **Pointe St-Hospice walk** from the Paloma beach circles a rocky peninsula below the villa gardens.

BACK TO NATURE

2 Monaco's **Jardin Exotique** has a wonderful collection of sub-tropical plants, including 10m (35-foot) Mexican cacti, able to grow successfully because of the very warm microclimate. Below ground there are impressive limestone caverns at the **Grotte de l'Observatoire**.

Sospel has a bohemian charm that inspires one to reach for paintbrush and canvas or camera

ⓘ Avenue Thiers, Nice

Leave Nice following the N98, the Corniche Inférieure, to Villefranche. Bear right for St Jean-Cap-Ferrat.

Cap Ferrat, Côte d'Azur

1 Cap Ferrat is a cape extending about 3km (2 miles) south of Beaulieu. All the capes along the Côte d'Azur are favoured residential areas, with imposing villas in discreet well-wooded grounds. At Cap Ferrat one of the most majestic of these, once the home of the Baroness Béatrice Ephrussi-de-Rothschild, was built early this century to house a massive collection of furnishings, tapestries, costumes, paintings and porcelain. The house and contents were left to the Académie des Beaux Arts and now form the **Musée 'Ile de France'**. It stands among 7 hectares (17 acres) of gardens in styles from different times and countries, and the collection, although it has a strong bias to the 18th century, includes Impressionist paintings and oriental *objets d'art*. St Jean-Cap-Ferrat, the resort village facing the towering cliffs that march to Monaco and the Italian frontier, is on an arm of the cape going off to the east. It has two promenades, the upper one on the roof of a line of shops, cafés and restaurants looking out to the yachts and cruisers bobbing in the harbour.

ⓘ Avenue Denis Seméria

Return to Villefranche and bear right on the D125, then follow signs through Beaulieu for Monaco.

Monaco

2 If you are a first-time visitor to Monaco, forget any idea that it is some kind of comic-opera place where only high-society millionaires feel at home. This is an ancient and

A fairytale palace where a fairytale princess once lived. The palace of Monaco is still very much the home of the Grimaldis, France's unofficial royal family

sovereign state, ruled by the Grimaldi family for over 700 years. The Grimaldis originated in Genoa in Italy, one of their number seizing the Rock of Monaco in 1297.

Despite being so tiny – no larger than many a farm – the vastly wealthy principality is divided into four main districts: Monte Carlo, where the casino and the sumptuous Hôtel de Paris are located; La Condamine, around the harbour with its tens of millions of pounds' worth of yachts; the lovely old town on Le Rocher, the original Rock of Monaco and Fontvieille, a new suburb.

Prince Rainier III's **palace** is reached from La Condamine up a steep ramp. It is mostly of the 16th and 17th centuries, and has several magnificent rooms open to the public, as well as a museum devoted to Napoleon, who was related to the Grimaldis. A fascinating archive collection documents centuries of Monagasque history. Throughout the palace and, indeed, throughout Monaco itself there are reminders of Princess Grace, the former film actress Grace Kelly whose fairytale marriage to Prince Rainier delighted the world. Also in the old town are the elegant **cathedral**, built in neo-Romanesque style in the 19th century and containing the tomb of Princess Grace, and the splendid **Musée Océanographique** (Oceanographic Museum), rising dramatically from the sea-cliffs. The latter, with an aquarium as well as fascinating museum exhibits, is directed by the famous underwater explorer Jacques Cousteau. Around it lie the beautiful **St Martin gardens**. They look down on the marina and Fontvieille, which is packed with housing and industry but has a large sports stadium and marina to its credit.

ⓘ Boulevard des Moulins

*Leave Monaco on the **N98** as for Menton. In Roquebrune bear right for Cap Martin. Follow 'Menton' signs to the shore road, then keep right along the seafront to Menton.*

Menton, Côte d'Azur

3 An old rhyme about the Riviera resorts claimed that 'Menton's dowdy, Monte's brass, Nice is rowdy, Cannes is class'. For years, Menton did have rather a faded air, brought about partly because its most faithful visitors were invalids and elderly people, from all corners of Europe. Famous visitors of the past include the writer Katherine Mansfield and the illustrator Aubrey Beardsley. Now Menton has revitalised itself, but, nevertheless retains a less hectic pace than most other Côte d'Azur resorts. In addition, it has a lovely climate and Italian-style architecture; the Italian border is in its eastern outskirts.

Menton has beautiful gardens including the **Biovès Gardens** in the town centre, a casino, fine museums, one of which is dedicated to the work of Jean Cocteau, and churches, promenades and squares. Around it lie the lemon groves – susceptible to very rare winter frosts – which give the town its most famous product. A Lemon Fair is held in February.

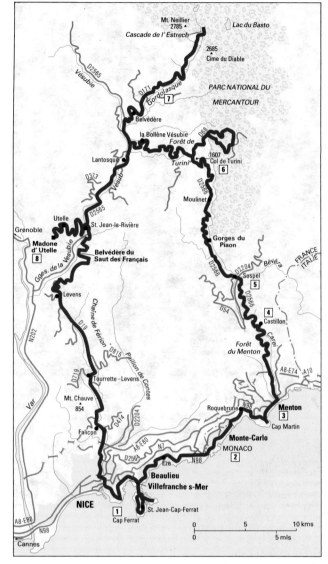

ⓘ Avenue Boyer

*Leave Menton on the **D2566** as for Sospel. Watch for the sharp right turn into Castillon.*

Castillon, Côte d'Azur

4 The original Castillon was wrecked in a 19th-century earthquake, and the rebuilt town destroyed during World War II. Their replacement is a charming modern village with lanes and stairways, a tiny square and a beautiful southern outlook, as well as shops and studios offering paintings, sculptures, ceramics, leatherwork, stained glass and jewellery.

*Return to the **D2566**, bearing right on it to the Col de Castillon. Go through the tunnel and turn right to Sospel.*

Sospel, Côte d'Azur

5 For a town in such an agreeable situation, at the junction of two river valleys surrounded by exhilarating mountain scenery, Sospel gives a scruffy impression to the visitor. However, there is an intriguing old quarter with houses alongside the River Bévéra which is crossed by an 11th-century toll bridge, and in the **Église St Michel** the town has a former cathedral whose grand baroque interior comes as a perplexing sur-

FOR HISTORY BUFFS

2 On a rocky promontory in Beaulieu, which lies between Cap Ferrat and Monaco, the **Villa Kérylos** is a modern replica of a Greek palace of the 5th century BC, created early in the 20th century by archaeologist Théodore Reinach. Its pillars, mosaics, frescos and furnishings, marble and alabaster benefit from their location by the deep blue Mediterranean, and there are some granite antiquities among the reproductions.

SPECIAL TO...

2 Monte Carlo's Casino is the most famous in the world, with lush interior decorations and a gloriously baroque architectural style. Visitors may enjoy the public rooms without gambling, but a passport or some other identification is necessary, and no one under 21 is admitted.

SPECIAL TO...

6 The **Col de Turini** is the most famous stage, every January, in the **Monte Carlo Rally**. You may see messages painted on the road – encouragement to top drivers from their fans.

SCENIC ROUTES

From the immaculate villas of the Cap de Nice, the **N98** swings round to open up a gorgeous view of Villefranche bay.

Leaving Menton, the **D2566** climbs past woodlands and soaring limestone ridges which stretch to the Italian border.

After the tunnel at the top of the Col de Castillon, be ready for a striking northwards view past dramatic wooded ridges to lonely skyline peaks.

Beyond Sospel the **D2566** cuts through a seemingly impenetrable mountain wall by hairpinning up the Gorges du Piaon. There is a remarkable view back down the ravine from the little Chapel of Notre-Dame de la Menour, reached by an arched staircase bridge across the road.

The Col de Turini descends a forested mountainside towards the red-roofed village of La Bollène-Vésubie.

As it rises, the hairpinned climb to Madone d'Utelle opens up more and more dramatic views.

BACK TO NATURE

6 Reached from the Col de Turini, the mountainous **Parc National du Mercantour** is home to chamois, ibex, ptarmigan and eagles. Alpine flowers and butterflies are at their best from June to August.

RECOMMENDED WALKS

7 In the valley of the Gordolasque, a long distance footpath on the east bank can be split into individual stretches for shorter walks. Look for the footbridges which cross the river and take you past scree-runs, boulder fields and thinning pinewoods on the other side.

La Bollène-Vésubie is an enchanting village encountered in the Col de Turini region. For all its sophisticated and playground-of-the-rich reputation, villages like this are the real south of France. Explore them on your own, and discover your favourites

prise. At the railway station a group of coaches in a siding form a **museum** about the Orient Express. On the outskirts, **Fort St Roch** is an astonishing underground artillery installation, part of the Maginot Line of defences built in the 1930s between the Belgian border and Corsica.

i Le Pont Vieux

Leave Sospel on the D2566 via Moulinet to the Col de Turini.

Col de Turini, Côte d'Azur

6 In the high pine and larch forests at 1,607m (5,270 feet) above sea-level, Turini is a winter sports resort and a cool bolt-hole in summer from the heat of the coast. Four roads radiate from the hamlet at the summit, one to the still-higher circuit of l'Authion, just inside the huge **Parc National du Mercantour**. There are magnificent viewpoints here, as well as ruins of military fortifications battled over during the Revolution and in the last bitter days of fighting in 1944.

Leave the Col de Turini on the D70 through La Bollène-Vésubie, where you should turn sharp right following 'St Martin' sign. Go right on the D2565 as for St Martin-Vésubie, then sharp right on the D71, follow signs to Belvédère and go right at the T-junction for Gordolasque. This is the narrow D171. Follow it to a car park before the bridge where the public road ends.

Vallon de la Gordolasque, Côte d'Azur

7 This dead-end valley road follows a rocky mountain stream past steep scree-slopes, crags and boulder-runs where the woodland cover peters out in scattered pines and larches. The public road ends at the 1,700m (5,575-foot) **Pont du Countet**, beside a relief map of the bare, impressive upper valley still to come. An easy stroll gives a grand view of the dashing falls at the **Cascade de l'Estrech**.

Return through Belvédère to the D2565 and turn left as for Nice. At St Jean-de-la-Rivière take the D32, the hairpinned climb past Utelle. Go left on the D132 to Madone d'Utelle.

Madone d'Utelle, Côte d'Azur

8 The silence, air of tranquillity and tremendous views make the journey to this remote hilltop well worthwhile. Madone d'Utelle has been a place of pilgrimage since the 9th century. The present church, with its many thanks-offerings, was built in 1806 and is the goal of four major pilgrimages every year. It shares the hilltop with a mountain 'refuge' and a domed orientation table which identifies the major summits among the all but unaccountable mountain peaks included in the glorious 360-degree skyline view.

Return to St Jean-de-la-Rivière and turn right on the D2565. After a 'Nice par Levens' sign, bear left on the D19 and follow it back to Nice.

Practical and beautiful: the Roman aqueduct at Pont du Gard

ⓘ Rue Auguste, Nîmes

Leave Nîmes on the D979 as for Uzés. Turn right on the D981, then watch for a right turn following it to Pont du Gard.

Pont du Gard, Languedoc-Roussillon

1 In civil engineering the Romans thought big. Their settlement at Nîmes needed water, and the magnificent three-tiered aqueduct at Pont du Gard, built around 20BC, was the most spectacular section of the 50km (30 miles) of channels which brought it from faraway springs. The first and second levels of arched bridges are simply supports for the topmost water channel which now, out of use, is open to pedestrians. In the modern world, few utilitarian structures have such abiding elegance.

Continue to Remoulins. Go straight on along the N86, then follow signs for Beaucaire.

Beaucaire, Languedoc-Roussillon

2 Road traffic here defers to the Canal du Rhône à Sète (Rhône-Sète canal). Beaucaire's one-way street system circles an attractive canal basin where barges and holiday cruisers are moored. The two great interests of the town are bull-fighting and music. Beaucaire was where the Camargue style of bull-fighting began, free from weapons and any taint of 'blood on the sand'. One statue in the town celebrates

THROUGH HISTORIC PROVENCE

Nîmes • Pont du Gard • Beaucaire • Tarascon
St Michel-de-Frigolet • Avignon • St Rémy-de-Provence • Les Baux
Arles • Méjanes • Musée Camarguais • Maison du Parc
Les Saintes-Maries-de-la-Mer • Aigues-Mortes • Nîmes

The Romans loved the blue skies, warmth and landscape of the south of France, and have left here, in the region they called Provincia – at Nîmes, Arles and Pont du Gard – some of their most imposing monuments. Avignon retains the architectural grandeur given it by popes in voluntary exile from Rome. In contrast, gypsies from all over Europe gather every year at Les Saintes-Maries-de-la-Mer. In the south, one of France's finest regional nature parks includes most of the Camargue, centred on the secret waters of the Étang de Vaccarès.

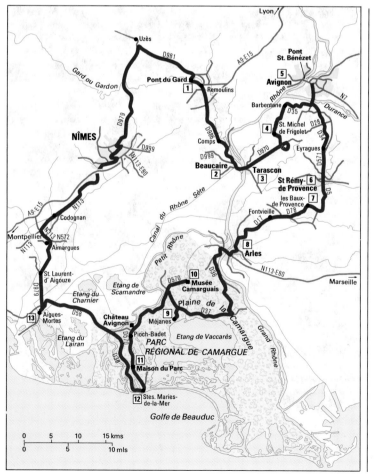

SCENIC ROUTES

North of Nîmes the **D979** crosses the limestone scrubland of the Garrigues, then descends to the gorges of the Gardon and continues through totally different country of fields and vineyards.

On the way to Frigolet and Barbentane, to the south of Avignon, the road runs through pleasant pinewoods with long stretches of scented picnic sites.

Beyond St Rémy, the **D5** climbs south towards the dramatic white skyline peaks of the Alpilles.

While the Camargue is as nearly dead-flat as makes no scenic difference, and there are no trees to form a clear horizon, roads like the **D37** offer a great deal to the observant traveller, as ponds, marshland and rice fields are glimpsed beyond the grassy wildflower-filled verges.

The Papal Palace, at Avignon, built when the Pope was a prince requiring splendour above all

Not only in the Camargue itself, but also in the inland towns, are regular and well-attended bullfights. However, these are not usually of the bloodstained Spanish variety you may find distasteful. Here the aim of the bullfighter (the rasetteur) is not to kill the bull but to get away unscathed with a rosette or some other favour that is tied to its horns. Bulls thus live to fight many times and become skilled operators.

RECOMMENDED WALKS

6 From the tourist office in St Rémy there is a walk through the outskirts of the town (finishing back on the main Boulevard Mirabeau), which visits the scenes of many of Vincent van Gogh's paintings – farms, poppy fields, plane and olive trees, and the quarry which appealed to him because of the Japanese-style arrangement of the rocks.

'Clairon' – not a famous bullfighter, but a bull! Classical and jazz concerts are held at various venues all over the town throughout the season. Beaucaire's part-ruined hilltop **castle** offers a good view over the lower Rhône, and the **town museum** holds many souvenirs of the days when traffic on the Roman highway – the *Via Domitia* – passed through between Italy and Spain. The town hosted a famous fair from 1217 to the mid-19th century and the museum has exhibits illustrating this.

ⓘ Cours Gambetta

Leave Beaucaire following signs to Tarascon.

Tarascon, Provence

3 The twin, and often the rival, of Beaucaire across the Rhône, Tarascon is famous for two fictional characters – the river monster called the Tarasqe, which is paraded through the town during the annual fair on the last Sunday in June, and Tartarin of Tarascon, the protagonist of *Aventures Prodigieuses de Tartarin de Tarascon* by Nîmes-born writer Alphonse Daudet. The hero of these 'prodigious adventures' features in a **musuem** in the town. Tarascon has cool plane-tree avenues where the summer sun is held at bay. Its 15th-century **castle** on a dramatic riverside site displays valuable 17th-century tapestries and houses regular art exhibitions. Close by, the **church** dedicated to St Martha has a very impressive crypt which is the traditional burial place of Martha herself, the sister of Mary and Lazarus in the Bible story.

ⓘ Rue des Halles

*Leave Tarascon on the **D970** as for Avignon. Turn right for St Michel-de-Frigolet, looping over the **D970** on an elevated bridge.*

St Michel-de-Frigolet, Provence

4 Among the trees, the spires and towers of a complex of **abbey buildings** suddenly comes into view. A religious community has lived here among the sweet scents of herbs and pinewood since as early as 1133, although there were some years in the 20th century when the monks were dispersed elsewhere. In the public areas of the abbey the buildings include a beautifully decorated basilica completed only in 1866. The old abbey farm is now a café; and the shop sells the modern version of Père Gaucher's Elixir, which featured in one of Daudet's best-known stories.

ⓘ Le Magasin

Continue to Barbentane, where you should ignore the 'Toutes Directions' sign and go straight on, following the 'Château' sign, then turn right and follow signs into Avignon.

Avignon, Provence

5 Avignon's heyday was in the 14th century, when the papacy moved the court here from Rome. The heart of the city is dominated by the grand 14th-century **palace complex** built by Popes Benedict XII and Clement VI and the towers, chapels, churches, cloisters and elegant courtyards which grew up to support it. What matters here is the architecture, since the restored buildings are mostly unfurnished, although Gobelin tapestries hang in the banqueting hall. Near by, the famous **bridge of St Bénézet** stretches its remaining arches across the Rhône. Visitors from all over the world come to stroll 'sur le pont d'Avignon', as in the old song.

The modern town has museums of all kinds, and a hectic summer programme of concerts, plays, dance, painting and sculpture exhibitions.

ⓘ Cours Jean-Jaurès

Return from Avignon on the N570 as for Arles. Turn left on the D571, then right for St Rémy on the D34, entering the town on the D571.

St Rémy-de-Provence, Provence

6 St Rémy is a place that knows how to cope with the relentless summer sun of Provence. There are virtual tunnels of shady plane trees, and cooling water runs down channels in the alleyways of the old town. The **Musée des Alpilles**, named after the limestone sierra that rises to the south, contains permanent exhibitions on St Rémy's history and domestic life. Among townspeople commemorated, is the 16th-century seer Nostradamus, whose birthplace can still be seen.

On the outskirts of St Rémy one road leads to a woodland lake at the foot of the Alpilles, another to the former Monastery of **St Paul de Mausole**, converted into the mental home where Vincent van Gogh spun out his last demented days. In the countryside you are likely to see amateur artists, serious under floppy hats, painting their own versions of the scenes van Gogh put on canvas.

South of the town lie the extensive ruins of the Greek and Roman settlement of *Glanum*. Many of the artefacts are displayed in **Le Musée Archéologique** in town.

i Place Jean-Jaurès

Leave St Rémy on the D5, then go right on the D27a to Les Baux.

Les Baux, Provence

7 On a ridge that towers above the southern plain, this hill settlement is split into two distinct parts, each of limestone masonry hard to distinguish at a distance from the living rock. The inhabited quarter, dating mostly from the 16th and 17th centuries, crams shops, museums, galleries, cafés, hotels and restaurants into its narrow lanes. The eerie 'Ville Morte' ('dead city') on the crown of the ridge was the medieval stronghold, which became famous for its 'Courts of Love', courtly rituals in which troubadours vied in composing ardent, flowery verses for aristocratic ladies. It is a now a ruin. In the 15th century Louis XIII crushed the power and influence of Les Baux, but the 'dead city' remains a haunting place with magnificent views over the surrounding countryside.

Just outside the town, on the D27, the **Cathédrale des Images** offers a majestic audio-visual presentation. In chilly halls cut into the old bauxite quarries (Les Baux was where that aluminium ore was first discovered), 40 projectors, using the walls as screens, continuously show historical and nature-based films.

i Hôtel de Manville

From Les Baux, follow the signs to Arles, entering the town on the N570.

Arles, Provence

8 Phoenicians, Greeks and Romans all established themselves here, but it is the Romans who made Arles the capital of *Provincia*, who have left the most abiding monuments. The elliptical amphitheatre

Below: The Seigneurs of Les Baux claimed descent from Balthazar, one of the Three Kings, and used the Star of Bethlehem as their coat of arms. Right: The windmill at Fontvielle has a compass with the names of the 32 different winds said to blow here!

FOR HISTORY BUFFS

8 In Fontvielle, 10km (6 miles) northeast of Arles, follow the 'Moulin de Daudet' signs to the restored windmill on an exhilarating viewpoint hill. This is the mill which featured in Alphonse Daudet's *Lettres de Mon Moulin*, required reading not only for generations of French schoolchildren, but also for those learning French abroad. It is now a museum devoted to Daudet's life and works. Many places on this tour – Beaucaire, Tarascon, Avignon and the Camargue among them – are mentioned in the 'Letters'.

BACK TO NATURE

9 All over the Camargue you will see the characteristic white horses, often ridden by gardians – the Camargue equivalent of cowboys. But look out for the foals. They are born black or grey, and may take as long as five years to grow a fully white coat.

11 Of the many species of birds which live in the southern part of the Camargue, the most often illustrated are the flamingos. In flight they rise like an exotic white and pink haze over the ponds and lagoons. Watch out also for herons and egrets standing motionless in the water before darting down to spear their prey. Bee-eaters are perhaps the most colourful of the Camargue's birds – look for them perched beside roadsides.

SPECIAL TO...

11 At Badet-Pioch, off the D570 before Les Saintes-Maries-de-la-Mer, is the **Musée Tsigane**, housed in a group of caravans. The museum tells the story of a thousand years of gypsy travel, history, music and crafts.

(Arènes) built by the Emperor Hadrian in the 1st century ad still survives, used, alas, for bullfights in the Spanish style as well as the bloodless style of the Camargue; and you can attend concerts and festivals in the semi-circular Augustan theatre (**Théatre Antique**). The town's summer calendar is crammed with events having an international flavour as well as those firmly rooted in the traditions of Provence. One of these is the parade of *gardians* – the Camargue 'cowboys' – on their white horses.

Arles is very well supplied with museums strong on paintings, sculptures and Provençal life. The former **cathedral and cloisters of St Trophime**, one of the finest cloisters in the south of France, are decorated with beautiful stone carvings. A favourite walk is along the tree-lined avenue of **Les Alyscamps**, flanked by ancient tombstones, the remains of Arles' once widespread necropolis.

There are more memories of van Gogh here; it was in Arles that, after a fight with his friend Gauguin, he slashed off his own ear. A memorial to his tormented spirit stands in the quiet and shaded public gardens.

ⓘ Boulevard des Lices

Leave Arles on the D570 as for Les Saintes-Maries-de-la-Mer. Go left on the D36, right on the D36b, then right on the D37. Turn left on the C5 to Méjanes.

Méjanes, Provence

9 In the very heart of the Camargue, and including some of the shoreline of the lagoon called **Étang de Vaccarès**, this estate doubles as a

---

France offers the best things in life, even if they are not always free! But nobody pays to enjoy simple sights of great beauty – the spring blossom and the growing vines of magical Provence

---

leisure centre and a farm. It has its own bull-ring, in which events are held every weekend during the summer, a restaurant and stables where horses may be hired for short or full-day rides.

Rejoin the D37. Turn right on the D570 to the Musée Camarguais.

Musée Camarguais, Provence

10 Based on an old sheepfold, the Camargue Museum is the best place to find out about the geology and history of this curious area and about the lives of the farmers and how intensive draining turned great areas of previously useless marsh into productive grazing and arable land. A walk from the museum follows the banks of a drainage canal dug as long ago as 1543, and shows the difference between reclaimed land and the original marsh. The museum is one of the main centres of the **Réserve zoologique et botanique de la Camargue** (Camargue Regional Nature Park) which covers more than 83,000 hectares (205,000 acres) of the Rhône delta.

Return along the D570 and watch for the Maison du Parc on the left of the road at Pont du Gau.

Maison du Parc, Provence

11 Complementary to the Musée Camarguais, this centre explains and illustrates the fascinating wildlife of the park, with an audio-visual theatre and a display on all the brands used on the Camargue horses. Throughout, the emphasis is on the fragility of this marvellous habitat. The good advice is offered that anti-mosquito creams are a wise precaution for anybody exploring the Camargue, particularly in September and October; but to avoid the insects, there is indoor wildlife watching here too. The picture windows at the rear of the

Aigues-Mortes has an intriguing history as its name suggests

centre overlook a pool where flamingos are often seen.

Close by, there is a privately owned **Parc Ornithologique** where many species of resident and migrant birds are on show.

Continue to Les Saintes-Maries-de-la-Mer.

Les Saintes-Maries-de-la-Mer, Provence

12 Often packed with summer visitors, the former fishing village of Les Saintes-Maries takes its name from the tradition that the three Marys from the Bible story, together with Martha (the sister of Mary and Lazarus), sailed here from Palestine and began evangelising the Camargue.

But for the gypsy people of Europe the significant figure in the story is Sarah. In one version an Egyptian or Ethiopian servant who accompanied the Marys; in another, a local woman who helped them ashore. Sarah is venerated as the patron saint of gypsies. Her statue, dressed in rich robes, is paraded through the town during two festivals in May and October. For the rest of the year it rests in the claustrophobic undercroft of the 9th-century **church**, illuminated by candles which also throw an eerie glow on a head of Sarah sculpted from Silesian coal.

Just south of the church, the **Musée Baroncelli** concentrates on local and natural history and folklore. On the outskirts of the town, the **Musée de Cire** has a glorious mixture of exhibits, from waxwork tableaux of local tales, comprehensive displays of old farming equipment and farmhouse furnishings, to a chamber of horrors with torture scenes, a victim on a rack ... and more that you can see yourself.

The **Musée Camarguais** shows the beauty of the Camargue through displays and films.

ℹ️ Avenue van Gogh

Follow 'Aigues-Mortes' signs from Saintes-Maries, keeping on the D38, D38c and D58.

Aigues-Mortes, Languedoc-Roussillon

13 This town is an amazing survival, extended hardly at all beyond the original rampart walls constructed in the 13th century by Louis IX of France – St Louis – who called from here on the seventh and eighth crusades. The walls, towers and fortified gateways remain in place. Inside them, a pleasant town retains the old medieval grid pattern of streets. A statue of St Louis looks down on the activity round the central square, just as his gilded statue graces the arcaded interior of the **church**. The best view of Aigues-Mortes is from the gallery of the **Tour de Constance**, once a political and religious prison, which overlooks the town and also puts it in a geographical context among the low-lying lagoons and lakes of the Camargue. But where is the sea? Over the years the Mediterranean has receded, stranding the town. In terms of the sea, Aigues-Mortes became what its name implies – the 'Dead Waters'. The history of the place is explained in the **Musée Jadis Aigues-Mortes**.

ℹ️ Porte de la Gardette

Return from Aigues-Mortes following 'Nîmes' signs on the D979, N313 and N113, avoiding the 'peage' signs, to Nîmes itself.

Nîmes – Pont du Gard 38 (24)
Pont du Gard – Beaucaire/Tarascon 25 (15)
Beaucaire/Tarascon – St Michel-de-Frigolet 12 (8)
St Michel-de-Frigolet – Avignon 15 (9)
Avignon – St Rémy-de-Provence 20 (12)
St Rémy-de-Provence – Les Baux 25 (15)
Les Baux – Arles 21 (13)
Les Arles – Méjanes 30 (19)
Méjanes – Musée Camarguais 13 (8)
Musée Camarguais – Maison du Parc 25 (15)
Maison du Parc – Les Saintes-Maries-de-la-Mer 5 (3)
Les Saintes-Maries-de-la-Mer – Aigues-Mortes 32 (20)
Aigues-Mortes – Nîmes 40 (25)

FOR CHILDREN

9 The easiest thing to arrange in the Camargue is an escorted ride on one of the mysterious Camargue white horses, with a *gardian* to act as guide. Sessions as short as half an hour are offered, and many visit farms where bulls are reared for the ring.

12 Just beyond Les Saintes-Maries-de-la-Mer, look for the sign to the pier where *Tiki III*, a little Mississippi-style sternwheeler, starts its cruises around the mouth of the Petit Rhône. This is an ideal way to wander past the grazings, well away from public roads, of Camargue horses and bulls.

RECOMMENDED WALKS

12 Eastwards from Les Saintes-Maries-de-la-Mer – and demanding sensible clothing on a baking hot summer day – the long breakwater which protects the lakes and ponds of the Rhône delta from the open sea is reserved for walkers and cyclists. Look for the famous flamingo nesting site on an island in the Étang du Fangassier.

80

THE ALPS TO ALSACE

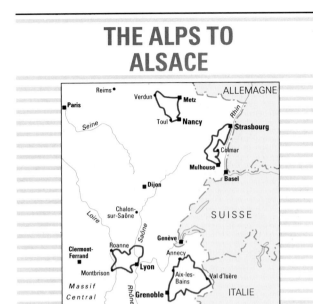

Near right: A funicular railway offers the most exciting view of Grenoble, especially by night – a modern industrial city, dedicated to superlative winter sports. Far right: A fountain with four horses guards the Place des Terraux in Lyon, France's second city

Alsace, Savoie, Burgundy, Lorraine – these towns include four provinces, each with its own independent heritage, separate for centuries from that of France. On the French-German border, Alsace and Lorraine were long contended territories, and even after they merged with France, they were lost again during the years of German occupation following the disastrous war of 1870 until the Allied victory in 1918.

The battlefields around Verdun and St Mihiel were the scene of indescribable carnage during World War I. There are few places in Europe where what actually happens in war – the paralysing noise, danger and the stench of death – comes home so vividly as at Verdun. This is not the sanitised version of war found in adventure stories and history books.

For 2,000 years and more, the Rhône/Saône valleys have been major highways, and it is still easy to drive quickly and unseeingly through them. However, off the main route, there is a jigsaw of medieval fishponds, and small towns of great interest.

East of Grenoble lie the majestic passes of the Alps and one of the highest roads in Europe. An exploration of the country of the lost duchy of Savoie, shows how France's massive hydro-electric schemes are landscaped so as not to spoil the glorious mountain scenery in which they are set.

Alsace is a different country once again, France with German names, sweeping vineyards and a strong preoccupation with storks. The Vosges mountains here may pale beside the Alps, but their forests and often cloudy upland ridges have an individual appeal.

Driving conditions are very varied. There are roads across the plains, among great acreages of arable land. Others wind through the vine-clad foothills. But on the Col de l'Iseran and the upper reaches of the Col de la Croix de Fer, you are in genuine Alpine country. The first of these passes can be swept by icy winds, the second can create a curious vertigo. All the roads, though, cope with summer tourist traffic.

There is splendid vineyard country here, producing wines as different as Burgundy and the Rieslings of Alsace. Many sophisticated gourmets consider that the country's finest 'table' is in Lyon.

The world's greatest motor museum is in Mulhouse. Colmar is one of the loveliest towns in Europe. And could there be a better place than Verdun to be preoccupied with peace?

Nancy
If you are expecting some modest provincial town, Nancy will come as a surprise. At the heart of this historic capital of Lorraine, richly-gilded Place Stanislas is one of the most elegant squares in France. Look for the lovely late Gothic Palais Ducal containing the Musée Historique Lorrain, for the Église des Cordeliers with the tomb of the dukes of Lorraine, for the superb medieval gateway and former prison of the Porte de la Craffe, and for the beautiful buildings of the old town. The Musée de Fer illustrates the history of iron, for generations a major industry in Lorraine. You can watch the glass-blowers in the crystal works of Daum.

Lyon
Lyon is a handsome city. It has sweeping quays on two rivers, the Rhône and the Saône, whose waters converge in the southern suburbs. Many notable buildings stand on the Presqu'île, the peninsula between the rivers. Here is the Musée des Beaux Arts with others devoted to textiles and decorative arts, printing and the history of banknotes. The 19th-century Basilica of Notre-Dame-des-Fourvière stands on the skyline above the streets of the old quarter in the loop of the Saône. A funicular links it with the lower town. Another climbs to twin Roman theatres still in use today.

The Lumière brothers, pioneers of moving film, worked in Lyon. There is a decorative mosaic, featuring famous figures such as Buster Keaton, near the Institut Lumière which regularly shows vintage films.

Grenoble
Grenoble, at the confluence of the Rivers Isère and Drac, is dominated by the soaring cliffs of the Massif de la Chartreuse. Cable cars whisk you to the viewpoint Fort de la Bastille, looking to the mountain ranges of Chamrousse and Vercors.

Beautifully sited, and with extensive parks and gardens, Grenoble offers music and drama, the Musée de Grenoble which contains paintings and sculpture, and has well-presented museums of science and technology, natural history, the Resistance and the region of Dauphiné.

Explore the gracious old quarter, admire Grenoble's modern architecture, and note its revived enthusiasm for the urban tram.

Strasbourg
Seat of the Council of Europe and the European Parliament, Strasbourg is also where Gutenberg, in the 15th century, invented modern printing. His memory is still revered.

The heart of the city is a river island, Look for the intriguing quarter called La Petite-France, where lovely old houses stand by the restored navigation canal.

Strasbourg has beautiful half-timbered and Renaissance buildings, a glorious cathedral and a cluster of museums in the 18th-century Château des Rohan. You

Capital of Alsace and sophisticated seat of government, there are other aspects to Strasbourg. Enjoy a relaxing stroll with your camera by the canals of La Petite-France

can take a river cruise, stroll through botanic gardens and enjoy the Parc de l'Orangerie created in 1804 for Napoleon's Josephine.

3 days – 300km (187 miles)

LORRAINE: VISIONS OF WAR & PEACE

Nancy • Parc de Haye • Liverdun Haut • Metz
Ville-sur-Yron • Verdun: Champs de Bataille • Verdun
St Mihiel • Butte de Montsec • Toul • Nancy

Except for part of the valley of the Moselle, this tour avoids the industrial districts of Lorraine in favour of the agricultural south around Nancy, the historic capital. There are peaceful rural landscapes here, but they have bitter memories. The Franco-Prussian War of 1870 ravaged Lorraine. So did the battles of the 20th century – this is, after all, the country of Verdun. Modern Lorraine is happily engaged, once more, with grain and fruit trees, livestock and vines.

FOR CHILDREN

1 The Parc de Haye has a children's play area and farm, mini golf and a miniature railway.

BACK TO NATURE

2 See how the currents of air sweeping up the wooded ridge from the Moselle suit the birds of Liverdun Haut. Kestrels nest in the old buildings and hunt above the woodlands. Kites are here too, as well as swifts, swallows and martins darting around the streets.

SPECIAL TO...

4 Along the **D903** near Verdun are certain kilometre stones which nominate the road the 'Voie de la Liberté' (Freedom Way). Allied troops swept the German forces along it in 1944.

i Place Stanislas, Nancy

Leave Nancy as for Paris on the A31. Take the 'Parc de Haye' exit.

Parc de Haye, Lorraine

1 This extensive leisure park is laid out on the site of a World War II American army camp; so it is appropriate that its **motor museum** should have both civil and military themes. You will see examples of Bugatti, Delahaye and Jaguar among the cars. The **Zoo de Haye**, with its deer and wild boar, rare domestic breeds and well-stocked aviary, is an unusual one. Almost all its wild animals and

Lorraine's capital Metz has been the prize of armies since Roman days

Green grass and white crosses cover the site of carnage at Verdun

birds are being cared for after accidents with cars, poisons or high-voltage lines and it is hoped they might be returned to their natural habitat.

*Turn right from the park exit following the **D400** sign, then right through Velaine and Aingeray. Go left over the bridge on the **D90b**, through traffic lights, then left for Liverdun Haut.*

Liverdun Haut, Lorraine

2 Crowning a bluff above a wooded curve of the Moselle, and providing lovely views over the river, this little medieval town was once the favoured summer residence of the bishops of Toul. Many old buildings survive. The tourist office is in the 16th-century fortified gateway, and there is an arcaded square of the same period. Dedicated to St Euchaire, the **church** is basically 12th-century. Look for the saint's tomb with his beheaded effigy. Euchaire was martyred at nearby Pompey in AD362.

i Porte Haute

*Return to the **D90b** and continue through Saizerais. Go right on the **D907** then, immediately after the 'Saizerais' board, turn left along Route de Villers. Go right at a give way sign, then left on the **N57** to Metz.*

Metz, Lorraine

3 Old fortifications are a reminder that Metz has been besieged, captured and relieved many times over the centuries, most recently in our own century. A memorial in the Place d'Armes recalls how, in 1918, Marshal Foch, Commander-in-Chief of the Allied armies on the Western front at the end of World War I, said that to see French troops on parade again at Metz was his greatest reward (the city had been in German hands for 47 years). Another memorial commemorates the liberation of Metz in 1944.

Despite being an industrial centre, Metz has a colourful selection of parks and gardens, a sizeable lake and attractive riverside promenades.

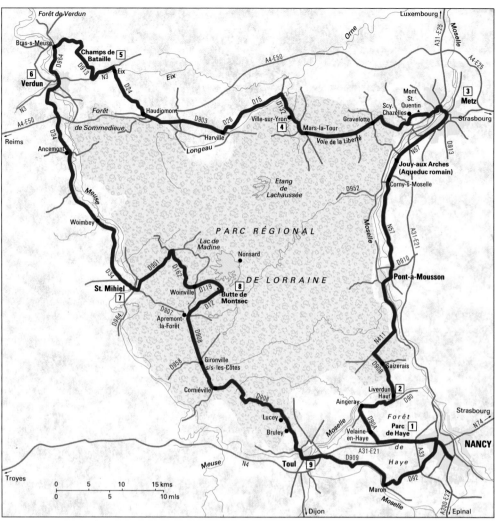

The **cathedral** (St-Étienne), of soft yellow stone, features a soaring interior with intricate stained glass including an impressive rose window. Archaeology, art and history are all to be found under one roof at the **Musée de Metz**. The Renaissance section is particularly enchanting, as is Roman Metz, displayed through sarcophagi, pottery and architecture.

i Place d'Armes

Leave Metz by the N3 through Longeville. At traffic lights in Le Ban St Martin, turn right on the D103w for Mont St Quentin, following the hairpinned Rue Fort. Down from Mont St Quentin, turn right at the Stop sign in the village (this is Scy-Chazelles), go left down Rue Leduchat and continue downhill at the next Stop sign. Pass Rue Robert Schuman on your left. At traffic lights turn right and follow 'Verdun' signs to Gravelotte, then go straight on along the D903 through Mars-la-Tour. Turn right on the D952, then left on the D132 to Ville-sur-Yron.

Ville-sur-Yron, Lorraine

4 In 1990, in this village tucked away among the fields, a fascinating **trail** was laid out which allows you to 'read' the architecture, building materials, history and way of life of a typical Lorraine agricultural settlement. It leads over the 19th-century bridge to the watermill, a landlord's and a labourer's farm, the 12th-century

church and the simple château built in 1762 by the bishop of Metz.

Continue on the D132, then go left on the D15, which becomes the D26 to Harville. Rejoin the D903 as for Verdun. Go right on the D24, then left on the D24a and left on the N3 into Verdun. Turn right at the traffic lights as for Paris, then watch for a sharp right turn following 'Champs de Bataille' boards. This is the D112. Go left at the crossroads on to the D913, follow 'Ossuaire' signs, then go left as for Verdun.

Verdun: Champs de Bataille, Lorraine

5 In 1916 the Germans launched a ferocious attack against the French lines northeast of Verdun: colossal artillery bombardments, mines, flame-throwers and poison gas were all employed. In the next few months, literally hundreds of thousands of troops died in the trenches, but the French essentially held the line. After the war, the ground of the battlefields was so ravaged that it was forested over.

Along the **D112** and the **D913** you will find forts, trenches, memorials and utterly devastated villages. The hilltop **Ossuaire (Ossuary) de Douaumont** is the last resting place for the bones of 130,000 soldiers on both sides, and offers a regular audio-visual programme on life in the trenches. As you walk to the

FOR HISTORY BUFFS

3 Jouy-aux-Arches on the N57 takes it name from the high masonry arches, built almost 1,900 years ago in the reign of the emperor Trajan as part of the Roman aqueduct to Metz. Metz was already an old town when Julius Caesar conquered Gaul. The Romans fortified it, their walls forming the battlefield fortifications.

4 Turn left along the Rue Robert Schuman in Scy-Chazelles, on the way from Metz to Ville-sur-Yron, to visit the modest home, now a museum, where the great French statesman (1886–1963) worked out his plans for a united Europe. Schuman played an important role in the creation of NATO, the Council of Europe and the European Coal and Steel Community, the first step towards the EU.

The **Musée Militaire** in Gravelotte recalls the disastrous Franco-Prussian War of 1870, which led to the downfall of Napoleon III.

SCENIC ROUTES

From the farming plain after Velaine there are long views all around, eventually including the beautiful setting of Liverdun above the far bank of the Moselle.

At Gravelotte you begin to cross the vast arable plains of Lorraine, then along the **D24** comes orchard country at the foot of low hills.

From Montsec, the **D12** runs through farm and orchard land, with occasional vineyards, below the wooded Côtes de Toul. After Toul, the **D909** before Maron offers pleasant glimpses of the curves of the Moselle.

RECOMMENDED WALKS

7 At Woinville, near Montsec, a roadside map will show you the network of local footpaths. Many are on the attractively wooded ridge of the Côtes overlooking the reservoir of Étang de Madine, and link up with other villages in the foothills.

9 On the return route to Nancy, from the **D909** and the **D92** before and after Maron, roads and tracks in the **Forêt de Haye** are linked up to make circular waymarked walks on the gentle gradients of the forest above the Moselle.

FOR CHILDREN

8 Turn left off the route at Woinville for Nonsard on the northeast shore of the reservoir called **Étang de Madine**. Here youngsters can enjoy mini golf, cyclocross and pedaloes, as relief from the grim memories of war all around.

SPECIAL TO...

9 On the **D908** approaching Toul, turn off for Lucey and Bruley. Lucey's **Maison du Polyculture** illustrates old farming methods and equipment. Grape juice is pressed for visitors at the vine harvest. At Bruley the **Centre du Promotion** lets you sample local produce such as smoke-cured meats, Côtes de Toul wines – especially the rosé – and the famous Mirabelle plums.

Peaceful agricultural countryside near Sion, in a region of France noted for the passionate intensity of its nationalism

Fort de Douaumont, you might wonder why the French high command in 1915 decided to leave this greatest underground stronghold in Europe virtually unguarded.

Continue to Bras and turn left to Verdun.

Verdun, Lorraine

6 Linked with other 'martyred towns' such as Hiroshima, Nagasaki, Coventry and Warsaw, Verdun is the Capital of Peace. Its vast underground citadel has tableaux of wartime scenes, and of the sombre moment in 1920 when France's Unknown Soldier was chosen. He now lies under the Arc de Triomphe in Paris.

Attractively sited on a curve of the Meuse, Verdun enjoys riverside quays, a fine Romanesque **cathedral** and the former **bishop's palace**, gardens and sports grounds, as well as prehistoric displays, paintings, furnishings and ceramics in the 16th-century **Hôtel de la Princerie**. Try the *dragées* – the sugared almonds which have been made in Verdun to a secret recipe since the 13th century.

i Place de la Nation

*Leave Verdun on the **D34** through Dugny, then go left on the **D901** to St Mihiel.*

St Mihiel, Lorraine

7 Best known in history for its strategic position in the St Mihiel salient – the defensive ring created by the Germans in 1918 – this little town also has the notable Benedictine **abbey church of St Michel**, with a 12th-century Romanesque portal and, in its light and airy interior, 80 beautifully carved choir stalls from the time of Louis XV. Here and in the **Church of St Étienne**, look for works by the local 16th-century sculptor Ligier Richier, a pupil of Michelangelo.

The Benedictines' library, itself a masterpiece of Lorraine design, survives with 8,000 valuable books and illuminated manuscripts.

i Place Jacques-Bailleux

*Leave St Mihiel as for Chaillon. Go right on the **D162** and left on the **D119** through Woinville to Montsec. Turn right on the **D12** then follow 'American monument' signs.*

Butte de Montsec, Lorraine

8 It was the Americans who smashed through the St Mihiel salient in September 1918. The **US 1st Army's memorial** is a massive rotunda on this beautiful viewpoint summit overlooking the **Étang de Madine**, with a relief map illustrating the course of the battle. Ironically, American troops had to fire on the memorial to subdue a German machine-gun post here in 1944. It was later completely restored.

*Return to the **D12** and turn right. Go left on the **D908** to Toul.*

Toul, Lorraine

9 Almost ringed by the Moselle, the Canal de l'Est and the canal linking the Marne with the Rhine, Toul once has the status of an independent enclave within the dukedom of Lorraine and as the heart of a diocese and a free imperial city was very important in medieval times. Old town gateways survive, as do the 17th-century walls, and the **cathedral** (St-Étienne) shows a splendid 15th-century Flamboyant frontage to the Place de Gaulle, and you should look at the decorated cloisters of the **Church of St Gengoult**. With all the water near by, Toul welcomes anglers, and the yacht basin is enlivened by the spray of a fountain in the centre.

i Parvis de la Cathédrale

*Leave Toul on the **N4** as for Nancy. Go under the bridge, then right on the **D909** to Maron. Turn left on the **D92** and return to Nancy.*

Château Varennes, Quincié, near Vaux-en-Beaujolais, heart of this celebrated wine-growing industry

ⓘ Place Bellecourt, Lyon

Leave Lyon on the D433 as for Neuville. Go through Caluire, then turn right at 'Musée de l'Auto-mobile' sign and follow 'Musée' signs along a complicated route to the Musée Henri Malartre.

Musée Henri Malartre, Rhône Valley

1 In the attractive, high-set **Château Rochetaillée** and the exhibition halls in its grounds, is an impeccably maintained collection of really rare cars. The Hugot, Thieulin, Noël Beret and the very early steam-powered Secretand, displayed in the Musée Henri Malarte, are the only survivors of these makes in the world. The separate hall displays several Gordini racing cars, built by the dogged but perpetually broke French constructor after whom it is named. Hitler's Mercedes is here, as well as examples of Packard, Lincoln and the 1912 Alco built by the American Loco-motive Corporation. Look for the bizarre gyroscope-equipped 1926 Monotrace tandem car, and the huge battery-powered Stela which ran as a taxi in Lyon till 1953. There is also a strong collection of cycles and motor-cycles (1898–1954).

Return by the same route to the D433 and turn left. Go right over the suspension bridge into Couzon, then left on the D51 into St Romain. Turn right on the D89. In St Cyr, go right on the D65. Continue straight on uphill at the Stop sign, then keep right on the D92 for Mont Cindre. After Mont Cindre, go straight on at a crossroads on the D90 signed 'Fortin du Mont Thou'. Return to the crossroads and turn right, then go right on the D73 to Poleymieux.

Le Mont d'Or, Rhône Valley

2 Follow the main route to Poleymieux over Le Mont d'Or ('Golden Hill') above Lyon, but be sure to stop off for occasional strolls, and to admire the views. There are several pleasant villages on the hill-sides, as well as farms and wood-lands. Mont Cindre, beside a telecommunications tower, is a favourite place for people from Lyon who take to the hills at weekends. Many of them enjoy the walk which starts at the hermitage. The best 360-degree panoramic view is from **Mont Thou**, as you walk over the grass-lands beside a hilltop military camp.

In Poleymieux bend right after gantry traffic lights, still on the D73, and continue via Curis to Neuville-centre on the D16. Go straight on along the D16e through Montanay, then left at the T-junction (this is the N83) through Mionnay. Turn right into the Parc des Oiseaux.

At Mont Brouilly there is a shrine to wine-growers. The vine is serious business here

SECRETS OF THE RHÔNE VALLEY

Lyon • Musée Henri Malartre • Le Mont d'Or • Parc des Oiseaux
Villars-les-Dombes • Châtillon-sur-Chalaronne •
Vaux-en-Beaujolais • Amplepuis • Roanne • Chazelles-sur-Lyon
Charbonnières-les-Bains • Lyon

Tourists rushing to and from the Riviera dash through the val-ley of the Rhône past Lyon. But the background to that great road and rail corridor is fascinating. The landscape changes from level plains scattered with ponds, to beautiful vineyards in the foothills and gentle forest passes. One of Europe's great motor museums is located here. Wildlife parks display water-fowl and spectacular birds of prey. There is a spa, and a village whose fictional antics made millions laugh. And one of the loveliest towns in the Lyonnais commemorates a saintly man whose life's work relieved the sufferings of the poor.

FOR CHILDREN

The **Parc de la Tête d'Or**, on the banks of the Rhône in Lyon, has a lake, a small zoo, go-cart track, botanical gardens and pony rides.

2 At the **Maison d'Ampère** in Poleymieux children are encouraged to try 18 of Ampère's original electrical experiments, including some with magnets. This is fun as well as a fine learning experience, and perfectly safe at the power levels employed.

FOR HISTORY BUFFS

2 In Poleymieux the Maison d'Ampère is devoted both to the brilliant and engagingly eccentric Lyon-born physicist André-Marie Ampère (1775–1836) – who gave his name to the standard unit of electric current – and to an amazing display of historic electrical equipment.

5 In Châtillon you can see the house where, in 1617, 'Monsieur Vincent' lived as the parish priest. Born in 1580, Vincent de Paul led an eventful early life, having been captured by corsairs on a voyage in 1605 and sold into slavery in Tunis. He was employed by the French royal family after his escape and before he came to Châtillon. Touched by the plight of the poor people of the town, he founded the first of his many charitable organisations, which led to the great Society of St Vincent de Paul (he was canonised in 1737).

Parc des Oiseaux, Rhône Valley

3 Far more than simply the ornithological park its name suggests, this public estate near Villars-les-Dombes takes full advantage of its situation in woodland circling an attractive lake. Eagles, vultures, parrots and parakeets have enclosures in the woods, and there is a tropical bird house, while pelicans, swans, geese and flamingos favour the water. The guided tour, by 'tourist train', takes 30 minutes. A walk round to see the park in all its details might occupy two hours. There is an adventure playground and a picnic area. At the entrance to the park, the **Maison de l'Artisanat** stocks high-quality ceramics, glassware and even boomerangs made by local craftworkers.

Continue to Villars-les-Dombes, eventually leaving the village on the D2 as for Châtillon.

Villars-les-Dombes, Rhône Valley

4 With a fine Gothic church, a road system which craftily keeps through traffic away from the narrow streets of the pleasant and colourful centre, and an excellent natural history bookshop, Villars is where to start any exploration of the curious plateau district known as Les Dombes.

Here there are a thousand pools, lakes or meres dug as fishponds from the 12th century onwards. They are now split between angling waters and commercial fisheries for carp, tench, roach and pike. Around 2,000 tonnes are taken every year, to make this one of the great inland fishery districts of France. Ask locally about dishes such as fillet of royal carp.

ⓘ Parc des Oiseaux

Continue on the D2 to Châtillon.

Châtillon-sur-Chalaronne, Rhône Valley

5 Few small towns in France have been awarded four stars in the national *villages fleuris* ('villages in bloom') competition, but Châtillon deserves every one. You should spend time admiring the blaze of blossoms in parks and gardens, beside the banks of the River Chalaronne and its tributary streams, in window boxes and hanging baskets, and decorating all the bridges.

Châtillon cherishes some beautifully maintained buildings to match the flowers. The covered **market hall** of 1670 is a gem, some of the old town **ramparts** survive, and the brickwork **Church of St André** dates from the 16th century. The

The Fourvières Basilica in Lyon offers a magnificent view from the top of the church tower

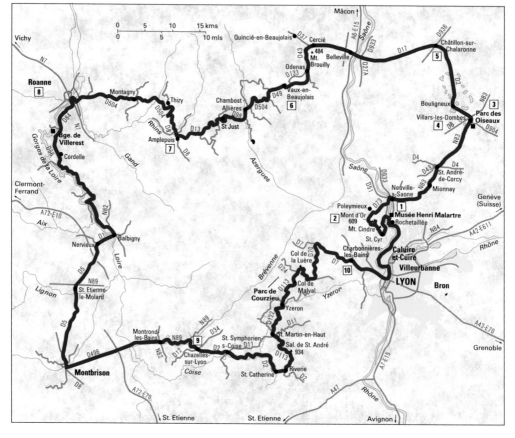

famous Châtillon **triptych** of 1527 is displayed in the dignified town hall. Its three Biblical scenes – the sleeping apostles, Christ taken from the cross and the Resurrection – are beautifully painted and restored.

Gathered in the intriguing old **Apothecairerie** is a fine collection of earthenware pots from which 18th-century pharmacists concocted their mixtures of gentians, sassafras, asafoetida and other plants. You can see where some of the prescribed salts ate away the painted surface of the pots!

☐ Place du Champ de Foire

*Leave Châtillon on the **D17**, which becomes the **D37** through Belleville and Cercié, then go left on the **D43** and left on the **D43e** to Mont Brouilly. Return to the **D43** and turn left. Turn right on the **D19**, then right on the **D49** to Vaux-en-Beaujolais.*

Vaux-en-Beaujolais, Rhône Valley

6 Gabriel Chevallier immortalised this village among the hillside vineyards as the fictional setting for his famous satirical novel *Clochemerle*, and several enterprises here continue the *Clochemerle* name. This is one of the most beautifully located of the Beaujolais wine-growing villages. There is a lively fraternity of enthusiasts for wine, and much of it may be tasted locally at the **Caveau de Clochemerle**.

However, *Clochemerle* is perhaps best remembered for the ceremonial inauguration of the public toilet. **La Pisotière de Clochemerle** stands on a terrace above the beautiful wine-planted valley, and is still popular with visitors today.

*Take the Lamure road, leaving Vaux on the 'Le Sottier poids lourds' road. This is the **D49**. Follow 'Lamure' signs – ignoring a left turn for Les Buissières – then go left on the **D44** to St Cyr. Turn right on the **D504** to Allières, left on the **D485**, then right on the **D98** and over the level crossing. Go straight on through St Just, then follow signs to Amplepuis.*

Amplepuis, Rhône Valley

7 In this little industrial town, the **Musée de la Machine à Coudre** celebrates a most heroic failure. Barthélèmy Thimonnier was an apprentice tailor here. In 1825, having seen the laborious work of the seamstresses, he invented the sewing machine.

He was spurned in Paris. London businessmen paid him an insulting sum for his design. Soon after his dejected return to France, the sewing machine revolutionised the production of clothes. But by then Thimonnier had died – still poor, still unappreciated and still unknown.

*Leave Amplepuis on the **D8**, then take the **D504** to Roanne.*

Roanne, Rhône Valley

8 Backing on to the Loire, Roanne is also on a well-maintained canal along which visitor cruises are run. It is an historic textile town, and old techniques of spinning and weaving are demonstrated at the **Écomusée**. If you enjoy ceramics, visit the elegant château of the **Musée Déchelette**, which has beautiful dis-

Quincié, at the centre of the wine-growing region of Beaujolais

BACK TO NATURE

4 Beyond Villars, the lakes and ponds of Les Dombes are havens for wildlife. On the Étang Forêt and the Étang du Château at Bouligneux you can expect to see teal and mallard, coots, herons and grebes.

RECOMMENDED WALKS

5 Three walks, mostly on country roads with occasional farm tracks, are suggested by the tourist office at Châtillon. One visits four of the little lakes for which the district is famous. The others go to the old castle ramparts and the banks of the Relevant stream.

SPECIAL TO...

7 The slopes of **Mont Brouilly**, between Vaux-en-Beaujolais and Amplepuis, are packed with vineyards whose geometrical lines, at different angles, create a beautiful pattern on the hillsides. Available locally, *Côte de Brouilly* is one of the fine crus of Beaujolais wine, with many individual producers.

SCENIC ROUTES

From **Mont Cindre** wonderful views open up of Lyon, the Rhône valley and the Alps.

After Châtillon there is a splendid outlook to the hillside vineyards of Beaujolais.

On the **D504** to Roanne, look for the gorgeous hilltop setting of **Thizy**.

The Lac de Villarest reservoir is very attractive from the **D56** between Roanne and Chazelles; a view of wooded gorges with an abandoned castle standing on a flooded rock.

There is a magnificent valley view to the right of the **D113** after Riverie, on the way from Chazelles to Charbonnières.

SPECIAL TO...

8 Many gourmet centres were originally on the main road from Paris to the Riviera. Roanne on the **N7** is now avoided by the traffic on the Autoroute de Soleil, but it remains a famous gastronomic town. The restaurant of the Troisgros brothers' hotel is classed as one of the finest tables in France.

FOR CHILDREN

9 The **Musée d'Allard** on the Boulevard de la Préfecture in **Montbrison**, on the way to Chazelles-sur-Lyon, has several individual themes, but is best known for its collection of dolls and puppets from countries all over the world.

BACK TO NATURE

10 Turn left at Col de Malval for the **Parc de Courzieu**. Here, not only are wolves, lynx and wildcats on show, but free-flying displays by eagles, vultures and falcons also take place in a thousand-seat auditorium.

RECOMMENDED WALKS

10 Stop off on the way to Chazelles and in St André-la-Côte, or from a left-hand bend on the route beyond it, take the waymarked path to the **Signal de St André**. In clear weather the dramatic view extends from a series of hill villages to the mountain wall of the Alps.

plays of French and Italian ware. Modern craftworkers congregate in the **Maison des Métiers d'Art**.

Roanne keeps a foothold in the wine business, although the great days when it shipped barge-loads of barrels to Paris are long since gone. You can taste some of the *Côte Roannaise* wine in the town-centre caveau, housed in a lovely little half-timbered building with a steeply pitched red-tiled roof.

ⓘ Cours de la République

*Leave Roanne on the **N7** as for Lyon. Go right on the **D43** as for Varennes then right on the **D84** as for Vernay. As soon as you enter Commelle-Vernay turn left as for Cordelle. Follow the **D56** and **N82** into Balbigny. Go right at the traffic lights to Nervieux, then left on the **D5** through St Étienne-le-Molard. Go left on the **D8** into Montbrison, left on the **D496**, then straight ahead on the **N89**. Go right to Chazelles-sur-Lyon.*

Chazelles-sur-Lyon, Rhône Valley

9 Off the main roads in the wooded hills north of St Étienne, Chazelles owes a great deal to the crusaders who brought back from the east the secret of making felt. Chazelles used this new-found expertise to turn itself into a great hat-making centre. The extensive **Musée du Chapeau** explains, with guided tours, audio-visual presentations and working machinery, all the techniques of preparation, manufacture and fashion, and has a gallery of more than 500 specimen felt hats of all styles, including a collection of chefs' *toques*. The museum also devotes space to the history of the town, from its days as a junction of Roman roads.

ⓘ Place J B Galland

Textiles, ceramics and wine, Roanne is an area of varied and colourful talents. The opulent countryside speaks more of its heyday as a major wine-producer when the canal carried barrels to Paris daily

*Leave Chazelles on the **D103**, which becomes the **D2**, to Ste Catherine. Go straight on as for Mornant, then turn left on the **D63** into Riverie and left on the **D113** via St André-la-Côte to St Martin. Follow signs to Yzeron, go left as for Plan d'Eau, left on the **D489** as for Duerne, then right on the **D113**. Continue straight on at Col de Malval, then at Col de la Luère go straight on along the **D24** as for Lyon. Watch for a sudden left turn on to the **D70**. Go through Poillonnay then turn right on the **D7** as for Lyon into Charbonnières-les-Bains, then left for Charbonnières-centre.*

Charbonnières-les-Bains, Rhône Valley

10 Lyon is one of several French cities to have a totally different-looking spa town just beyond its outskirts, well away from the familiar busy streets. The first mineral spring here was traditionally discovered by a donkey on its last legs, which regained its vigour by drinking from it.

Whatever its origins, Charbonnières developed into a full-scale spa and health resort with thermal baths, a pump house, a casino and elegant villas in discreetly wooded grounds. It has good sports facilities, shaded footpaths and a fine array of shops.

ⓘ Parc Thermal

Follow 'Lyon-centre' signs and return to Lyon.

4 days – 472km (294 miles)

The reality of the picture postcard is to be found in delightful Alpine villages like Notre Dame de Bellecombe

PEAKS & LAKES: THE FRENCH ALPS

i Rue de la République, Grenoble

Leave Grenoble for Le Sappey on the D512, then continue to St Pierre-de-Chartreuse. Turn left and follow signs to the Musée de la Grande Chartreuse, using the one-way system.

La Grande Chartreuse, Rhône-Alps

1 High on the west side of the Massif de la Chartreuse stands La Grande Chartreuse, the grand mother house of the Carthusian monks. It has been established in this remote location, on ground under snow for more than half the year, since its founder St Bruno built the first monastery here in 1084.

The monks lead an austere life of study, meditation, solitude and prayer. No visitors are allowed in La Grande Chartreuse itself, and cars may not use the road to it. However, a fine **museum** has been created at La Correrie, by the end of the public road. It explains and illustrates the monastic life, as well as the history of the Order and the difficulties experienced by the monks here, (they were expelled from the monastery during the Revolution, and again between 1903 and 1940).

The famous Chartreuse liqueurs, the profits from whose sales fund the Order's charitable works, are distilled elsewhere.

Return to St Pierre-de-Chartreuse and turn left to rejoin the D512. Follow this road and the D912 to Chambéry.

Annecy is a deservedly popular town at the top end of the enchanting Lac d'Annecy

Grenoble • La Grande Chartreuse • Chambéry
Aix-les-Bains • Annecy • La Clusaz • Le Beaufortain
Bourg-St-Maurice • Val d'Isère • Col de l'Iseran
Modane • St Jean-de-Maurienne
Col de la Croix de Fer • Défilé de Maupas • Grenoble

While it starts in the valley city of Grenoble and visits the lakeside resorts of Aix-les-Bains and Annecy, this is essentially a mountain tour among the wild and magnificent landscapes of the French Alps. Check the *ouvert-fermé* (open/closed) signs – in most years the route is not fully open till mid-June – and be ready for some steep gradients and exposed hairpinned climbs. You can learn about one of the most famous monasteries in Europe, sample the traditional cheeses of Savoie, and pass through the dramatic scenery – territory of marmots, chamois, ibex and eagles – of the vast Parc National de la Vanoise.

SCENIC ROUTES

From Grenoble to Chambéry the route, runs over a massif of hills, forests, deep-cut valleys and towering limestone cliffs.

On the **D34**, after Aix-les-Bains, look for the dramatic valley of the Chéran, overlooked by the rock pillars called the Fairies' Chimneys.

The superlative mountain landscapes beyond La Clusaz include glimpses on the eastern horizon of **Mont Blanc**.

Even the spectacular climb to the Col de la Croix de Fer is surpassed by the descent through precipitous gorges to the **N91**.

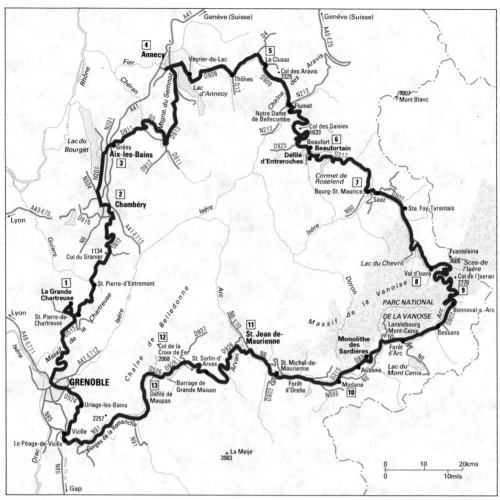

BACK TO NATURE

3 Approaching Aix-les-Bains, the N201 runs beside the shore of **Lac du Bourget**. Just before Tresserve, stroll over to look down on the reed beds and watch the comings and goings of a large population of great crested grebes. Coots, pochards and little grebes can also be seen on the water, and there are grey herons around the margins.

SPECIAL TO...

5 Before La Clusaz you will begin to see signs to the farms where the delicious traditional Savoie cheeses are produced. Most popular is Reblochon – check for the green 'fermier' label guaranteeing that it is farm-made. Look also for *Tomme de Savoie* and the strong goat's-milk *Chevrotin des Aravis*.

FOR HISTORY BUFFS

6 At the breezy summit of the **Col des Saisies**, on the stretch between La Clusaz and Beaufort, look for the **monument** to the daring exploit in August 1944, when a daylight wave of RAF planes parachuted arms and ammunition to the Resistance fighters of Savoie.

Chambéry, Rhône-Alpes

2 Why the elephants, you may wonder, on the great **fountain** the pleasant centre here? They commemorate the Duc de Boigne, who made his military reputation and his fortune in the East, before retiring to Chambéry to indulge his passion for town planning.

Wander through the arcaded streets, intriguing alleyways and courtyards of the old quarter. Above them stands the castle of the dukes of Savoie. The guided tour explains how Savoie was once an independent state whose territory stretched from Lake Geneva to the Mediterranean and included regions of modern Italy.

The Italian connection persists in the **Musée des Beaux-Arts**, which has a splendid display of Italian paintings. Local history collections are housed in the **Musée Savoisien**.

In the **cathedral** (look for more elephant motifs), some interior details such as the apparently vaulted ceiling are actually 19th-century attempts at *trompe l'oeil* paintwork. If nothing more, they have achieved some historical curiosity value of their own.

ⓘ Boulevard de la Colonne

Leave Chambéry for Aix-les-Bains on the N201.

Aix-les-Bains, Rhône-Alpes

3 Starting at the banks of the Lac du Bourget, the most extensive mountain lake in France, the town rises from a cruise-boat harbour and a lakeside promenade to a very stylish town centre. Aix-les-Bains is an elegant and well equipped spa resort. Its springs were known to the Romans, and later patrons were Napoleon's family and Queen Victoria. Colourful gardens, old and new-style fountains and pleasant woodland walks are scattered around. Top-class sports facilities are provided, especially winter sports on the lake, and the mountains are always in view.

Relics of Roman times include a **Temple of Diana** and a restored archway facing the Thermes Nationaux. Guided tours – on which you are encouraged to wear a toga – explore the Roman remains, the original baths and the statues preserved in the **Musée Lapidaire**.

On a hillside boulevard, the Musée Faure houses a valuable art collection. Look for fine paintings and sculpture by Degas, Pissarro, Rodin and Corot.

ⓘ Place Mollard

Continue on the N201, then go right on the D911. Turn left on the D31, right on the D5 and go straight on as for Le Châtelard on the D911. Turn sharp left on the D912 over Col de Leschaux. Go left on the N508 to Annecy.

Annecy, Rhône-Alpes

4 You can see how dearly the Annéciens love their pure and beautiful mountain-rimmed lake (Lac d'Annecy). They have spurned any encroachment on the lakeside parks and gardens which are areas of general relaxation as well as wonderful mountain viewpoints; and they make an attractive feature of the rivers and canals which thread through the lovely old quarter of the town.

Lake cruises are a favourite excursion here, but in a place ideally laid out for aimless strolling around, or for clip-clopping along in the calèches (open carriages) which ply for hire, there are also specific attractions on land. Visit the castle museum, for instance. Go to prison – or, at least, to the Palais de l'Ile, the old jail, mint and courthouse (which now houses a small history museum). The château (restored) houses a local museum.

In the evenings, the old town (pedestrianised) is lively and chattering as its pavement restaurants and cafés fill up. Then the lights reflect in the waters lapping quietly by.

ⓘ Centre Bonlieu, rue Jean-Jaurès

*Leave Annecy for Veyrier-du-Lac on the **D909**. Continue through Thônes to La Clusaz.*

La Clusaz, Rhône-Alpes

5 Here is the first of many Alpine ski resorts on this tour, occupying a valley site crammed between jagged peaks. In summer when, as throughout the region, the weather can be very changeable, La Clusaz seems to be waiting impatiently until the snows return, bringing with them thousands of winter sports enthusiasts.

However, summer visitors are by no means neglected. The Bureau des Guides will introduce you to rock-climbing in half-day courses, and grass skis are available for hire. You can also, briefly or at length, try your hand at canoeing, fishing, skating, tennis, horse- or pony-riding, fencing, archery, pistol-shooting and pottery. Folklore groups enliven the evenings.

In among the typical shops, chalets, bars, cafés, hotels and restaurants of a ski resort, La Clusaz has a most attractive modern church. Look for the beautiful stained-glass windows, illustrating work in the mountains, fields and forests.

ⓘ Parc de l'Église

*Continue on the **D909** over the Col des Aravis to Flumet, then go straight ahead on the **D218B** over the Col des Saisies and follow signs to Beaufort. Go through Beaufort as for Bourg-St-Maurice.*

Le Beaufortain, Rhône-Alpes

6 At Beaufort, a village in a spruce-clad mountain valley, you may wonder where the road can possibly go next. In fact, it slices through the amazing rock cleft of the Défile d'Entreroches, then up a hairpinned pass with magnificent views of the valley left behind.

A good excursion centre, Beaufort is the heart of the Beaufortain district. In its co-operative you can watch the making of 'the prince of Gruyères' – Beaufort cheese, produced with milk from the upland farms – and even help in the process.

Eastwards, the Lac de Roselend reservoir lies in a deep depression among the mountains. Then the

Summer or winter, La Clusaz has something to offer

road battles up through 10 hairpin bends towards a notch in the skyline. This is an exciting landscape of mountain torrents, scree slopes and high snow-filled gullies. Wildflowers put on their brave summer display.

ⓘ On the **D925** in Beaufort

Continue to Bourg-St-Maurice.

Bourg-St-Maurice, Rhône-Alpes

7 Bourg-St-Maurice lies in a spectacular setting overlooked by cliffs and tiers of chalets. Green in summer, the hill slopes to the southeast are in the easily-reached skiing area of Les Arcs, upgraded for the 1992 Winter Olympics.

Down in the town itself there is a **woodland park** beside the compensation reservoir of a hydro-electric scheme. Bourg-St-Maurice is keen on sports such as white-water canoeing and rafting. Horse and pony trips can also be arranged. There is a minerals and crystals display, and another co-operative where Beaufort cheese is made.

The satellite village of Vulmis, along a steep road to the southwest, has a **chapel** with beautiful 15th-century frescos. And at Hauteville-Gondon to the south, you will find a costume museum and an unexpectedly baroque 17th-century church.

ⓘ Place de la Gare

*Leave Bourg-St-Maurice on the **N90** to Séez. Go right on the **D902** to Val d'Isère.*

FOR CHILDREN

5 La Clusaz has a summer toboggan run called the **luge d'été**. Youngsters (and adults) have a choice of two smooth metal pistes sweeping down the hillside for 800m (2,620 feet). Here also, on summer evenings, there are free shows in the village by jugglers, clowns and puppeteers.

7 Bourg-St-Maurice has installed a modern **funicular railway**. Children will enjoy the ride as the train climbs above the river then plunges into a mountain tunnel on its way up to the ski areas of Les Arcs.

RECOMMENDED WALKS

5 La Clusaz has a network of summer walks, some from the top stations of cable-car and chairlift lines. Ask at the tourist office, where you can also book for guided walks to lakes and mountain viewpoints, good areas for alpine flowers and the secret trails of the old *contrebandiers* (smugglers).

BACK TO NATURE

10 Pause after Sardières, on your way to Modane, to look at the *monolithe*, a huge isolated limestone pillar soaring to 83m (272 feet) in the heart of a pinewood. This strange weathered feature is not uncommon here. You will see more of them among the pines further on.

SPECIAL TO...

11 Transhumance – the bringing down of sheep from the lush summer mountain pastures – is still practised in the Maurienne. However, nowadays, the flocks arrive by train.

Val d'Isère, Rhône-Alpes

8 The resort of Val d'Isère lies 1,850m (6,068 feet) above sea level and is one of the most famous locations on the European ski-racing calendar. Cable cars climb from its narrow valley setting to reach spectacular viewpoint summits such as Bellevarde at 2,827m (9,270 feet). The eastern mountain ridge, marking the frontier with Italy, soars to over 3,350m (11,000 feet).

Val d'Isère is simply a series of long lines of apartment blocks, chalets, shops, hotels and restaurants. Many of the latest buildings, though, are quite sensitively designed in traditional mountain-country idiom.

Summer sports facilities are more for weekly residents than for transients, although horse and pony hire, archery and tennis lessons and mountain biking may be tackled in shorter bursts.

[i] Maison de Val d'Isère

*Continue on the **D902** to Col de l'Iseran.*

Col de l'Iseran, Rhône-Alpes

9 When the road over the Col de l'Iseran was opened in 1937, it had taken 20 years to build. At 2,770m (9,085 feet) in the wildest country, it was the highest road in Europe. Today, only a handful surpass it. The Iseran is usually under impenetrable snow till mid-June, but even a month later chill winds may sweep down from the still higher glaciers and snowfields.

In clear weather the Iseran is exhilarating, although the climb is on a broken surface. There is a summit shop. An austere, four-square chapel stands a little way apart. This is the

The village of Beaufort clusters round a fine 17th-century church. Near by, two lakes produce hydro-electric energy for the region

only through road which penetrates the huge nature reserve of the **Parc National de la Vanoise**. The mountain scenery is magnificent, and the descent is fortunately on a much better-surfaced road.

*Continue on the **D902**. In Bessans follow the 'Chambéry' sign. Go through Lanslevillard, then, in Lanslebourg, join the N6 as for Chambéry. In Sollières, turn right on the **D83**. In Sardières, go right as for Hôtel du Parc, then left past La Monolithe. Turn right at the T-junction, rejoining the **D83** to Aussois, then go straight ahead on the **D215** to Modane.*

Modane, Rhône-Alpes

10 This is where the busy road and rail tunnels to Bardonecchia in Italy begin. The 12.8km (8-mile) road tunnel opened in 1980. Go to the old ornamental rail tunnel entrance above the town, and you will see the coats of arms of the main cities on the Calais-Paris-Rome line.

Modane had a hard time in World War II. It was heavily bombed by the Allies in 1943, in an attempt to disrupt the German-Italian rail supply system, and the Germans fired colossal demolition charges at the rail tunnel entrance in 1944. You can still see a concrete blockhouse, intact but flung askew by the tremendous force of the explosion.

There is a glorious view from here, over Modane in its deep winding valley to the skyline of the Vanoise peaks. The town is an access point to the mountain footpaths of the Vanoise. Local walks include a hairpinned climb to the **Fort du Replaton** which you will see directly across the valley. Another excursion worth making is to the complex of forts at l'Esseillon, built in the 1820s to defend the forgotten kingdom of Piedmont-Sardinia against possible invasion from France.

[i] Place du Replaton

*Leave Modane on the **N6**, then turn left into St Jean-de-Maurienne.*

St Jean-de-Maurienne, Rhône-Alpes

11 Although the world's most modern aluminium factory is sited here, it is well away from the charming heart of St Jean-de-Maurienne. As you approach, you will see, rising above the town, a great sweep of pasture land dotted with higher and higher hamlets and farms.

The town square dips down to a fine modern war memorial outlined against the northern mountains. During the holidays, schoolchildren act as earnest and well-informed guides to the **cathedral** and the one-time **bishop's palace** whose elegant salon and connecting rooms house a comprehensive **local museum**. Displays include traditional women's dresses from villages round about, showing how each place had its individual style.

The Opinel company based here exports its wooden-handled clasp knives all over the world. The factory

Modane is a departure point for Italy, the site of the first-ever tunnel through the Alps

museum shows how its extensive range is produced.

ⓘ Place de la Cathédrale

Leave St Jean for Col de la Croix de Fer on the D926.

Col de la Croix de Fer, Rhône-Alpes

12 Take care in the five rock tunnels above the stunning Arvan gorge, with the needle peaks of the Aiguilles d'Arves on the skyline. Alpine meadows towards Entraigues, and the little ski resort of St Sorlin, come and go.

Then comes the narrow and dizzying zigzag road up the boulder fields to the summit of the pass. Here you can relax by the little restaurant, note the cross of iron which gave the col its name, and marvel at the outlook over a sea of Alpine summits. To the south-southeast, the 3,983m (13,065-foot) peak of La Meije is just in view.

Beyond the col, turn left as for Grenoble.

Défilé de Maupas, Rhône-Alpes

13 The final exposed climb to the Croix de Fer may have left you wondering what lies on the other side. In fact, the descent is on a road of a much higher standard, although the grandeur of the mountain scenery and of the majestic gorge which takes the route back down to a lower level is even more impressive.

Pause at the **Barrage de Grand'Maison**. Displays here explain how this is the top reservoir of the most powerful hydro-electric scheme in France, fed by cascades from the permanent snowfields.

Continue downhill. Avoid the road for Le Verney and take the road signed 'Hydrolec'. Turn left as for Grenoble, then join the N91. Go through Le Péage de Vizille, then turn right to Vizille-centre on the D101. Continue to Uriage on the D524 and return to Grenoble.

Grenoble – La Grande Chartreuse 27 (17)
La Grande Chartreuse – Chambéry 42 (26)
Chambéry – Aix-les-Bains 15 (9)
Aix-les-Bains – Annecy 47 (29)
Annecy – La Clusaz 30 (19)
La Clusaz – Le Beaufortain 55 (34)
Le Beaufortain – Bourg-St-Maurice 5 (16)
Bourg-St-Maurice – Val d'Isère 29 (18)
Val d'Isère – Col de l'Iseran 18 (11)
Col de l'Iseran – Modane 55 (34)
Modane – St Jean-de-Maurienne 30 (19)
St Jean-de-Maurienne – Col de la Croix de Fer 27 (17)
Col de la Croix de Fer – Défilé de Maupas 13 (8)
Défilé de Maupas – Grenoble 59 (37)

FOR HISTORY BUFFS

13 On the return route to Grenoble, the 17th-century **château** at Vizille houses a comprehensive **museum of the French Revolution**. In 1788, a year before the Revolution, the three Estates – nobles, clergy and commoners – met in this castle to denounce Louis XIV's suppression of parliament and proclaim individual liberty. With tableaux, sculptures, paintings and posters as well as weaponry, the museum stresses the artistic environment of revolutionary France no less than the events and personalities.

3/4 days – 420km (260 miles)

ALSACE –
THE GERMAN CONNECTION

Strasbourg • Mont Ste-Odile • Ste Marie-aux-Mines
Thann • Mulhouse • Écomusée d'Alsace
Guebwiller • Colmar • Kaysersberg • Riquewihr
Sélestat • Strasbourg

From the Rhineland plain south of Strasbourg to the breezy viewpoint roads high in the Vosges mountains, this tour explores some of the most beautiful areas of Alsace. There have been vineyards in the eastern foothills of the Vosges since Roman times. At higher altitudes lie great forests and upland pastures covered by the winter snows. Alsace has passed several times from French to German control and back again. To this day, many names have German spellings and French pronunciation. This is a region which offers you colourful villages, some astonishingly well-endowed museums and, at Colmar, one of the most dazzling towns in Europe.

RECOMMENDED WALKS

1 At **Mont Ste-Odile** you can step into the network of waymarked trails which explore this beautifully wooded hill. Some were originally pilgrims' paths, others follow the Pagan Wall, and all offer splendid views to the valleys

ⓘ Place de la Cathédrale.Strasbourg

*Leave Strasbourg for Eckbolsheim on the **D45**. Continue to Ergersheim, then take the **D30** to Molsheim. Follow the 'Strasbourg' sign, then take the **D422** and **D35** through Rosheim to Ottrott. Turn right in Ottrott on the **D426**, then follow the **D426a** to Ste-Odile.*

The fortified church at Hunawihr bears witness to a turbulent past

Mont Ste-Odile, Alsace₅

1 You may be surprised by the press of traffic on this out-of-the-way woodland hilltop. The cluster of buildings here is one of France's great pilgrimage centres: the historic **convent** which guards the tomb of Odile, the patron saint of Odile.

Odile died around the year 720, as abbess of the original religious house of this splendid site. The present buildings, in fine order, are from much later centuries, including our own. With cloister and courtyard gardens, an excellent paved walk around viewpoint terraces, a pilgrims' hall and several individual chapels, this is a place of beauty, dignity and repose. The site appealed to earlier civilisations, too. As you approach the summit, look for carefully worked masonry of the imposing **Mur Païen** (Pagan Wall) constructed in prehistoric times.

*Return downhill, bear slightly left and follow signs to Champ du Feu. Go straight ahead there and follow signs to Villé. Turn right on the **D39** as for St Dié. In Fouchy, go left on the **D155** to Col de Fouchy, then follow signs to Lièpvre and go right to Ste Marie on the **N59**. Approaching Ste Marie, avoid the tunnel.*

Ste Marie-aux-Mines, Alsace

2 From the 16th century onwards, this little town was famous for the richest seams of silver in France. You can join a guided tour of the old **St Bartélemy mine**. Safety helmets and waterproof capes are provided, and you start by walking in through a hillside tunnel to the levels and galleries beyond.

There is also a fine **Musée Minéralogique** in the town, and the **Maison du Pays** (not quite the 'country house' which the local English translation suggests) mounts displays on the mining era and on the spinning, dyeing, weaving and hosiery which, combined, formed Ste Marie's other 'boom' industry.

Look for the restrained baroque style of the **Church of La Madeleine**, for intriguing old buildings such as the towered **Pharmacie** by the main square, and for the little public gardens which include one, beside the town hall, with a floral peacock on display.

ⓘ Rue Wilson

*Leave Ste Marie-aux-Mines as for Le Bonhomme. Turn right at Col des Bagenelles to Col du Bonhomme. Turn left on the **N415**. At the roundabout go right on the **D48** to Orbey, then follow signs 'Les Lacs' and 'Lac Blanc'. Go left on the **D418** to Col de la Schlucht. Turn right on the **D417** as for Épinal and almost immediately left on the **D430** to Le Markstein. Continue straight ahead on the **D431** to le Grand Ballon, then follow signs to Thann.*

Fortified Kientzstein is a charming place to stop, browse and find refreshment

Thann, Alsace

3 On the banks of the fast-flowing River Thur, overlooked by a hillside Cross of Lorraine, Thann was wrested back from German control by Marshal Joffre's troops in 1914. The text of his emotional proclamation is carved on a war memorial. Thann's history is even more complex than that of other places in Alsace, as it was Austrian territory from 1324 to 1648.

The splendid collegiate Church of **St Thiébaut** features immensely detailed sculptured façades and portals, polychrome roof tiling and superb carved-oak choir stalls. Look there for the figures of the gossip, the fiddler and the spectacled man.

Thann's **local history museum** is in the arcaded corn market (Halle aux blés) of 1519. Two towers survive of its medieval ramparts, and several fine buildings from the 16th century onwards remain.

ℹ️ Place Joffre

Leave Thann on the N66. Go over the autoroute and continue to Mulhouse.

Mulhouse, Alsace

4 Despite its parks and gardens, zoo and yacht basin and attractive old quarter, 'Moo-loose' is an industrial town which may take some time to grow on you. Then look round its museums, and you will realise that this is one of the most amazingly well-endowed towns in Europe as regards museums of technology.

History, fine arts, painted wall-coverings and printed fabrics all have extensive museums of their own, but the **Musée des Beaux-Arts** is an excellent starting-point. Railway enthusiasts should head for the excellent **Musée Français du Chemin de Fer**. Close by, the **Musée du Sapeur-Pompier** has a fine display of fire engines.

However, the pride of Mulhouse is the **Musée National de l'Automobile**, the most stupendous motor museum in the world. On display are over a hundred Bugattis, whole collections of Rolls-Royces, Alfa Romeos, Maseratis, Mercedes-Benz, Gordinis and the rest – more than 500 splendid vehicles of almost 100 different makes. The fine tradition continues, as new Peugeots are also made in Mulhouse.

ℹ️ Avenue Maréchal-Foch

Leave Mulhouse as for Guebwiller on the D430. Turn on to the D430bis and follow 'Éco-musée' signs.

Écomusée de Haute Alsace, Alsace

5 Occupying a roomy site on the Alsace plain, here is a fascinating replica village of more than 60 traditionally styled buildings – houses,

SPECIAL TO...

1 Molsheim, to the southwest of Strasbourg, was the home of Bugatti, the marque which epitomises pur sang (the thoroughbred ideal) in car design. Cars are no longer built in what is now the Messier-Bugatti factory, but Bugatti owners regularly make the pilgrimage to Molsheim.

SCENIC ROUTES

Early on, the **D45** opens up long views over villages and vineyards to the forested range of the Vosges.

On the way to Thann, the **D48** rises through beautiful miniature landscapes in the valley of the Petite Lièpvre. After the Col de la Schlucht, admire the 'top of the world' views over the deep western valleys from the 'Route des Crêtes', then on to the descent of Le Grand Ballon.

From the approach to Guebwiller, you are in the delicious foothills country of the 'Route du Vin'. The flat return to Strasbourg is enhanced by unexpectedly bright and flower-filled villages.

FOR CHILDREN

3 At **Le Grand Ballon**, the highest point in the Vosges mountains, the youngsters will enjoy a whoosh down the *luge d'été* summer toboggan ride; but in chilly weather make sure they wrap up well.

BACK TO NATURE

3 To the right of the **D430** after the **Col de la Schlucht**, the university-run **Jardin d'Altitude du Haut-Chitelet**, at nearly 1,228m (4,030 feet), displays hundreds of mountain plant species from all over the world.

Beyond the Col de la Schlucht, watch for buzzards soaring over the open ground. The pine forests are home to the bulky capercaillie. Biggest of the grouse family, it is reduced to something like 160 pairs in the whole of the Vosges. Several species of woodpecker are found in the forests, along with crested tits and Bonelli's warblers.

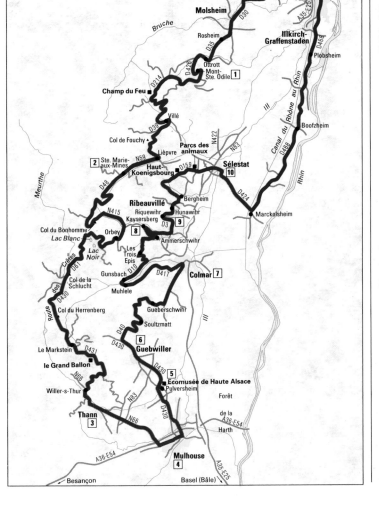

Capital of the region, Colmar has many delights – 'Little Venice', bordering the River Lauch, is one of them. Summer folklore events are a speciality, with a Wine Fair in mid-August and a Fête de la Choucroute (sauerkraut) in September

farms, barns and workshops – created to show the domestic life of past generations, as well as the work of the blacksmith and cart builder, baker, clog-maker and weaver, and all the half-forgotten farming trades.

Favourite local dishes are cooked for the restaurants, and Alsace wines are served. There is a keen interest in wildlife conservation: storks, for instance, are encouraged to nest.

During the 1990s a major project is the restoration of the potassium mine whose derelict buildings you will see on the approach road.

Return to the D430 and continue to Guebwiller.

Guebwiller, Alsace

6 A place full of squares, and bright with window-boxes, Guebwiller is partly built of a soft local stone which gives the Église St-Léger, for instance, a warmer 'feel' than most French churches. St-Léger also has stately arcaded aisles and some worthwhile stained-glass windows.

Overlooked by hillside vineyards, the town enjoys some beautiful parkland. The Parc de la Marseillaise features fine examples of cypress, lime, cedar and sequoia trees.

Guebwiller was the birthplace of the 19th-century ceramic artist Théodore Deck. Examples of his work, and historical mementoes of the district, are on display in the Musée du Florival.

i Place St-Leger

Continue on the D430 as for Le Markstein. Turn right on the D40 to Soultzmatt, left on the D18bis to Osenbach, then right on the D40 again. Bear right to Gueberschwihr, turn left as for Hattstatt, then join the N83 for Colmar, and enter it on the D30.

Colmar, Alsace

7 In colour, design, construction, layout and state of preservation, Colmar is one of the world's most beguiling towns. The narrow streets, some darting off at eccentric angles, are lined with colour-washed half-timbered houses of the 16th and 17th centuries, most of them banked with flowers.

Look in particular for the balconied Maison Pfister of 1537, the riverside houses of the Quai de la Poissonnerie and 'La Petite Venise' (Little Venice) to which they lead, and for the lovely cluster of buildings by the pastry shop at the corner of Rue Kléber. The 15th-century Koïfhus – the old customs house, used as the town hall – is topped by glorious polychrome roof tiling.

Colmar has a museum and art gallery in the old Dominican convent of Unterlinden (Musée d'Unterlinden), noted for its 16th-century altarpiece by Matthias Grünewald – the Isenheim Altarpiece. The sculptor Auguste Bartholdi was born here, in a courtyard house which is now a museum recalling that his most famous work was the Statue of Liberty.

i Rue des Unterlinden

Leave Colmar as for Épinal on the D417. Turn right to Gunsbach, then right at the crossroads on the D10. Go left on the D11 to Trois-Épis, then right to Ammerschwihr. Take the first left under the archway, follow the 'Toutes Directions' sign, then turn left and continue to Kaysersberg.

Kaysersberg, Alsace

8 As you stroll through this attractive little flower-decked medieval 'city', past the caves of wine growers and liqueur distillers, you will encounter many houses, gateways, bridges, towers and chapels of the 13th to 15th centuries.

The Église Ste-Croix has a magnificent altarpiece of 1518. Other works of religious art are displayed in the local museum.

Kaysersberg is twinned with Lambaréné in Gabon because of the town's links with Dr Albert Schweitzer. The Nobel Peace Prize winner was born in Kaysersberg in 1875 and spent most of his working life at his hospital in West Africa. A room in his birthplace is preserved in his memory.

ℹ Place de la Mairie

Leave Kaysersberg as for Ribeauvillé on the D28. Go left at the roundabout and left on the D3 to Riquewihr.

Riquewihr, Alsace

9 Enclosed in 16th-century ramparts, this charming old town is the 'pearl of the Alsace vineyards'. Wine cellars stock the produce of its Riesling, Muscat, Tokay and Gewürztraminer grapes.

Local history is the concern of the **Musée Dolder**. The **Tour des Voleurs** (Thieves' Tower) houses an 'authentic' torture chamber. Installed in a princely palace, the **Musée d'Histoire des PTT d'Alsace** includes lavish displays of stage coaches, maps, models, uniforms, electric and wireless telegraphy systems, telephones, teleprinters and a miniature of the Ariane space rocket, telling the story of 2,000 years of message deliveries since Gallo-Roman times.

ℹ Place de la 1ère Armée

Leave Riquewihr for Ribeauvillé and Bergheim. In Bergheim, go left on the D42 as for Haut Koenigsbourg. Turn right on the D159 and continue to Sélestat, entering it on the N83.

Sélestat, Alsace

10 Unremarkable in its suburbs, Sélestat becomes much more interesting as you explore its historic centre. Here there are beautiful medieval, Renaissance and 18th-century houses and public buildings, the Romanesque **Church of Ste-Foy** and the later Gothic **Church of St-Georges**. The town's water towers are unexpectedly ornate.

Sélestat is the main centre where modern Alsace artists show their paintings, and its 15th-century **Bibliothèque Humaniste**, housed in the old corn market (Halle aux blés), is one of the most valuable libraries of books and manuscripts in France.

ℹ Boulevard Leclerc

Leave Sélestat on the D424 as for Marckolsheim. At the roundabout, turn left on the D468 and return to Strasbourg.

Strasbourg – Mont Ste-Odile 42 (26)
Mont Ste-Odile – Ste Marie-aux-Mines 52 (32)
Ste Marie-aux-Mines – Thann 105 (65)
Thann – Mulhouse 24 (15)
Mulhouse – Écomusée d'Alsace 13 (8)
Écomusée d'Alsace – Guebwiller 10 (6)
Guebwiller – Colmar 35 (22)
Colmar – Kaysersberg 41 (25)
Kaysersberg – Riquewihr 10 (6)
Riquewihr – Sélestat 25 (16)
Sélestat – Strasbourg 63 (39)

A fountain in a courtyard in Kaysersberg bears an inscription which has wise advice for lovers of the grape: 'Too much water at table chills the stomach; better to drink an old and subtle wine and leave my water to me'

FOR HISTORY BUFFS

10 On the way to Sélestat, turn left off the D159 for the spectacular hilltop castle of **Haut-Koenigsbourg**. The 12th-century fortress was destroyed in the 17th century, and was completely restored early this century on the orders of Kaiser Wilhelm II. It looks like a film set, and was in fact used by the great director Jean Renoir for *La Grande Illusion*.

On the return route to Strasbourg, turn right into Marckolsheim then left on the D10 to the **Musée de la Ligne Maginot**, the French defensive line bypassed by the Germans in 1940, but the scene of fierce fighting in 1944.

FOR CHILDREN

10 Off the D159 on the way to Sélestat, the **Montagne des Singes** allows 300 Barbary apes to roam in 20 hectares (50 acres) of forest. At the nearby **Volerie des Aigles**, in the grounds of a castle, eagles, vultures, kites and falcons give flying displays.

THE NORTH, BURGUNDY & CHAMPAGNE

Many visitors to France arrive at Calais, the busiest of all Channel ports. This area of northern France, just back from, or along the coast, could give you an enjoyable holiday on its own, as there is plenty to see and do.

It has been fought over all too often, and frequently devastated by war. Here you will find historic battlefields, such as Crécy, Valmy and Sédan, and more from the terrible World War I Somme campaign, whose British and Commonwealth victims are remembered in dignified parkland memorials such as Vimy Ridge.

Huge areas of land are occupied by arable farms. This is the country's bread-basket, and the source of many of its fine vegetables. Here and there, on these arable plains, modest woodlands break up the view, and the high points are more likely to be the water towers known grandly as *châteaux d'eau*.

Elsewhere, there are full-scale state forests, including some of the most beautiful in France. The forest around Fontainebleau at first attracted the royal and imperial courts. Then it was the turn of the 19th-century artists to enjoy both the forest and the atmospheric towns and villages close by. Some of France's most lavish state residences are here: Fontainebleau, Rambouillet, Pierrefonds.

Near the border, France shares with Belgium the lovely winding, wooded river valleys of the Ardennes. Other hill country includes quiet areas off the Paris-Riviera autoroute and the mazy lanes of the Morvan.

You can hardly miss the vineyards in the foothills of the Côte d'Or and the great champagne estates round Reims.

On the coast you will find resorts as different as the stylish Le Touquet and simple Le Crotoy by the Somme. Inland towns, such as Pierrefonds, Compiègne and Moret-sur-Loing, have their following too.

You will encounter the long-lost melding of French and English history. Richard the Lionheart, for instance, conferred with the French king at Vézélay before they set off to lead their joint army in the Third Crusade. And you can learn how Revolutionaries pursued and captured the fleeing Louis XVI, how artists such as Millet shrugged off the studios of Paris and came to paint from real life in the countryside, and how the French are progressing with the massive Channel Tunnel project, after so many false starts in the past, to link Britain physically with Europe.

Calais
Under English occupation for more than 200 years, Calais has always looked across the Channel. The Dover-Calais route was the first Continental service to be operated by a steamship, the *Rob Roy*, in 1821. One of the most famous sights is Rodin's great statue of the Burghers of Calais, who pleaded with Edward III of England to spare the town after its surrender in 1347. There is a confidently ornate town hall, a fine arts museum displaying the lacework for which Calais is famous, and a little parkland museum of the town's travails in World War II.

Amiens
Amiens is centred on the majestic Cathédrale Notre-Dame, largest of all the Gothic churches in France. Even its grubby exterior cannot hide the wonderful fretted upper reaches. Inside, there are beautifully carved oakwood choir stalls.

Museums and galleries concentrate on local art and history: Amiens is the capital of Picardy. Quaysides and inlets of the Somme thread through the northern suburbs, and there is an eastern quarter of market gardens first cultivated in medieval times.

Reims
Reims is not just outwardly the city of champagne. Millions of francs' worth lies in cellars underground. Visitors are welcome at the champagne houses which even commissioned stained-glass panels of the different vineyard areas for the cathedral. Two of the old city abbeys have been turned into museums. You can see where the German capitulation order was signed in 1945. And Reims has a major motor museum devoted entirely to French marques.

Chalon-sur-Saône
Baseball in France? Yes, in a beautiful park at Salon-sur-Saône, which also features a magnificent riverside garden with 25,000 roses from Europe, America, Japan and the Himalayas.

By the Saône, visit the museum commemorating the pioneer of

*Left: The imposing façade of the cathedral at Chalon-sur-Saône.
Above: Rodin's moving statue in front of Calais' town hall commemorates the courage of the six burghers who surrendered their city to Edward III in 1347*

photography, Nicéphore Niepce. Exhibits range from his first camera of 1822 to the Apollo equipment taken to the moon.

There is an exhibition centre for the 44 vineyard villages known collectively as the Côte Chalonnaise. On the little St Laurent island, the topmost gallery of the Tour du Doyenné is an unusual viewpoint over the town.

Chartres
Chartres is, first and foremost, its cathedral, Notre Dame, whose twin towers are seen for miles across the plain. Connoisseurs consider that the stained-glass windows at Chartres are the finest in the world. An art gallery concentrates on stained glass of classical and modern designs, and there are studios where present-day artists work.

Look for the Maison Picassiette with its décor picked out in fragments of glass and china. Admire the paintings, sculptures and tapestries in the fine arts museum, and stroll by the quays, mills and wash-houses on the River Eure.

3 days – 272km (170 miles)

THE ENGLISH CONNECTION

**Calais • Sangatte • Cap Blanc-Nez • Boulogne
Le Touquet • Domaine du Marquenterre • Le Crotoy
Crécy • Montreuil • Desvres • Calais**

Coast and country are the two faces of this tour from Calais, busiest of all the French car ferry ports. It visits resorts both sophisticated and family-style, some popular with generations of British visitors. The chalk headlands match the white cliffs of Dover, which can be seen on a clear day, glistening in the sun. Behind the coast there are inland river valleys where quiet villages doze in the shelter of gently wooded hills.

ⓘ Boulevard Clemenceau, Calais

Leave Calais on the D940 through Sangatte.

Sangatte, Pas de Calais

1 Here is the huge landward base of the French **Channel Tunnel**. At the information centre a comprehensive display explains what massive

Cross-Channel ferries use Boulogne daily, but it is also home to these smaller craft and the largest fishing port in France

SPECIAL TO...

1 West of Calais there are several smaller fishing ports. One local speciality is *moules* (mussels), often sold from stalls outside the fishermen's homes.

3 The Pas de Calais district played a great part in World War II, and there are several museums about the conflict. Two on the route are at Ambleteuse and in a former German blockhouse at Audinghen.

BACK TO NATURE

2 The chalk cliffs around Cap Blanc-Nez and Cap Gris-Nez are a nesting ground for gulls and fulmars which skim the waves and soar on the upcurrents of air. Kestrels also nest here, and you may be lucky enough to see one hovering over the grassy cliff-tops before plunging on its prey. The clifftop flora is outstanding during the summer months.

The Hôtel de Ville in Calais, a town which suffered devastation in two wars but has been reborn

investment and civil engineering expertise were need for the opening.

ⓘ Rue du Vigier

Continue on the D940 to Cap Blanc-Nez.

Cap Blanc-Nez, Pas de Calais

2 This sweeping chalk headland is introduced by a fine windswept statue of the pioneer French aviator, Hubert Latham, who was famous, like Blériot, for his 'audacious flights' above the Channel. Turn right for the splendid viewpoint memorial to the French sailors of the World War I Dover Patrol. Turn left for the **Musée du Transmanche** devoted to the history of the Channel Tunnel plans from the earliest hare-brained schemes involving horse-drawn carriages.

Continue on the D940 through Audinghen, where the D191 on the right leads to Cap Gris-Nez. Beyond Wimereux the left turn signed 'vers A16' leads towards the Colonne de la Grande Armée. The D940 continues to Boulogne.

Boulogne, Pas de Calais

3 France's most important fishing port has a bustling and complex harbour front. Every morning fishermen's stalls offer the freshest possible produce of the sea.

Turn uphill through the busy shopping streets, and you will come to one of the best-preserved historic citadels in the north of France. The **castle museum** covers a bewildering variety of subjects including archaeology, ethnology, painting and sculpture and local souvenirs from the time of Napoleon. A pleasant stroll round the towers and fortified gateways of the preserved 13th-century ramparts, which enclose the medieval Haute Ville, gives views of the catamarans below discharging and loading.

ⓘ Quai de la Poste

Leave Boulogne on the N1, then take the D940 and N39 to Le Touquet.

Le Touquet, Pas De Calais

4 Le Touquet grew up in the 19th century, largely as a haven for British gamblers taking advantage of the more lenient French gambling laws. Developed jointly by French and British interests Le Touquet has unparalleled facilities for all kinds of sport, including a huge annual motorsport 'enduro' race on its extensive sands. Three well-kept **golf courses** occupy the southern outskirts. The beaches are glorious.

You may think that some of the seafront apartment blocks contrast hideously with the few remaining 19th-century buildings there. The heart of the town, however, retains its elegant shops, cafés and restaurants. Discreet wooded footpaths are threaded through the pine- and birch-woods of the handsome residential suburbs.

☐ Palais de l'Europe

Leave Le Touquet following Berck and Hesdin signs, and rejoin the D940 as for Rue. Turn right, following signs to Domaine du Marquenterre.

3 On the outskirts of Boulogne, the **Colonne de la Grande Armée** is a towering monument topped by a statue of Napoleon in characteristic pose. He assembled his army here in 1803 for an invasion of Britain which never took place.

This small orderly harbour lies between Le Touquet, with its casino glamour, and the fishing port of Etaples – except for the trees and the sunshine, it could almost be the south coast of England

Domaine du Marquenterre, Picardy

5 Reached by a rather rough approach road, this private estate is one of the finest bird reserves in Europe. **La parc ornithologique de Marquenterre** was created behind a screen of pine trees on land reclaimed as recently as the 1970s from the estuary of the Somme. Residents and migrants include ducks, geese, swans, gulls and waders, hoopoes, avocets, spoonbills, storks and dozens of other species of shore, lake and saltmarsh. Entry is free and you may rent binoculars.

Return from the Domaine and follow signs to Le Crotoy.

Le Crotoy, Picardy

6 Very much a French family resort, Le Crotoy has a good beach, fishing and yacht harbours by the River Somme. Fresh fish and shellfish are available from roadside stalls and in the restaurants. You should take care before imitating the locals' casual-seeming gumbooted strolls

SCENIC ROUTES

After the **D940** climbs out of Sangatte it swoops up and down hill through immaculately tended farmland.
Further south, bypassing Rue, the **D940** crosses lovely pastoral country given artificial horizons by line upon line of stately poplars.

FOR CHILDREN

4 **Aqualud** on the seafront at Le Touquet is a modern swimming pool complex. Its water fountains and a 90m (98-yard) curving chute are great fun for the children; adults might enjoy the sauna.

5 On the **D940** south of Le Touquet, the extensive fun park at **Bagatelle** features a roller-coaster ride which finishes with a belly-flop into a lake, a monorail, a mirror maze, roundabouts, an aviary and a zoo.

RECOMMENDED WALKS

6 Local tourist offices have maps of the network of walks inland from Le Crotoy, in the lovely pastureland behind the Somme estuary. They wander past fields, woodlands and water channels in what was unproductive marshland just a few generations ago.

7 Eight waymarked paths explore the sun-dappled beech and oak woods in the **Forest of Crécy**, once a hunting ground of the French kings. Look for the map beside the **D111** after Nouvion.

FOR HISTORY BUFFS

7 At Nolette, between Le Crotoy and Crécy, one of the most unusual cemeteries in France commemorates the 96,000 members of the Chinese Labour Force employed by the Allies during World War I. Its base was near by, and 870 of the Chinese, who died in an epidemic, are buried here.

Another hero of the Battle of Crécy was the blind King John of Bohemia, brother-in-law of the French king, Philippe VI. A cross marks the spot on the battlefield where he is said to have fallen. A tradition that this king's emblem was adopted by the Black Prince as the Prince of Wales' Feathers is a romantic fiction.

The old quarter of Boulogne mercifully escaped wartime bombs

across the tidal inlets. Make sure not to be caught by the incoming tide. The old station is a terminus for the summer railway whose steam-hauled trains explore the pleasant countryside inland.

Leave Le Crotoy by 'Sortie Ville' signs. Turn right on the D940, then left on the D140 to Noyelles. Turn left over a level crossing, then left on the D111 through Nolette to Crécy.

Crécy, Picardy

7 On the exit from the village a view-point tower (**Le Moulin Édouard III**) stands at Edward III's traditional vantage point over the battlefield of Crécy in 1346, when his English archers routed the French cross-bowmen in one of the most decisive battles of the Hundred Years' War. Edward's son, the Black Prince, who was then little more than a boy, won his spurs here.

Continue on the D111 to Dompierre, then go left on the D85 to Valloires. After the Abbaye de Valloires turn sharp right to Maintenay, right at a roundabout and left on the D139 to Montreuil.

Montreuil, Pas De Calais

8 Formerly Montreuil-sur-Mer, the town is now 14km (9 miles) from the sea. It retains many picturesque houses on cobbled and steeply cambered streets; some of the action of Victor Hugo's *Les Misérables* is set

here. A statue of Sir Douglas Haig is a reminder that the British commander-in-chief in World War I made his headquarters near by. Montreuil's historic ramparts provide a beautiful hour-long walk, partly edged with trees and giving splendid sunset views. The **abbey church** dates back to the 11th century.

ⓘ Place Darnétal

Leave Montreuil on the N39, then take the N1 as for Boulogne. Bear right off the N1 for Ixent, then follow the D127 to Desvres.

Desvres, Pas de Calais

9 The square here is the site of regular morning markets, but since the 18th century the main business of the town has been in faience or glazed pottery. Several workshops welcome visitors, and there is a purpose-built **pottery museum**.

ⓘ Rue Jean Macé

Leave Desvres on the D127. Turn right on the N42 and then take the D224 to Ardres. In Ardres turn left on the N43 and return to Calais.

TOWNS & COUNTRYSIDE OF PICARDY

The soaring grace and exquisite craftsmanship of Amiens Cathedral

ⓘ Rue Catelas, Amiens

Leave Amiens on the N235 through Picquigny, then go right on the D191 following signs to Samara.

Samara, Picardy

1 Laid out among scrubland, marsh and ponds, Samara is a fascinating historical park which takes as its theme thousands of years of human life and activity in the valley of the River Somme. There are accurate representations of ancient dwellings and demonstrations of prehistoric trades such as flint cutting and bronze casting. You can see a fowler's hut where the hunter awaits the dawn flight over the marshes; or a peat-cutter's cabin with the tools of a once-traditional trade. There is a botanical garden and arboretum. Along the pathways you will find an excavated Celtic town and a modern pavilion whose exhibits look not only into the distant past but also at what life may be like for generations to come.

ⓘ 1a Chaussée Tirancourt, Picquigny

Continue on the D191 to St Sauveur, go left on the D97 at 'Grottes de Naours' sign, left on to the D933 to Flesselles, straight on along the D117 to Naours, right on the D60, then sharp left to the Grottes de Naours.

Picardy brings remembrance of that generation of young men of all nations who died here. The Vimy Parc Memorial honours 75,000 Canadians who gave their lives in 1917

**Amiens • Samara • Grottes de Naours
Battlefields of the Somme • Arras • Vimy Parc Memorial
Douai • Centre Historique Minier • Laon
Blérancourt • Pierrefonds • Compiègne
Ermenonville • Beauvais • Amiens**

Centred on the cathedral city of Amiens, this tour is through districts often missed by visitors to France. It features wide rural landscapes in areas such as the Picardy plateau, goes through the fringes of the northern industrial belt and takes in elegant towns nearer Paris with wooded and spacious suburbs. There are also reminders of the two World Wars. Theme parks and museums here have a remarkable variety: you will find an open-air 'eco-museum' showing crafts of 5,000 years ago, a mining museum on the site of a former coal pit and – on the outskirts of a little country town – a museum which celebrates 200 years and more of co-operation between France and the United States of America.

SCENIC ROUTES

West of Amiens the **N235** towards Picquigny runs above pools and light woodlands by the River Somme.

From St Sauveur to Albert the attractive countryside features gently rolling farmland planted with well-mixed crops, copses and lines of skyline trees.

Around World War I battlefields and cemeteries after Albert you may find it almost impossible to believe that the peaceful, settled countryside was once the scene of such carnage.

SPECIAL TO...

6 The belfry at Douai houses the largest **carillon** in France, using no fewer than 62 individual bells. Douai's official carillonist is the 34th in a line which started in 1391. Douai also owns the first mobile carillon in France, with 50 bells. This glorious instrument is often on parade at outdoor events in July and August.

Grottes de Naours, Picardy
2 Burrowed into a wooded hillside above the village, the Underground City of Naours (Grottes de Naours) is one of the most amazing places in France. About 30 tunnels and 300 separate rooms – including chapels and stables – have been used as refuges in times of danger and invasion from the Gallo-Roman era to the 18th century. Then they were the haunt of salt smugglers and, as late as World War II, stores for the British Army and a secret communications base for the Germans.

Return from the car park, go left at the Stop sign and follow the D60 to Contay. Turn right on the D919, immediately left on the D23 to Franvillers and left on the D929 through Albert. Go left on the D20, right on the D151 to Thiepval, left on the D73 and follow signs to Beaumont-Hamel memorial park.

Battlefields of the Somme, Picardy
3 The whole countryside hereabouts is scattered with war graves and monuments recalling the catastrophic first day of July 1916, the opening of the Battle of the Somme. Among the most impressive are Sir Edward

Lutyens's massive brick-and-stone **memorial** at Thiepval; the recently restored **Ulster Tower** also near Thiepval; and the heart-rending but beautifully landscaped **Newfoundland Memorial Park** at Beaumont-Hamel, where almost the whole of the 1st Newfoundland Regiment were mown down by enemy machine-gun fire and shrapnel. A bronze caribou silhouetted on a rock-garden mound bellows defiance to the sky.

Continue on the D53 to Mailly-Maillet. Turn right on the D129, then right on the D919 to Arras.

Arras, Picardy
4 If only stone-cleaning were an enthusiasm of the French! Arras, the capital of Artois, would be a finer place if its two most spectacular squares - la Grand Place and la Place de Héros – had gleaming stonework to match the elegance of their arcaded buildings. The **Hôtel de Ville** (town hall) is a handsome affair, and there is a generous view from its belfry. Part of the former Benedictine **Abbaye de St-Vaast** is now a cathedral (18th- to 19th-century); in the south wing of the abbey, between two elegant cloisters, is a well-stocked **fine arts**

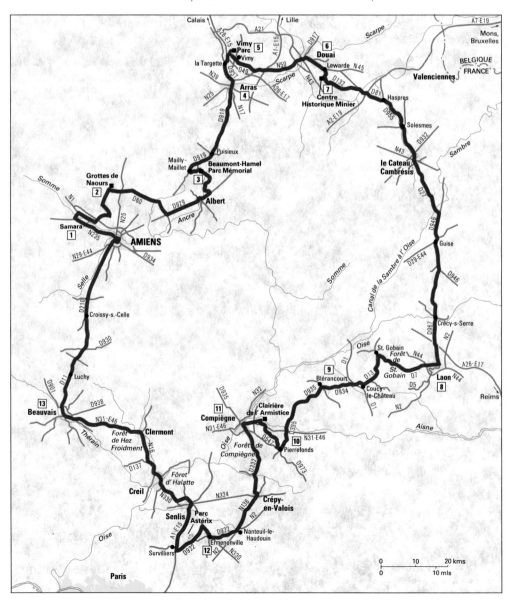

museum with extensive collections of French and Flemish paintings, medieval wood carvings and a superb display of local porcelain and tapestry. The fame of Arras tapestry dates from medieval times. In the 17th-century citadel of Arras, a sombre memorial (la Mur des Fusillés) commemorates members of the Resistance shot during World War II.

ⓘ Place des Héros

> *Leave Arras on the N425, then take the D937 as for Béthune. Turn right on the D55 following the 'Memorial Canadien' sign to Vimy Parc.*

Vimy Parc Memorial, Picardy

5 One of the largest and most meticulously maintained war memorial areas in France, Vimy Parc commemorates, in particular, the tremendous assault of 9 April 1917 when all four divisions of the Canadian Corps, in a copybook attack, stormed the German defences on Vimy Ridge. The open trenches are a stunning reminder of how close the opposing front lines were – within speaking, let alone shouting distance of each other. Keep to the paths, as there is still a chance of encountering unexploded shells and ammunition. Guided tours explore the underground galleries. On the crown of the ridge, a wonderful limestone memorial, the **Mémorial et Parc Canadien**, whose soaring pillars bear the maple leaf of Canada and the fleur-de-lys of France, is the most majestic of all the monuments raised after the Great War.

> *From the memorial, return down the D55 as for Arras, then go left at the first junction following the 'Gendarmerie' sign. Turn right on the N17 to Thélus, left on the D49, right on the D33, go under a bridge, then turn left and join the N50 dual carriageway to Douai.*

Douai, Picardy

6 An industrial town brightened by judiciously placed gardens, flowery roundabouts and avenues of trees, Douai is, at its heart, an island bounded by the River Scarpe and its associated canals, lined with old quaysides. The most impressive building is the ornate Gothic belltower, completed in 1410 in an era when these were status symbols in the towns of northern France. Escorted tours show visitors the view from the top, over the town, and also the fine interior of the historic **Hôtel de Ville** (town hall). In the old Carthusian convent (**Chartreuse**) – a mixture of three centuries of architectural ideas – more than a dozen exhibition halls show off French, Flemish and Italian Renaissance paintings as well as sculptures, earthenware and ivories. There is a splendid antique map of Douai, drawn in 1709 to Louis XIV's command.

ⓘ Place des Armes

> *Leave Douai on the N45. In Lewarde turn right on the D135 and follow 'Centre Historique Minier' signs on to the D132.*

For 200 years until AD987, Laon was actually capital of France. The Museum passes a pleasant hour

Centre Historique Minier, Picardy

7 On the site of the old Delloye pit (**Fosse Delloye**) near Lewarde, you will find an extensive indoor, outdoor and underground museum dedicated to coal-mining in the north of France. Former miners guide visitors round displays about the geology and exploitation of the coal-seams, the machinery and processing plant used in the mines, and the working conditions of miners through the centuries. Finally, you can descend into one of the original pits where 450m (490 yards) of galleries have been reconstructed as they would have been in their heyday.

> *Continue on the D132 to Bouchain. Go right on the D943, left on the N30, then right to Haspres. In Haspres, go left for Saulzoir and right before the FINA station, leaving Haspres on the D955 to Solesmes. Then follow signs to Le Cateau. Leave Le Cateau on the D12, which becomes the D27, then follow the D946 and the D967 to Laon.*

Laon, Picardy

8 The attractions of Laon are partly in its situation, partly in the architecture of the old city (Ville Haute) surrounded by medieval ramparts and imposing entrance gates. Laon lies on a long narrow ridge which dominates the surrounding plain and is an excellent natural viewpoint. The many-towered 12th- to 14th-century cathedral, one of the great Gothic edifices of France, has a nave of immense grandeur and some beautiful medieval stained-glass windows. Beside an old garden chapel of the Knights Templar (**Chapelle des Templiers**), the museum holds extensive archaeological and arts collections.

ⓘ Place de la Cathédrale

> *Leave Laon on the D7 for St Gobain. Go left on the D13, then right on the D5 to Coucy. Join the D937 as for Folembray, then turn left on the D934 to Blérancourt.*

SPECIAL TO...

From the D7 west of Laon, there are beautiful views of the hillier parts of the **Forest of St Gobian**. The D13 is another attractive road through the forest, leading to the historic town gate of Coucy.

Both main and minor roads around the **Forest of Compiègne** provide lovely shaded woodland drives. The last part of the tour crosses the open rural landscape of the Picardy plateau.

BACK TO NATURE

8 Between Amiens and Laon there is little in the way of extensive woodland cover, but the **Forêt de St Gobian** alongside the **D7** has lovely beech, oak and birch groves, with individual trees identified.

RECOMMENDED WALKS

10 Ask at the tourist office in Pierrefonds for the *Itinéraires circuits pédestres* booklet describing four way-marked walks in the eastern part of the **Forêt de Compiègne**. One follows an ancient Roman road, another goes past the Empress Eugénie's hunting pavilion.

11 After leaving the Clairière de l'Armistice, turn left on the **D130**, then left again for two more walks included in the same booklet. They follow part of the **Allée des Beaux-Monts**, an avenue leading to the castle of Compiègne, and take in several fine viewpoints over the river valleys which border the forest.

FOR HISTORY BUFFS

11 Marshal Foch, whose impressive statue overlooks the site, accepted the German surrender on 11 November 1918 in an atmospheric forest clearing near Compiègne, now called the **Clairière de l'Armistice**. The documents of surrender were signed in a railway carriage similar to the one now fitted out as a **museum** (the Germans destroyed the original during World War II). A grim worded memorial recalls the Germans' 'criminal pride'.

In Compiègne the **Musée de la Figurine Historique**, in the Flamboyant Gothic town hall, houses a marvellous collection of model figures in miniature tableaux of military and historic scenes from the time of the Revolution to the present day.

Joan of Arc was finally captured here, the French royal court played here for generations, and in a nearby forest two world wars ended with an armistice. History has not ignored Compiègne

Blérancourt, Picardy

9 Headquarters during World War I of the American volunteer ambulance corps, the pavilions, restored ground floor and gardens of the largely dismantled **Château de Blérancourt** are now the national **Museum of Franco-American Cooperation**. Notable Americans such as George Washington, Benjamin Franklin, John Paul Jones and Thomas Jefferson are honoured. There is a substantial library, as well as many documents and souvenirs of battles in which the two nations fought side by side, notably in the two World Wars.

Leave Blérancourt on the D935, which becomes the D335, to Pierrefonds.

Pierrefonds, Picardy

10 Drive slowly down the hill into Pierrefonds, so as not to miss the first stunning glimpse of the massive castle which towers over this engaging island resort. Handsome villas in discreet wooded grounds overlook a lake, which rowing boats and pedaloes share with the coots and mallards. The **Parc Rainette** is home to a herd of stately fallow deer. However, it is the **château** which dominates the town. Napoleon I bought it in ruins, but it was Napoleon II who commissioned the great architect Viollet-le-Duc to oversee its transformation into a grand imperial residence. Guided tours show off the whole lavish project; one room is dedicated to the architect himself, but the château itself is his memorial.

[i] Place de l'Hôtel-de-Ville

Leave Pierrefonds on the D973 as for Compiègne. Go right on the D547 to Vieux Moulin, then left on the N31 and right on the V4 to Clairière de l'Armistice. Then follow signs to Compiègne.

Compiègne, Picardy

11 Here is a dignified and spacious town with a fine riverside frontage on the River Oise, spreading parkland and suburbs to south and west where villa gardens drift into the glorious Forêt de Compiègne. Louis XV and Louis XVI commissioned the building of a **palace** here, facing a wide cobbled square. It was completed in the fateful year of 1789. After the Revolution, Napoleon I had it rebuilt, and later still it was the favourite residence of Napoleon III and Empress Eugénie.

Open to the public, the royal and imperial apartments recall all these personages, and there is a separate **Musée du Second Empire**. Elsewhere in the complex of buildings a first-class motor and carriage museum (**Musée National de la Voiture et du Tourisme**) includes splendid exhibits of vehicles from the horse-drawn age, and cars which are a reminder that, although Germany was the birthplace of the automobile, the French were livelier designers and experimenters.

Another memorable museum in Compiègne is the **Musée Vivenel**, which includes exceptional collections of archaeological items and classical ceramics. But do not spend too much time indoors. The parks and gardens, riversides and forest glades are waiting.

[i] Place de l'Hôtel de Ville

Leave Compiègne on the D332 as for Meaux. In Crépy-en-Valois follow 'Paris' signs and take the D136 into Nanteuil, ignoring the bypass. Watch the navigation here. About 55m (60 yards) after a Fiat garage, turn right following the sign 'Ermenonville Tourisme'. Go left on the D922, then right on the N330 through Ermenonville.

Ermenonville, Picardy

12 Ermenonville has been done no favours by the planners, who have signposted the road here as being a convenient way to bypass other towns. Traffic is usually heavy. However, the town itself includes one haven of tranquillity. To the left of the main road there is a **park**, introduced by a carved stone which says 'here begins the course of a sweet and rustic leisure' with woodland paths, ponds and streams.

Beyond Ermenonville there is a small zoo (**Zoo Jean-Richard**). The **Abbey of Chaalis**, 2.5km (1½ miles) north of the town, in a gracious parkland which contains one of France's finest rose gardens, is a classical 18th-century château on the site of an old Cistercian monastery. Here there are paintings, sculptures and a museum (**Musée Jacquemart-André**) devoted to Jean-Jacques Rousseau the philosopher, who died at Ermenonville in 1778.

Turn sharp left for Mortefontaine. Join the D922 and in Plailly follow the blue and white 'A1' signs. Join the A1 autoroute as for Lille. Parc Astérix is reached by the first exit. After Parc Astérix take the next autoroute exit as for Senlis. After the toll booths follow the 'Creil' sign on the N330, then the Beauvais signs via Clermont into Beauvais itself.

The Château at Coucy survived 600 years to be blown up in 1918

Beauvais, Picardy

13 One victim of World War II was the tapestry industry at Beauvais, removed elsewhere and never brought back here. The **Galérie Nationale de la Tapisserie**, a gallery of French tapestries from the 15th century onwards, is nevertheless one of the sights of the town. Stained glass was another Beauvais interest, and fortunately much of it survives, both in the **Church of St-Etienne** and as a feature of the superb interior of the **cathedral (St Pierre)**, which has a tremendous height for the area of its base. Bring binoculars to admire the glass closely. The cathedral's **astronomical clock**, gilded and astonishingly complicated, was completely restored in 1989. There are regular audio-visual displays about its amazing complexities.

Beside the cathedral, the old bishop's palace houses the **Musée Départementale de l'Oise**, the principal museum in the *départment* of the Oise region. There are wide-ranging displays of classical and contemporary art, art nouveau and art deco, as well as a glorious exhibition of ceramics.

ℹ Rue Beauregard

Leave Beauvais on the D901 as for Abbeville, then take the D149 as for Crèvecoeur and the D11/D210 back to Amiens.

Amiens – Samara 19 (12)
Samara – Grottes de Naours 16 (10)
Grottes de Naours – Battlefields of the Somme 45 (28)
Battlefields of the Somme – Arras 37 (23)
Arras – Vimy Parc Memorial 13 (8)
Vimy Parc Memorial – Douai 27 (17)
Douai – Centre Historique Minier 10 (6)
Centre Historique Minier – Laon 105 (65)
Laon – Blérancourt 45 (28)
Blérancourt – Pierrefonds 26 (16)
Pierrefonds – Compiègne 21 (13)
Compiègne – Ermenonville 46 (29)
Ermenonville – Beauvais 86 (54)
Beauvais – Amiens 57 (36)

FOR CHILDREN

12 The **Mer de Sable**, north of Ermenonville, is a fun park with roundabouts, a Ferris wheel, camels and pony rides, on the side of a huge sand dune. **Parc Astérix**, off the A1, on the way from Ermenonville to Beauvais, is an expensive but massive theme park based on the adventures of the ancient Gauls – Astérix, Obélix, Toutafix and the rest – made famous by the Goscinny and Underzo comic strips.

BACK TO NATURE

13 If you approach Beauvais at a time of heavy traffic, you may welcome a pause in the cool shade of the **Forêt de Hez-Froidemont** on the N31. Picnic tables are provided among stands of beech and oak, but you have to go further, and very carefully, into the forest to catch a glimpse of its roe deer. Woodpeckers, Bonelli's warblers and buzzards are among the other forest residents.

108

3/4 days – 386km (240 miles)

A TASTE OF CHAMPAGNE

Reims • Montagne de Reims • Châlons-sur-Marne
Valmy • Ste Menehould • Varennes-en-Argonne
Parc de Vision de Belval • Sedan • Charleville-Mézières
Musée de la Forêt • Rethel • Reims

Although Reims itself is the heart of the champagne country, in the early part of the tour you will find many growers whose vineyards occupy sloping fields on the edge of the Montagne de Reims, south of the city. Elsewhere, you will see where Louis XVI, trying to reach the still-loyal Army of the East, was arrested by townspeople in the grip of revolutionary zeal; and the battlefield where victory over the Prussians led directly to the proclamation of the French Republic. Great arable plains stretch north to the beautiful hill and river country which France shares with Belgium in the Ardennes.

FOR CHILDREN

2 In Châlons-sur-Marne, there is a **circus school** which sometimes allows visitors to watch clowns, jugglers and other performers. Ask at the tourist office.

ⓘ Place Guillaume de Machault, Reims

Leave Reims on the N31 as for Soissons. Turn left on the D27 to Gueux, then left on the D26 through Vrigny. Turn right into Ville Dommange, follow

Trepail, on the slopes of the Montagne de Reims, in the heart of champagne country

'Courmas' sign, then go right to the Chapelle St Lié.

Montagne de Reims, Champagne-Ardenne

1 From the viewpoint below the Chapelle St Lié there is a glorious outlook down over the vineyards on the lowest slope of the wooded hills south of Reims, and of the city itself, separate on the plain. Many of the villages are the home of champagnes little known abroad – Rilly for *Vilmart*, Ludes for *Blondel*, Villedommange immediately below for *Champagne de la Chapelle*. St Lié itself, a church on the summit of a wooded hill sacred from pagan days, is being sympathetically restored.

The hilly woodlands and the villages are all included in the **Parc Naturel Régional de Montagne de Reims**. Many waymarked walks have been laid out in it. St Lié is on the **sentier petite montagne** which meanders along the north-facing slopes.

Return to the D26 and turn right. Follow this road, not always numbered on signs, through Villers-Allerand, Ludes, Rilly and Verzenay to Verzy. In Verzy, watch for a right turn on the D34 to Louvois and Condé. Go left on the D1 to Châlons-sur-Marne.

Châlons-sur-Marne, Champagne-Ardenne

2 An old-established town – the main street in on the line of the Romans' Via Agrippa from Milan to Boulogne – Châlons sometimes calls itself Châlons-en-Champagne. It does have extensive champagne cellars to be visited. The largely 13th-century cathedral (St Étienne) with lovely stained glass which you can easily admire, because it is at less than usual neck-craning angle, has a march of flying buttresses and a later north front uncomfortably out of tune with the rest. You may find **Notre-Dame-en-Vaux** just as interesting. In a **cloister museum** reached by a lane beside this multi-towered church, more than 50 carved columns featuring saints, prophets and medieval personalities are on display. Châlons has many waterfronts along the River Marne and the canals connected with it. Look for the series of parks and formal gardens called the **Jards**.

ⓘ Quai des Arts

Leave Châlons on the N3 as for Metz. After Auve, watch for a left turn signed for Valmy. This is the D284. Turn right for Moulin de Valmy.

Valmy, Champagne-Ardenne

3 The reconstructed windmill (*moulin*) on the hilltop at Valmy, with its elevated views of fields, spinneys and faraway avenues of trees, marks the site of the most significant engagement in the war which

A picturesque mill still in operation at Verzenay, in fertile vine-growing farmland

Revolutionary France fought against the Prussians and Austrians. Plaques show the line-up of troops on 20 September 1792, when General Kellermann's inexperienced French army faced the battle-hardened Prussians under the Duke of Brunswick.

Expecting an easy victory, the Prussians were in fact repulsed, and the young Revolutionary forces proved they could defend the homeland. Within a few hours, the Republic was proclaimed.

The French troops, and Kellermann himself (by a spirited statue) are commemorated near by. There is a **museum** of the battle on the **D31** in the little village of Valmy, and other reminders of it later on the route.

ⓘ Maison du Meunier

Continue on the D284, follow signs to Braux-Ste-Cohiere, then follow sign 'Vers N3'. Go left on the N3 to Ste Menehould.

St Menehould, Champagne-Ardenne

4 A statue of Dom Pérignon recalls the fact that this Benedictine monk, to whom we owe the modern method of blending different wines into champagne, was born here in the 17th century. Incongruously, perhaps, you will find many shops selling a quite different speciality – pigs' trotters. It was at the now-restored **Maison de Poste** that the ill-fated Louis XVI and Marie Antoinette were recognised, to be arrested later.

At Ste Menehould you will see a river flowing in different directions. Thanks to canal works, the Aisne splits into two channels which encircle the town and join up again after it. Since the Auve joins the Aisne here, Ste Menehould has many pleasant waterways.

Its plateau location and a woodland fringe keep the old upper town almost out of sight, but a good self-guided walk links it with the lower town, whose elegant public buildings were raised after a disastrous fire in 1719.

ⓘ Place Leclerc

Continue on the N3. In Les Islettes turn left for Varennes, following the D2 and then the D38.

The pleasing profile of the aqueduct at Conde-sur-Marne draws the eye

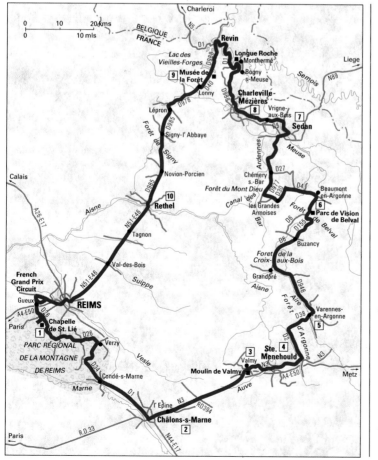

known to have lived in them within the last 2,000 years.

Because the red, roe and fallow deer, the wild boars, the mouflons (wild sheep), the bison and the other animals all live in semi-freedom inside the boundary fence, visitors drive slowly along the viewing roads, follow a fenced-in walking route or travel on the little 'tourist train', whose locomotive is a thinly-disguised tractor.

The only animal kept in a separate secure enclosure is a brown bear, which might otherwise become testy if annoyed!

*Continue on the **D4** through Beaumont, then go straight on to the **D30** as for Le Chesne. Beyond Les Grandes-Armoises, after the bend sign, take the first right to pass an '8t' sign. Turn right at the Give Way sign. This is the **D977**. Follow the signs to Sedan.*

Sedan, Champagne-Ardenne

7 Some quarters of the town are fairly depressing, but Sedan can barely dispel the memories of its past. This is where Napoleon III capitulated to end the Franco-Prussian War of 1870. In World War I the huge **Château-Fort**, in area the biggest castle in the whole of Europe, was a brutal forced-labour camp. And in the next war, this was where the Germans burst through the French lines in the invasion of 1940. Now the castle houses a **museum** on Sedan's military history, and there is a guided tour.

Away from these melancholy recollections, Sedan is famous for its high-quality woollen rugs; the workshop where rugs are still made as they were a century ago is open to visitors. There are pleasant promenades by the River Meuse, some medieval walls and arcades, and a high-level walk with viewpoints over the town.

[i] Rue Rousseau

*Leave Sedan for Floing on the **D5** and continue on this road to Charleville-Mézières. Avoid the autoroute.*

Charleville-Mézières, Champagne-Ardenne

8 Two once-separate towns around loops of the River Meuse have merged here. Mézières to the south is virtually on two islands. Within its 16th-century ramparts, the Flamboyant Gothic **Church of Notre-Dame d'Espérance** will surprise you with its abstract and geometrical stained-glass windows by René Dürrbach, a collaborator of Picasso's.

At Charleville the elegant, arcaded **Place Ducale** remains virtually as it was completed in 1628 (pity about the faded and obsolete shop signs).

The grand watermill (Vieux Moulin) on the Meuse is a local museum (**Musée Ardenne**), partly dedicated to the poet Arthur Rimbaud, who was born at Charleville in 1954. A foot-bridge leads to parkland and the quay from which river cruises start, and also to walks on the wooded 'Mount Olympus'.

[i] Place Ducale

FOR HISTORY BUFFS

5 At Lachalade, on the **D2** between Ste Menehould and Varennes, look for the memorials to the *Garabaldiens* – Italian troops who fought alongside the French in 1914–15, never imagining that in the next war the two countries would be enemies.

10 In Novion-Porcien, on the **D985** before Rethel, the sudden appearance of an American World War II tank marks the entrance, through a bar, to a war museum largely dedicated to the Battle of the Ardenne (the Battle of the Bulge) in late 1944.

SCENIC ROUTES

From the beautifully kept village of Gueux, the **D26** runs along the foothills of the Montagne de Reims, through vineyards below the forest ridge.

Beyond Varennes the route follows a pleasant rural landscape, sometimes on the shallow valley floor. The D6 gives long views over fields and wooded hills.

After Monthermé the deep, sinuous and thickly wooded valley of the Meuse gives the finest scenery in the French Ardennes.

Sedan, dominated by a fortress, has had a turbulent military history – often tragic. Any connection between the town and the 17th-century origin of the famous Sedan chair remains a mystery, however

Varennes-en-Argonne, Champagne-Ardenne

5 In June 1791, when Louis XVI and his family fled secretly from Paris to try to join loyal troops at Metz, it was in Varennes that their coaches were stopped. Arrest, trial and the guillotine followed. The **Musée d'Argonne** is an excellent local museum, which describes the drama, and gives a balanced account of a king who forcefully supported the Americans in the War of Independence but made many political blunders at home. It also has intriguing displays on the old crafts and industries of the Forest of Argonne, and on the devastating effect on the district of World War I.

French and American flags fly at the entrance to the little grassy park leading to the pillared **Pennsylvania Monument**. It was troops from that US state who liberated Varennes in 1918.

[i] Musée d'Argonne

*Leave Varennes on the **D946**. Turn right on the **D6** to Buzancy, left on the **D947**, then right and left on the **D155** to Fossé, taking care on the bumpy roads. Go left on the **D55**, left on the **D4** and follow it right as for Beaumont, to the Parc de Vision de Belval.*

Parc de Vision de Belval, Champagne-Ardenne

6 In 350 hectares (865 acres) of woodland and clearings, with a lake to accommodate its ducks and geese, this extensive wildlife park houses around 400 wild animals belonging to species which either still live in the northern forests or are

Leave Charleville on the D988 and follow signs to Monthermé along the D989. In Monthermé watch for a sharp left turn on the D1 to Revin. Go left on the D988 as for Les Mazures, then join the D40 as for Renwez and turn left at the junction with the D140 into the Musée de la Forêt.

Musée de la Forêt, Champagne-Ardenne

9 As much a museum 'in' the forest as 'of' the forest, this 5-hectare (12-acre) area of woodland is devoted to showing – partly with the aid of cheery wooden sculptures – the traditional crafts and harvesting methods of a few unmechanised generations ago.

Strolling round, you will see how birchwood brushes were made, how oak bark was peeled, how charcoal burners went about their trade, the kind of huts woodcutters used to live in, and a selection of axes and single- and two-man saws.

The museum holds occasional wood-chopping contests, where competitors test their speed and accuracy as they axe their way through felled logs.

Continue on the D40. Go straight through Lonny. Turn right into Sormonne and left on the D978 as for Laon. Go left on the D985 and continue to Rethel.

Rethel, Champagne-Ardenne

10 An inscription at the bridge over the River Aisne here is a simple

list of seven years between 1411 and 1940 – the years when war came to Rethel. In the 1930s the town hall was proudly re-created in Renaissance style; then in May 1940 more than three-quarters of the buildings in Rethel were flattened. But the town bobbed up again, as it always has. The fine old **Church of St-Nicholas** was restored. The local **museum** was restocked, although it has very restricted opening times. Walks along the river and the nearby canal were opened up, including the tree-lined Promenade des Isles.

There are sports facilities here for everything from tennis and rugby to show-jumping and archery, and the modern **swimming pool** is partly under cover, partly in the open air.

ⓘ Avenue Gambetta

Leave Rethel on the N51 to Reims.

Route	km (miles)
Reims – Montagne de Reims	17 (11)
Montagne de Reims – Châlons-sur-Marne	54 (34)
Châlons-sur-Marne – Valmy	34 (21)
Valmy – Ste Menehould	10 (6)
Ste Menehould – Varennes-en-Argonne	28 (18)
Varennes-en-Argonne – Parc de Belval	45 (28)
Parc de Belval – Sedan	47 (29)
Sedan – Charleville-Mézières	20 (12)
Charleville-Mézières – Musée de la Forêt	45 (28)
Musée de la Forêt – Rethel	47 (29)
Rethel – Reims	39 (24)

Monthermé is in a region of narrow valleys and thickly-wooded hills chiefly famous for 'The Battle of the Bulge' fought around here in December 1944

RECOMMENDED WALKS

7 After joining the D977 for Sedan, turn right on the D230 into the **Forêt de Mont-Dieu**. The **Circuit de la Chartreuse** walk wanders through the forest and overlooks the historic monastery of Mont-Dieu in its clearing among the fields.

9 In Monthermé, after Charleville-Mézières, cross the Meuse bridge, take the D989 uphill, then turn left for the car park at the start of the ridgetop path to Longue Riche, a stunning viewpoint over the winding valley.

SPECIAL TO...

10 Local gastronomic specialities in the northern part of the route include the salty *Rocroi* cheese and, in Rethel, *boudin blanc*, a white sausage made from pork, eggs, shallots and seasoning. The town has an annual fair to celebrate it.

FOR CHILDREN

8 Charleville-Mézières is the world capital of puppetry. Its **Institut International de la Marionette** has details of the summer puppet festival.

10 Before Rethel turn left off the D978 after Lonny for a neat little karting centre with two circuits for children of different ages. Low-powered karts are available for the real youngsters, and first-time drivers are patiently shown how to go about it.

BACK TO NATURE

10 Ask at the tourist office in Rethel for the leaflet about two nature trails along the banks of the River Aisne and the Ardennes Canal. It identifies the bird species to be seen, and locates a heronry high in the canalside trees.

3 days – 408km (255 miles)

THE HEART OF BURGUNDY

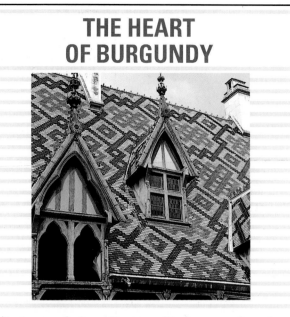

Chalon-sur-Saône • Beaune • Flavigny-sur-Ozerain
Semur-en-Auxois • Avallon • Vézelay • St-Brisson
Château-Chinon • Autun • Chalon-sur-Saône

At one time, this tour would have been within the realm of the independent duchy of Burgundy. North of Chalon-sur-Saône, it runs through the famous Burgundy vineyards. Then it crosses upland areas off the usual tourist track, and wanders through the farm and forest country of the extensive Parc Naturel Régional du Morvan. Fortified towns are scattered along the route. One of the most gracious basilicas in France is a former hilltop pilgrimage site. You can learn about the dogged Resistance fighters of the Morvan and – unexpectedly – about the gifts lavished by foreign dignitaries on the President of France.

No contention that Beaune is a prestigious wine-producer!

ℹ️ Square Chabas, Chalon-sur-Saône

Leave Chalon on the N6 as for Beaune. Turn right on the N74, left on the C2 to Puligny-Montrachet, the take the D113b to Mersault. Go straight ahead on the D23, turn right on the D17, continue through Pommard and go left into Beaune.

Beaune, Burgundy

1 Hundreds of thousands of visitors come every year to the historic ramparted capital of Burgundy. Many go to the Hôtel-Dieu, opened in 1443 as a charitable hospital. Containing displays in richly decorated salles which show how the nuns looked after their aged patients in years gone by, as well as Rogier van der Weyden's stunning 15th-century altarpiece of the Last Judgement (commissioned for the chapel), the building itself is a ravishing mixture of polychrome tiling, intricate window details and appealing galleries. Beaune is honeycombed with wine cellars, some of them in the town walls. The **Musée du Vin** occupies an old town mansion of the dukes of Burgundy, while the **Athenaeum** is a cultural centre linking wine, literature and local history.

Magnificent tapestries hang in the **Church of Notre-Dame**. Beaune also has a **fine arts museum** and, in the **Musée Marey**, a tribute to Beaune-born pioneer of moving pictures, Étienne Jules Marey.

ℹ️ Place de la Halle

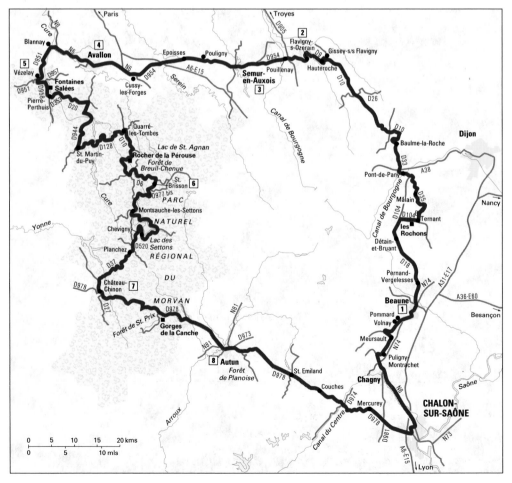

Leave Beaune on the **D18** going north, passing Pernand-Vergelesses. Continue on the **D18** through Changey, turn right on to the **D8**, then take the **D25F** and the **D25** to Bruant. Go left on the **D8** again, fork right on the **D104**, right on the **D104b** to Ternant, then take the **D35** to Pont-de-Pany. Go left on the **D905**, and immediately after leaving Pont-de-Pany turn right over the autoroute to Mâlain. Continue through Baulme-la-Roche. Turn left on the **D10** to Gissey. Bear left at the roundabout, past Café de l'Oze, on to the **D10e** to Hauteroche. Turn sharp right and follow signs to Flavigny, entering it on the **D9**.

Flavigny-sur-Ozerain, Burgundy

2 History has moved on, isolating this little medieval hilltop town. Park outside, study the labyrinthine medieval street plan and feel the centuries drift away as you stroll through an ancient gateway, along narrow streets and alleyways, to the 13th-century **church** in the square.

Products of the local farms are sold here. Guided tours are arranged of an eerie 8th-century crypt. And there are farm-track walks on the plateau, one to a site said to be a Roman camp from Julius Caesar's time.

ⓘ Place de l'Église

*Continue on the **D9** and **D954** to Semur-en-Auxois.*

Semur-en-Auxois, Burgundy

3 Semur occupies a pinched-in red granite promontory at a hairpin bend on the River Armançon. Its 18th-century Pont Joly looks to banked up houses and massive ram-

You can still walk the ancient ramparts at imposing Semur-en-Auxois and gaze at the river way down in the ravine

part towers of a former castle. You can visit the **Tour de l'Orle d'Ore**.

The 13th-century **Church of Notre-Dame** features an eccentrically narrow nave and good stained-glass windows including a rather frank account of the work of the butchers' guild. There are medieval houses and a rampart walk. From the Pont Joly, Semur probably looks its best floodlit or at sunset.

ⓘ Place Gaveau

*Continue on the **D954** and **N6** to Avallon.*

Avallon, Burgundy

4 Those Burgundians who fortified Avallon would be surprised that so many of their rampart walls, towers, bastions and gateways survive in the very agreeable old town today. Perimeter walks and stairways look down on the attractive valley of the River Cousin, with its woods and terraced gardens.

Avallon is packed with fascinating old buildings, such as the clock tower of 1456, formerly a town gate, through which a street leads to the well-endowed **Musée de l'Avallonnais** and the 12th-century **Church of St-Lazare**. Part of St-Lazare houses the etchings for 20th-century artist Georges Rouault's harrowing but highly regarded series of prints entitled *Miserere*.

ⓘ Grande Rue Aristide-Briand

*Continue on the **N6** as for Auxerre, then turn left on the **D951** to Vézelay.*

SPECIAL TO...

1 Puligny-Montrachet, Meursault and Pommard are vineyard villages of the Côte d'Or, whose white burgundies are held in high regard. More than a dozen grand crus and premiers crus come from Puligny-Montrachet, while the Meursault growers are keenest on welcoming visitors.

Details of wine tours in the Côte d'Or are available from the tourist information in Beaune.

2 A waft of liquorice in the air at Flavigny hints at its most famous product. The old **abbey** makes aniseed in many forms – sweets, candies and flavourings. The genuine article – véritable marque des anis – is on sale in local groceries.

8 During August, Autun's strong links to its Roman heritage are celebrated, with great displays by legionnaires (in full costume) and chariots racing in the remains of the Roman theatre.

BACK TO NATURE

4 The district around Avallon is a hunting-ground for birds of prey. Stop beside the **N6**, for instance, and look to see if kites are wheeling overhead.

6 After Vézelay, turn left off the **D958** for the **Fontaines Salées**, where excavations have uncovered 2,000-year-old Gallo-Roman baths built over natural saline springs.

FOR HISTORY BUFFS

2 Look for the **dolmens** in the woodland left of the **D104b** before Ternant. These great balanced-stone chambers remain impressive and mysterious after 6,000 years.

4 At Époisses, on the **D954** on the way to Avallon, pause to visit the dry-moated **château**, with its dovecote exhibition and 13th-century parish church. Madame de Sévigny was a frequent visitor to the château. Even when the château itself is closed, an English-language leaflet welcomes you to its grounds, which form a Burgundy village in miniature.

6 See how Quarré-les-Tombes (on the way to St-Brisson) justifies its name – dozens of lichen-covered **sarcophagi** surround the parish church. They date from before AD900, when this area may have been a centre of monumental sculpture.

RECOMMENDED WALKS

5 Ask at the tourist office in Vézelay about the seven waymarked walks in the lovely countryside 'under the hill'. Each is described in an individual leaflet which includes a map, walking directions, information and a picture postcard.

6 Turn right off the **D10** before Les Larvaults along a one-way circuit of forest roads, which leads to the walks at the 609m (1,997-foot) **Rocher de la Pérouse**. There are splendid views over the forest to the valley of the River Cure.

SCENIC ROUTES

Between Beaune and Pont-de-Pany on the Burgundy Canal lies high farming country ignored by most visitors, who rush past on a triangle of autoroutes.

After Mâlain, look for the limestone cliff towering over Baulme-la-Roche. Beyond it, a watershed plateau splits the rivers between the Mediterranean and the English Channel.

Pause on the **D353** after Vézelay to admire the cliffs and wooded valley of the Cure.

The roads to Quarré-les-Tombes and Montsauche wander by rolling hills, farms and woodlands characteristic of the Morvan.

FOR CHILDREN

7 Lac des Settons beside the **D193** is a fine recreational reservoir with wooded bays, beaches and picnic sites. The youngsters can try out pedaloes and generally splash around.

At the post office at Château-Chinon, children can amuse themselves watching the antics of a gloriously eccentric mechanical fountain. Coloured sculptures are set in constant motion by spurts of water sent out by old redundant industrial machinery.

Vézelay, Burgundy

5 Climbing sinuously to a hilltop, the main street of this little town passes artists' studios, galleries and displays of semi-precious stones before it reaches the **Basilica of Ste-Madeleine**, one of the all-time glories of Romanesque design. The church, a great pilgrimage goal when it was believed to contain the remains of Mary Magdalen, survived fire, plunder and virtual destruction during the Revolution, to be completely restored in the 19th century. Look for its splendid doorways, intricately carved capitals, impressive crypt and the view from the tower, but most of all for the mellow light that pours into the interior, subtly changing through the day.

☐ Rue St Pierre

*Leave Vézelay on the **D957** to St Père, then go right on the **D958** to Pierre-Perthuis. Turn left on the **D353** and immediately right following 'Les Ponts' sign. Go through Précy-le-Moult, then turn right on the **D36** which becomes the **D20**. At a crossroads, turn right on the **D944**. In St Martin, watch for a sharp left turn to Quarré. In Quarré-les-Tombes, turn right through Les Levaults on the **D10**, then right on the **D211**. Go straight ahead on the **D6** to the Maison du Parc.*

St-Brisson, Burgundy

6 On the edge of St-Brisson, a fine old red-roofed farm complex is the headquarters of the **Parc Naturel Régional du Morvan**, the Morvan being the wooded mountain region between the rivers Loire and Saône. The **Maison du Parc** illustrates wildlife, crafts, conservation and the rural way of life. The grounds include a herb garden, animal enclosures, a waterfowl pond with pochard, mallard and shelduck, and pathways down to the lake. Near by, the **Musée de la Résistance** tells the story of the Morvan's secret war in World War II.

☐ Maison du Parc

Return from Maison du Parc, take the first left, go left at the T-junc-

The message at Volnay is quite clear as to how you might pass some time enjoyably

*tion through St-Brisson, then bear right on the **C1** and continue to Montsauche. Go left on the **D37**, then left on the **D193**. Keep Lac des Settons on your right, then watch for a sharp right turn following the 'Rive Gauche' sign. At the give way sign turn left on the **D520** and continue to Château-Chinon.*

Château-Chinon, Burgundy

7 Capital of the Morvan, Château-Chinon rises to a parkland with walks and drives and gorgeous views over the surrounding countryside.

The **Musée du Costume** also has displays on local arts and traditions. In the **Musée du Septennat** ('seven-year term museum') you will find an amazing exhibition of the ceremonial gifts lavished at home and abroad on François Mitterand during his first term as President of France. Previously a local politician here, he donated them all to the département.

☐ Place Gudin

*Leave Château-Chinon on the **D978** to Autun.*

Autun, Burgundy

8 Founded by the Emperor Augustus as *Augustodunum*, Autun retains Roman archways such as the **Porte St André** and the **Porte d'Arroux**, still used by traffic and pedestrians. The **Musée Rolin**, housed in a 15th-century mansion, specialises in Roman exhibits, and the original riverside theatre is still in use. In this dignified town, look for the majestic portal of the 12th-century **Cathédrale St-Lazare**, the medieval **rampart walk**, the immaculate **military academy**, and the 18th-century **Lycée Bonaparte** where Napoleon was a pupil.

☐ Avenue Charles de Gaulle

Leave Autun following signs to Chalon-sur-Saône.

Chalon-sur-Saône – Beaune 35 (22)
Beaune – Flavigny-sur-Ozerain 80 (50)
Flavigny-sur-Ozerain – Semur-en-Auxois 16 (10)
Semur-en-Auxois – Avallon 34 (21)
Avallon – Vézelay 19 (12)
Vézelay – St-Brisson 74 (46)
St-Brisson – Château-Chinon 56 (35)
Château-Chinon – Autun 40 (25)
Autun – Chalon-sur-Saône 54 (34)

The Auberge du Père Ganne in Barbizon, the village that inspired a school of painters

ⓘ Place de la Cathédrale, Chartres

Leave Chartres on the N154. At the traffic lights, turn right for St Prest and continue on the D6 to Maintenon. Turn right to Épernon. Turn right on the D176, then continue through Droue to Émancé. Go as for Orphin, turn left on the D62 to Gazeran, then follow the signs to Rambouillet.

Rambouillet, Île-de-France

1 This is France's 'presidential town'. Its elegant château, standing among extensive woodlands, lawns and water gardens, is an official residence of the president, but is open to visitors most of the year. Louis XVI commissioned two intriguing buildings in the grounds – the ornamental dairy called the **Laiterie de la Reine**, and the **Chaumière des Coquillages** ('Cottage of Shells') with its wall covering of seashells, mother-of-pearl and tiny pieces of marble. Also in the grounds you will see the **Bergerie Nationale**, famous for its pedigree Merino rams. There is a **museum** here on the husbandry and breeding of sheep. Rambouillet's racecourse is southeast of the town. Beyond it (take the **D27**), a wildlife reserve shelters red, roe and fallow deer.

ⓘ Place de la Libération

Moret-sur-Loing is a favourite escape for Parisians at 'le weekend'

THE HISTORIC CENTRE OF FRANCE

Chartres • Rambouillet • Milly-la-Forêt • Barbizon Fontainebleau • Moret-sur-Loing • Grez-sur-Loing Pithiviers • Chartres

Many strands of French life and history combine in this tour from the cathedral city of Chartres. The palace of Fontainebleau and the castle at Rambouillet recall the sumptuous ease of the aristocracy in years gone by while their parks, like most of the magnificent forest which circles Fontainebleau, are beautiful strolling-grounds. Barbizon gave its name to one of the most famous schools of 19th-century French artists. Moret-sur-Loing is a delightful once-fortified town. You will find pleasant roads which run through cool shady woodlands, and others which cross skyline-to-skyline arable plains, wide open to the summer sun.

RECOMMENDED WALKS

1 After you have left Rambouillet, where the **D24** crosses the D91, turn left, following the 'Cascades' sign to the woodland walks, to the left of the road, leading by a jumble of rocks down to a river ravine and its falls.

4 On the 'Fontainebleau par route forestière' road, stop at the **Gorges d'Apremont** picnic area. Pathways explore the beautiful wooded tablelands and valleys and the parched area called the **Désert d'Apremont**. Later, watch for the right turn off the D301 towards the sandy birchwood paths of the Gorges de Franchard.

SPECIAL TO...

2 In Le Perray, after Rambouillet, the **Musée des Vieux Métiers** is a working forge with a collection of traditional blacksmith's tools and equipment. You can hardly miss the 9m (30-foot) model of the Eiffel Tower.

5 Moret-sur-Loing is famous for its delicious barley sugar – the *sucre d'orge* sold in many local shops. The still-secret recipe originated with the Benedictine nuns who settled here in 1638
On Saturday evenings during the summer, locals stage *son et lumière* pageants illustrating the histroy of the town.

SCENIC ROUTES

From Chartres to Maintenon you will drive through a pleasant area of riverside and fishponds, farms and woodlands separating the villages.
You reach Étampes over a wide arable plain with traditional tree-lined roads, and approach Milly-la-Forêt seeing avenues of trees on the skyline, then sweeping woodlands.

Leave Rambouillet as for Paris, join the N10 dual-carriageway and turn off through Le Perray on the D910. Go right on the D24 and continue to Cernay-la-Ville. Turn left on to the D306, then sharp right on the D72, left on the D61, then right D72 again to Clairefontaine. Go left on the D27 and follow 'Dourdan' signs, turning right on the D149. Go left on the D836 to Dourdan, then take the D116 before rejoining the D836 and taking the N191 through Étampes. Go right on the D837 and into Milly-la-Forêt.

Milly-la-Forêt, Île-de-France

2 Expertly trimmed, shade-providing trees; a 15th-century market hall, red-tiled houses; and a wondering stream with wash-house quays: all these combine to give this village a peaceful, attractive and timeless appearance.
The artist, poet and dramatist Jean Cocteau is buried in the little 12th-century chapel of **St-Blaise-des-Simples**, which he had previously decorated. The *simples* are medicinal herbs, which remain a preoccupation of Milly today. On the Nemours road you can visit the Conservatoire National of medicinal and aromatic plants and plants used by industry.

Follow 'Fontainebleau' signs on the D837. In Arbonne, bear left as for Melun. Turn right on the D64 to Barbizon.

Barbizon, Île-de-France

3 In the mid-19th century, a group of landscape artists centred on the painter Théodore Rousseau, made this village their base. They were to become known as the Barbizon School. Greater figures, such as the Realist painter Jean François Millet, whose *Angelus* was painted near by, were also Barbizon men.

Like Robert Louis Stevenson, make time to enjoy the gracious tranquillity of Grez-sur-Loing

In Rousseau's house, fascinating maps and illustrations shows the village as it was then. Upstairs in his north-light studio is a collection of little gems of landscape art.
The artists' often frugal meals were taken at the village inn run by old Monsieur Ganne. Now the **Auberge du Père Ganne** houses an atmospheric museum in which it is easy to imagine that the next person at the door is a hungry painter, ready for dinner after a day's sketching in the forests or fields.

i Grande Rue

Leave Barbizon by the Grande Rue and enter the Forêt de Fontainebleau. Turn right at a T-junction following the 'Fontainebleau par route forestière' sign. Go right at the Stop signs for Franchard (this is the D301), then left on the N152 and at the busy roundabout take the N6 for the town of Fontainebleau.

Fontainebleau, Île-de-France

4 Everything else in this elegant town defers to the spectacular

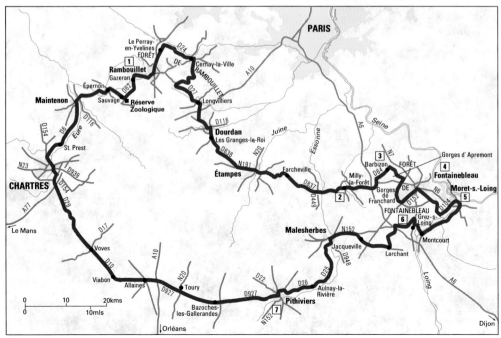

palace in its parkland of lakes, wooded and formal and landscape gardens. A discreet plaque acknowledges John D Rockefeller Jr's generous funding of the palace restoration. The Musée Napoléon houses a massive exhibition on the Bonaparte family. Do not confuse this with the **Musée Napoléonien d'Art et d'Histoire**, in the town itself, which features grand displays on French military through the ages.

i⃞ Rue Denecourt

Return to the busy roundabout and take the D58 as for Bourron-Marlotte. Go straight ahead on the D148, then turn left on to the D104 to Moret-sur-Loing.

Moret-sur-Loing, Île-de-France

5 This very appealing little place is an 'ancient and royal city' which once stood on the French frontier, fortified against Burgundy on the far side of a beautiful stretch of the River Loing. Fine medieval gateways, Renaissance and later buildings survive.

By the river, **La Grande Batelière** is the home of the Clemenceau family, open at weekends to tell the story of France's famous World War I president. Moret also celebrates its connection with the Impressionist painter Alfred Sisley.

i⃞ Avenue Jean-Jaurès

Leave Moret on the D302, then immediately turn right at traffic lights for Nemours. Watch for another right turn as for Nemours along the D40. Go right on to the D40d, then left into Grez-sur-Loing.

Grez-sur-Loing, Île-de-France

6 Here is a lovely stretch of the Loing with gardens, boathouses, weeping willows and flotillas of geese and mallards. Swallows and damselflies dart above the water, swifts in the higher air. Beyond the old arched bridge rises a pale 12th-century tower.

In the 1870s, having tried Barbizon, Robert Louis Stevenson joined the Bohemian summer colony at Grez. Later, Frederick Delius composed much of his music here.

Stroll to the austere and lofty medieval **church**, and along the hollyhock lane from the little Place

Fontainebleau is a great palace rich in history, but its studied proportions and surrounding forest make it humanly appealing

Jolivet. The artists have gone, but the appeal of this charming village never fades.

Leave Grez as for La Chapelle-la-Reine, taking the D104. After the junction sign watch for a left turn to Larchant. Go right as for La Chapelle on the D16. Turn left on to the D36 and follow signs to Jacqueville. Bear right then left following the 'Malesherbes' sign on the C7. Take care at the level crossing. At the give way sign, go left on to the N152 to Malesherbes. Take the D948 as for Puiseaux, then go right on the D25 through Pinçon and Briarres. Continue through Aulnay-la-Rivière to Pithiviers.

Pithiviers, Île-de-France

7 Famous for its cakes, Pithiviers has a good local museum (in the former Hôtel-Dieu) which explains the local cuisine and its cooks' pioneering use of saffron – the region was once of European importance for saffron-growing.

Historic steam locomotives from as early as 1870 run on the last 4km (2½-mile) stretch of a light railway opened in 1892. An exhibition displays some elegant old coaches and tells the story of France's branch lines.

i⃞ Mail Ouest

Leave Pithiviers on the D927 to Allaines. Go right at the Stop sign, then left on to the D12 and join the D10 to Voves. Turn right on to the D17 as for Auneau and enter the one-way traffic system in Voves. At the two-way sign turn into a side road on the left. Go right at the Stop sign and return to Chartres.

BACK TO NATURE

4 Planted with pines, oaks, birches, chestnut trees, hornbeams and – especially – glorious beechwoods, the **Forêt de Fontainebleau** is one of the most beautiful and most carefully protected woodlands in Europe. It covers about 25,000 hectares (61,775 acres), most of them open to the public.

FOR CHILDREN

6 As you approach Grez-sur-Loing, look on the right for **Tacot des Lacs**, a full-scale railway, whose trains like the 1900 steam locomotive *Clémentine* run weekend trips through scrubland and across the River Loing.

FOR HISTORY BUFFS

7 Malesherbes, on the way to Pithiviers, has two castles worthy of a visit on its outskirts. The **Château de Malesherbes**, off the Puiseaux road, is furnished as it was immediately before the Revolution. Off the D132, the many-turreted **Château de Rouville** overlooks the wooded valley of the Essone.

INDEX

References to captions are in *italic*.

A

Abbatiale Sainte Marie 53
Abri Pataud 52
accidents on the roads 6
Aigues-Mortes 79, *79*
Aix-les-Bains 90
Alée Couverts 23
Alsace 80, 94–7
   tour map 95
Ambert 31
Amboise 42, 43
Amiens 98, 103, *103*
Amplepuis 87
Angers 41
Angoulême 36
Annecy *89*, 90–1
Antibes *66*, 67
Aquitaine 48–53, 54–5
   tour maps 49, 52
Arcachon 48
Arles 77–8
Arras 104–5
Arromanches 10
Aubagné 65
Aubusson 34, *34*
Autun 114
Auvergne 28–31
   tour map 29
Avallon 113
Avignon 76, *76*

B

Badet-Pioch 78
Bagnères-de-Bigorre 57
Bagnères-de-Luchon 57–8
Bagnoles de l'Orne 13
Bandol 63, *63*
banks 5
Barbizon *115*, 116
Barbotan-les-Thermes 50
Barneville-Carteret 12
Barrage de Grand'Maison 93
Barrage de Treignac 34
Battlefields of the Somme 104
Baugé 40
Bayeux *10*, 10–11
Beaucaire 75–6
Beaufort 91, *92*
Beaugency 45
Beaulieu 73
Beaumont-Hamel 104
Beaune 112, *112*
Beauvais 107
Beauval 43
Beauvoir 20
Bergerac 55
Bergerie Nationale 115
Besse-en-Chandesse 30
Beynac 55
Bibliothèque Humaniste 97
Biot 67, *67*
Biscarrosse 49
Blérancourt 106
Blois *44*, 45
Bordeaux 46, *47*, 48
Boulogne *100*, 100–1, *102*
Bourg-St-Maurice 91
Bourganeuf 32
Bourneville 17
Boyardville 36
breakdowns 6
Brest 24
Brittany 8, 18–25

tour maps 18, 23
Brouage 36
Bruley 84
Burgundy 112–14
   tour map 112
Butte de Montsec 84

C

Caen 8, 10
Calais 98, *99*, 100, *100*
Camaret-sur-Mer 23
Cancale 20
Cannes 60–1, 66
Cap d'Antibes 66–7
Cap Blanc-Nez 100
Cap Canaille 62, 63
Cap de Carteret 12
Cap d'Erquy 20–1
Cap Ferrat 72
Cap Fréhel 20, 21
Cap Sizun 23
car hire 7
Cascade de l'Estrech 74
Cassis 62, *62*, 63
Castellane 69, *69*
Castelleras 69
Castelnaud 55
Castillon 73
Caudebec-en-Caux 15
Cauterets 59
Centre Historique Minier 105
Chaalis 107
Chalon-sur-Saône 98–9, *99*, 112
Châlons-sur-Marne 108
Chambéry 90
Chambord 45, *45*
Champagne-Ardenne 108–11
   tour map 109
Chanteloup 42
Charade 28
Charbonnières-les-Bains 88
Charleville-Mézières 110, 111
Chartres 99, 115
Chartreuse de la Verne 65
Château Garreau 50
Château de Gourdon 68
Château Meillant *28*
Château de Robert-le-Diable 17
Château Sully *42*
Château de Terre-Neuve 37, *37*
Château Yquem 51, *51*
Château-Chinon 114
Château-Fort 110
Châtillon-sur-Chalaronne 86–7
Chazelles-sur-Lyon 88
Chenonceau 42
Cherbourg *8*
Cholet *38*, 38–9
Cimitière des Martyrs 38
Cirque de Gavarnie 58
Clécy 13
Clermont-Ferrand 26, *26*, 28
Clisson 38
Cognac 36
Col de la Croix de Fer 93
Col de la Croix St Robert 30
Col de Guéry 29
Col de l'Iseran 92
Col du Tourmalet 58
Col de Turini 72, 74
Collobrières 65
Colmar 96, *96*
Combourg 18
Compiègne 106, *106*
Conde-sur-Marne 109
Corniche Angevine 41
Côte d'Azur 66–70, 72–4
   tour maps 67, 73
Coucy 107
Coudroy 45
Coulon 37
Courchons 69
Courseulles 12
Crécy 102
credit cards 5
currency 5

customs regulations 4–5

D

Défilé de Maupas 93
Desvres 102
Devil's Island 35
Dieppe 8–9, 14, 15
Dinan *4*, 21, *21*
Dinard 20
Domaine de Marquenterre 101
Domme 54–5, *55*
Douai 104, 105
Douarnenez 22, 22–3
Doué-la-Fontaine 38, 39
Draguignan 71
Dune de Pilat *48*, 49
Dunes de la Slack 100

E

École National d'Equitation 39
Écomusée de Haute
   Alsace 95–6
embassies 6
emergencies 5
entry documents 4
Epoisses 113
Erigné 40
Ermenonville 107
Erquy *20*, 20–1
Esquibien 24
Étang de Madine 84
Étang du Puits 44
Étretat 14–15

F

Fayence 71
Fécamp 14, *14*
Ferme St-Michel 24
Flavigny-sur-Ozerain 113
fly/drive 7
Fontainebleau 116–17, *117*
Fontaines Salées 113
Fontenay-le-Comte 37, *37*
Fontevieille 77, *77*
Forêt de Bercé 40
Forêt de Chandelais 39
Forêt de Compiègne 105, 106
Forêt de Fontainebleau
   116, 117
Forêt de Fougères 19
Forêt de Hez-Froidment 107
Forêt de Mont-Dieu 111
Forêt de St Gobian 105, 106
Forêt des Saumonards 37
Forêt des Singes 54
Forêt de la Teste 50
Fort de Douaumont 84
Fort de la Latte 20
Fort St Roch 74
Fosse Delloye 105
Fougères 18–19
Fourcès 49
French National Stud Farm 32

G

Gassin *62*, 64
Gavarnie 58–9
Gien 44, *44*
Gimel-les-Cascades 33
Gorge d'Enfer 52
Gorges d'Apremont 116
Gorges du Verdon 71
Gouffre de Padirac 54
Gourdon 68, *68*
Gramat 54
Grande Cascade 58
Granville 12, *12*, 13
Grasse 68, *68*
Gravelotte 83, 84
Grenoble 80, *80*, 89
Grez-sur-Loing *116*, 117
Grimaud 65
Grotte du Grand Roc 52
Grottes de Bétharram 59
Grottes de Naours 104
Guebwiller 96

ACKNOWLEDGEMENTS

The Automobile Association would like to thank the following photographers, libraries and associations for their help in the preparation of this book, and P & O European Ferries and La Fedération Nationale des Logis de France who assisted the photographer, Barrie Smith.

BARRIE SMITH took all the photographs not listed below in this book (AA PHOTO LIBRARY).

J ALLAN CASH PHOTO LIBRARY 102 Boulogne, 103 Amiens.

SPECTRUM COLOUR LIBRARY 13 Pointe du Hoc, 17 Church of St-Ouen, 19 Mont St-Michel, 20 Erquy, 22 Pointe du Raz, 28 Meillant Château, 33 Château Pompadour, 107 Château Coucy.

WORLD PICTURES 8/9 Cherbourg, 14 Fécamp, 98 Chalon-sur-Saône, 101 Picardy.

ZEFA PICTURE LIBRARY UK LTD Cover Mont St-Michel, 1 near Carcassone, 4 Le Croisic, 4/5 Dinan, 9 Cathedral Quimper, 26 Clermont-Ferrand, 27 La Rochelle, 46 Bordeaux skyline, 47 Dordogne Valley, 61 Marseille, 81 Grenoble, 81 Strasbourg, 81 Lyon, 100 Calais, 100 Boulogne.

Copy editors: Audrey Horne, Dilys Jones